Credit, Market, Operational, and Liquidity Risk

Applied CQRM Book Series

Volume V

Applying Monte Carlo Risk Simulation, Strategic Real
Options, Stochastic Forecasting, Portfolio Optimization,
and Data and Decision Analytics

IIPER Press

IIPER
Press

Johnathan Mun, Ph.D.

California, USA

ROV CMOL Risk

For Jayden, Emma, and Penny.

In a world where risk and uncertainty abound, you are the only constants in my life.

Dedicated in loving memory of my mom.

Delight yourself in the Lord and He will give you the desires of your heart.

Psalm 37:4

The Applied CQRM Book Series showcases how the advanced analytics covered in the Certified in Quantitative Risk Management (CQRM) certification program can be applied to real-life business problems. In Volume V, we show how Credit, Market, Operational, and Liquidity (CMOL) Risks can be modeled using the CMOL software, Risk Simulator, and Modeling Toolkit.

Pragmatic applications are emphasized in order to demystify the many elements inherent in risk analysis. A black box will remain a black box if no one can understand the concepts despite its power and applicability. It is only when the black box methods become transparent, so that researchers can understand, apply, and convince others of their results, value-add, and applicability, that the approaches will receive widespread attention. This transparency is achieved through step-by-step applications of quantitative modeling as well as through presenting multiple cases and discussing real-life applications.

This book is targeted at those individuals who have completed the CQRM certification program but can also be used by anyone familiar with basic quantitative research methods—there is something for everyone. It is also applicable for use as a second-year MBA/MS-level or introductory PhD textbook. The examples in the book assume some prior knowledge of the subject matter.

Additional information on the CQRM program can be obtained at:

www.iiper.org

www.realoptionsvaluation.com

www.rovusa.com

ABOUT THE AUTHOR

Dr. Johnathan C. Mun is the founder, chairman, and CEO of Real Options Valuation, Inc. (ROV), a consulting, training, and software development firm specializing in strategic real options, financial valuation, Monte Carlo risk simulation, stochastic forecasting, optimization, decision analytics, business intelligence, healthcare analytics, enterprise risk management, project risk management, quantitative research methods, and risk analysis located in northern Silicon Valley, California. ROV has partners around the world including Argentina, Beijing, Chicago, China, Colombia, Ghana, Hong Kong, India, Italy, Japan, Malaysia, Mexico City, New York, Nigeria, Peru, Puerto Rico, Russia, Saudi Arabia, Shanghai, Singapore, Slovenia, South Africa, South Korea, Spain, United Kingdom, Venezuela, Zurich, and others. ROV also has a local office in Shanghai.

Dr. Mun is also the chairman of the International Institute of Professional Education and Research (IIPER), an accredited global organization staffed by professors from named universities from around the world that provides the Certified in Quantitative Risk Management (CQRM) and Certified in Risk Management (CRM) designations, among others. He is the creator of many powerful software tools including Risk Simulator, Real Options SLS Super Lattice Solver, Modeling Toolkit, Project Economics Analysis Tool (PEAT), Credit Market Operational Liquidity Risk (CMOL), Employee Stock Options Valuation, ROV BizStats, ROV Modeler Suite (Basel Credit Modeler, Risk Modeler, Optimizer, and Valuator), ROV Compiler, ROV Extractor and Evaluator, ROV Dashboard, ROV Quantitative Data Miner, and other software applications, as well as the ROV risk-analysis training DVD. He holds public seminars on risk analysis and CQRM programs. He has over 21 registered patents and patents pending globally. He has authored over 23 books published by John Wiley & Sons, Elsevier Science, IIPER Press, and ROV Press, including multiple volumes of the Applied CQRM Series (IIPER Press, 2019-2020); *Modeling Risk: Applying Monte Carlo Simulation, Strategic Real Options, Stochastic Forecasting, Portfolio Optimization, Data Analytics, Business Intelligence, and Decision Modeling,* First Edition (Wiley, 2006), Second Edition (Wiley, 2010), and Third Edition

(ROV Press, 2015); *The Banker's Handbook on Credit Risk* (2008); *Advanced Analytical Models: 250 Applications from Basel Accord to Wall Street and Beyond* (Wiley 2008 and Thomson–Shore 2016); *Real Options Analysis: Tools and Techniques,* First Edition (2003), Second Edition (2005), and Third Edition (2016); *Real Options Analysis Course: Business Cases* (2003); *Applied Risk Analysis: Moving Beyond Uncertainty* (2003); and *Valuing Employee Stock Options* (2004). His books and software are being used at over 350 top universities around the world, including the Bern Institute in Germany, Chung-Ang University in South Korea, Georgetown University, ITESM in Mexico, Massachusetts Institute of Technology, U.S. Naval Postgraduate School, New York University, Stockholm University in Sweden, University of the Andes in Chile, University of Chile, University of Hull, University of Pennsylvania Wharton School, University of York in the United Kingdom, and Edinburgh University in Scotland, among others.

Currently a risk, finance, and economics professor, Dr. Mun has taught courses in financial management, investments, real options, economics, and statistics at the undergraduate and the graduate MS, MBA, and PhD levels. He teaches and has taught at universities all over the world, from the U.S. Naval Postgraduate School (Monterey, California) and University of Applied Sciences (Switzerland and Germany) as full professor, to Golden Gate University (California) and St. Mary's College (California), and has chaired many graduate research MBA thesis and PhD dissertation committees. He also teaches weeklong Risk Analysis, Real Options Analysis, and Risk Analysis for Managers public courses where participants can obtain the CRM and CQRM designations on completion. He is a senior fellow at the Magellan Center and sits on the board of standards at the American Academy of Financial Management.

He was formerly the Vice President of Analytics at Decisioneering, Inc., where he headed the development of options and financial analytics software products, analytical consulting, training, and technical support, and where he was the creator of the Real Options Analysis Toolkit software, the older and much less powerful predecessor of the Real Options Super Lattice software. Prior to joining Decisioneering, he was a Consulting Manager and Financial Economist in the Valuation Services and Global Financial Services practice of KPMG Consulting and a Manager with the Economic Consulting Services practice at KPMG LLP.

He has extensive experience in econometric modeling, financial analysis, real options, economic analysis, and statistics. During his tenure at Real Options Valuation, Inc., Decisioneering, and KPMG Consulting, he taught and consulted on a variety of real options, risk analysis, financial forecasting, project management, and financial valuation issues for more than 100 multinational firms (current and former clients include 3M, Airbus, Boeing, BP, Chevron Texaco, Financial Accounting Standards Board, Fujitsu, GE, Goodyear, Microsoft, Motorola, Northrop Grumman, Pfizer, Timken, U.S. Department of Defense, U.S. Navy, Veritas, and many others). His experience prior to joining KPMG included being department head of financial planning and analysis at Viking Inc. of FedEx, performing financial forecasting, economic analysis, and market research. Prior to that, he did financial planning and freelance financial consulting work.

Dr. Mun received a PhD in finance and economics from Lehigh University, where his research and academic interests were in the areas of investment finance, econometric modeling, financial options, corporate finance, and microeconomic theory. He also has an MBA in business administration, an MS in management science, and a BS in biology and physics. He is Certified in Financial Risk Management, Certified in Financial Consulting, and Certified in Quantitative Risk Management. He is a member of the American Mensa, Phi Beta Kappa Honor Society, and Golden Key Honor Society as well as several other professional organizations, including the Eastern and Southern Finance Associations, American Economic Association, and Global Association of Risk Professionals.

In addition, he has written many academic articles published in the *Journal of Expert Systems with Applications; Defense Acquisition Research Journal; American Institute of Physics Proceedings; Acquisitions Research (U.S. Department of Defense); Journal of the Advances in Quantitative Accounting and Finance; Global Finance Journal; International Financial Review; Journal of Financial Analysis; Journal of Applied Financial Economics; Journal of International Financial Markets, Institutions and Money; Financial Engineering News;* and *Journal of the Society of Petroleum Engineers.* Finally, he has contributed chapters in dozens of books and written over a hundred technical whitepapers, newsletters, case studies, and research papers for Real Options Valuation, Inc.

JohnathanMun@cs.com

San Francisco, California

...powerful toolset for portfolio/program managers to make rational choices among alternatives...
>Rear Admiral James Greene (Ret.), Acquisitions Chair
>Naval Postgraduate School (USA)

...unavoidable for any professional...logical, concrete, and conclusive approach...
>Jean Louis Vaysse, Vice President, Airbus (France)

...proven, revolutionary approach to quantifying risks and opportunities in an uncertain world...
>Mike Twyman, President, Mission Solutions,
>Cubic Global Defense, Inc. (USA)

...must read for anyone running investment economics...best way to quantify risk and strategic options...
>Mubarak A. Alkhater, Executive Director, New Business,
>Saudi Electric Co. (Saudi Arabia)

... pragmatic powerful risk techniques, valuable theoretical insights and analytics useful in any industry...
>Dr. Robert S. Finocchiaro, Director,
>Corporate R&D Services, 3M (USA)

...most important risk tools in one volume, definitive source on risk management with vivid examples...
>Dr. Ricardo Valerdi, Engineering Systems,
>Massachusetts Institute of Technology (USA)

...step-by-step complex concepts with unmatched ease and clarity... a "must read" for all professionals...
>Dr. Hans Weber, Product Development Leader,
>Syngenta AG (Switzerland)

...clear step-by-step approach...latest technology in decision making for real-world business...
>Dr. Paul W. Finnegan, Vice President,
>Alexion Pharmaceuticals (USA)

...clear roadmap and breadth of topics to create dynamic risk-adjusted strategies and options...
>Jeffrey A. Clark, Vice President Strategic Planning,
>The Timken Company (USA)

...clearly organized and tool-supported exploration of real-life business risks, options, strategy...

    Robert Mack, Vice President, Distinguished Analyst,
    Gartner Group (USA)

...full range of methodologies for quantifying and mitigating risk for effective enterprise management...

    Raymond Heika, Director of Strategic Planning,
    Northrop Grumman Corporation (USA)

...a must-read for product portfolio managers...captures risk exposure of strategic investments...

    Rafael Gutierrez, Executive Director Strategic Marketing Planning,
    Seagate Technologies (USA)

...complex topics exceptionally explained...
can understand and practice...

    Agustín Velázquez, Senior Economist,
    Venezuela Central Bank (Venezuela)

...constant source of practical applications with risk management theory...simply excellent!

    Alfredo Roisenzvit, Executive Director/Professor,
    Risk-Business Latin America (Argentina)

...the best risk modeling book is now better...
required reading by all executives...

    David Mercier, Vice President Corporate Dev.,
    Bonanza Creek Energy [Oil & Gas] (USA)

...bridge of theory and practice, intuitive,
understandable interpretations...

    Luis Melo, Senior Econometrician,
    Colombia Central Bank (Colombia)

...valuable tools for corporations to deliver value to shareholders and society even in rough times...

    Dr. Markus Götz Junginger, Lead Partner,
    Gallup (Germany)

CONTENTS

BANKING RISK

This book looks at some practical tools—quantitative models, Monte Carlo risk simulations, credit models, and business statistics—utilized to model and quantify regulatory and economic capital, measure and monitor key risk indicators, and report all the obtained data in a clear and intuitive manner. It relates to the modeling and analysis of asset liability management, credit risk, market risk, operational risk, and liquidity risk for banks or financial institutions, allowing these firms to properly identify, assess, quantify, value, diversify, hedge, and generate periodic regulatory reports for supervisory authorities and Central Banks on their credit, market, and operational risk areas, as well as for internal risk audits, risk controls, and risk management purposes.

In banking finance and financial services firms, *economic capital* is defined as the amount of risk capital, assessed on a realistic basis based on actual historical data, the bank or firm requires to cover the risks as a going concern, such as market risk, credit risk, liquidity risk, and operational risk. It is the amount of money that is needed to ensure survival in a worst-case scenario. Financial services regulators such as Central Banks, Bank of International Settlements, and other regulatory commissions should then require banks to hold an amount of risk capital equal at least to its economic capital times some holding multiple. Typically, economic capital is calculated by determining the amount of capital that the firm needs to ensure that its realistic balance sheet stays solvent over a certain time period with a prespecified probability (e.g., usually defined as 99.00%). Therefore, economic capital is often calculated with *Value at Risk* (VaR) type models.

Capital modeling in banks has surged as a necessity for the larger international financial institutions, which have discovered that the regulatory approaches taken by regulators were too basic and mainly not risk based. For example, credit risk capital requirements under Basel I were just a percentage (8% times another multiplier) of the volume of operations. This measure, which was very easy to calculate, was not risk sensitive, other than the differentiation of broad asset types. Therefore, complex banks found these capital requirements to be very inefficient in terms of capital planning, pricing, and leveraging limits and targets. With the evolution of the use of statistical models and available data—especially in market risk measurement—regulators started accepting internal capital models developed by the big international financial institutions. Accordingly, in 1996, an amendment was introduced to the Basel Accord (still Basel I) that allowed certain qualifying banks to calculate and hold capital in line with their internal models. To differentiate these measures of capital, banks started calling these internal calculations "economic capital," because it had a very close relationship with the real economics of the business, whereas "regulatory capital" was the requirement mandated by regulators. As the business evolved, and regulations became more ample, complex financial institutions started relying more on their economic capital models for the measurement and management of risks, while simultaneously having to hold regulatory capital. In most cases, the differences between these two kinds of capital for the same risk were very significant. This fact was one of the primary motivators of Basel III/IV, prompted mainly by a request from the more complex banks that the International Standards and, hence, banking regulations allow them to use their economic capital models to allocate regulatory capital. In other words, one of the outright motivations for the Basel III/IV reforms was to close the practical gap between economic and regulatory capital.

As Basel III/IV started to be implemented in most countries, the new regulatory paradigm established that banks—not just complex international financial institutions—must have IMMM processes for all material risks, and calculate and allocate economic capital for each and every one of these risks. For any given bank, these risks are defined by regulations as identified in the Basel Core Principles: credit, market, operational, liquidity, interest rate, strategic, reputational, securitization, and so on. In this light, banks of any size, in virtually every country, need to identify, measure, monitor, and mitigate all these risks, and calculate, evaluate, and allocate economic capital for each. This chapter discusses a set of simple approaches with straightforward tools that allow banks of any size and complexity to generate information for the management (the IMMM process) of these risks, and for the calculation of economic capital based on available balance sheet and regulatory information. In light of these International Standards, which are now formal regulations in virtually every country in the world, we utilize a spectrum of basic and more complex approaches to generate an economic capital model calculated on the formally defined risk drivers in each case and providing for risk-sensitive capital results for each relevant risk. Additionally, for each risk, through a set of basic information, a set of key risk indicators is generated and combined with the capital model results to produce relevant risk reports. Since regulations still require many instances of regulatory capital, such calculation is still provided along with Basel Standards as another useful output of the software tools. Finally, The Basel Committee differentiates credit, market, and operational risks from the rest, defining these three as the most relevant in any given financial institution. According to the Three Pillar design of Basel III/IV, these are known as Pillar I risks. Under Basel III/IV, economic and regulatory capital can be unified for Pillar I risks. In other words, for these three risks (credit, market and operational), economic capital models are given by the Basel Accord as a way to generate some standardization of methodologies and comparison among banks and countries.

For credit risk, the traditional approach for Basel I regulatory capital (still available as a basic choice in Basel III/IV) is to calculate 8% of outstanding loan volume, multiplied by a factor depending of the type of asset treated (100% for uncollateralized loans, 50% for mortgages, 20% for interbank, etc.). This approach, however, does not differentiate by risk within each category. In order to create a more risk-sensitive approach, Basel III/IV incorporated the main logic of portfolio models, where capital is the amount required to cover unexpected losses. Unexpected losses, in turn, are calculated as the residual given by the difference between the mean and the confidence interval of a loss distribution function.

Figure 1.1 illustrates the ROV PEAT software's ALM-CMOL module for Credit Risk—Economic Regulatory Capital (ERC) Global Settings tab. This current analysis is performed on credit issues such as loans, credit lines, and debt at the commercial, retail, or personal levels. To get started with the utility, existing files can be opened or saved, or a default sample model can be retrieved from the menu. However, to follow along, we recommend opening the default example (click on the menu icon on the top right corner of the software, then select *Load Example*).

The number of categories of loans and credit types can be set as well as the loan or credit category names, a *Loss Given Default* (LGD) value in percent, and the Basel credit type (*residential mortgages, revolving credit, other miscellaneous credit*, or *wholesale corporate and sovereign debt*). Each credit type has its required Basel III/IV model that is public knowledge, and the software uses the prescribed models per Basel regulations. Further, historical data can be manually entered by the user into the utility or via existing databases and data files. Such data files may be large and, hence, stored either in a single file or multiple data files where each file's contents can be mapped to the list of required variables (e.g., credit issue date, customer information, product type or segment, Central Bank ratings, amount of the debt or loan, interest payment, principal payment, last payment date, and other ancillary information the bank or financial services firm has access to) for the analysis, and the successfully mapped connections are displayed. Additional information such as the required VaR percentiles, average life of a commercial loan, and historical data period on which to run the data files to obtain the *Probability of Default* (PD) is entered. Next, the *Exposure at Default* (EAD) analysis periodicity is selected as is the date type and the Central Bank ratings. Different Central Banks in different nations tend to have similar credit ratings but the software allows for flexibility in choosing the relevant rating scheme (i.e., Level 1 may indicate on-time payment of an existing loan whereas Level 3 may indicate a late payment of over 90 days, which, therefore, constitutes a default). All these inputs and settings can be saved either as stand-alone settings and data or including the results. Users would enter a unique name and notes and save the current settings (previously saved models and settings can be retrieved, edited, or deleted; a new model can be created; or an existing model can be duplicated). The saved models are listed and can be rearranged according to the user's preference.

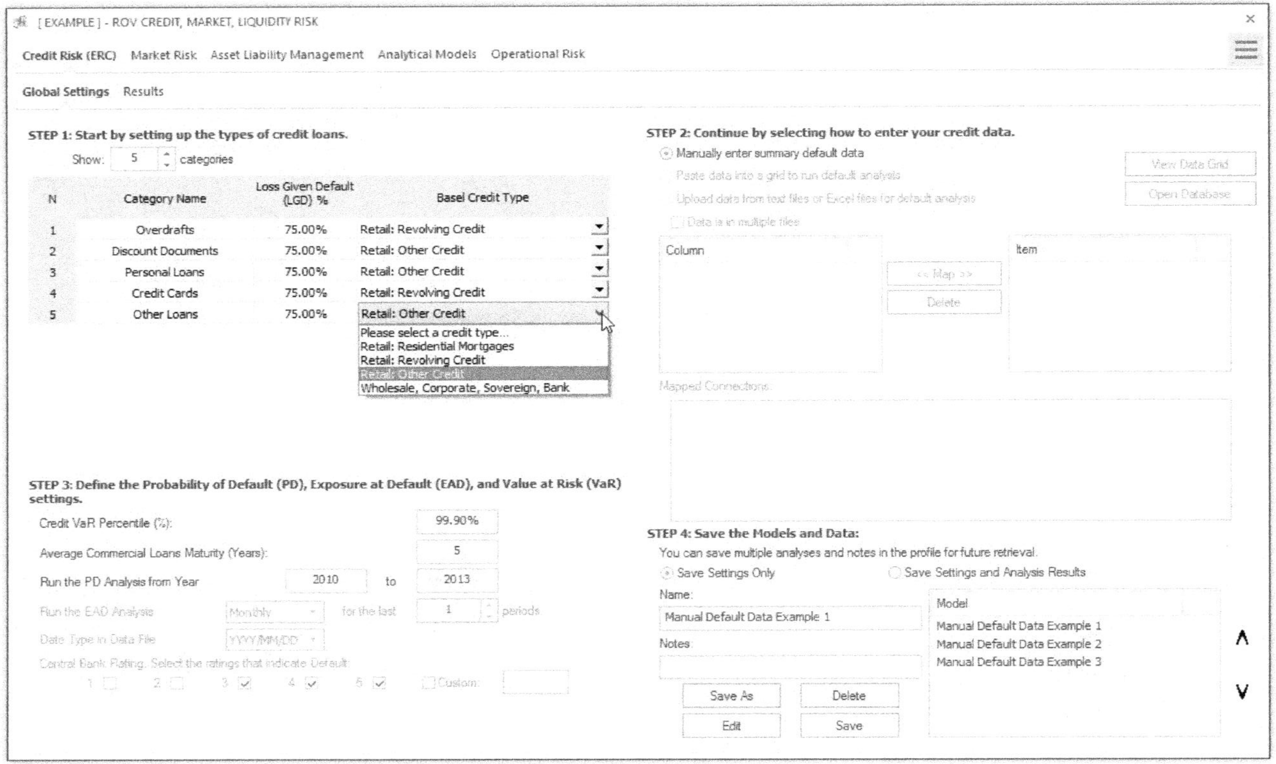

Credit Risk (ERC)   Market Risk   Asset Liability Management   Analytical Models   Operational Risk

Global Settings   Results

STEP 1: Start by setting up the types of credit loans.

Show: 5   categories

N	Category Name	Loss Given Default (LGD) %	Basel Credit Type
1	Overdrafts	75.00%	Retail: Revolving Credit
2	Discount Documents	75.00%	Retail: Other Credit
3	Personal Loans	75.00%	Retail: Other Credit
4	Credit Cards	75.00%	Retail: Revolving Credit
5	Other Loans	75.00%	Retail: Other Credit

Please select a credit type...
Retail: Residential Mortgages
Retail: Revolving Credit
Retail: Other Credit
Wholesale, Corporate, Sovereign, Bank

STEP 3: Define the Probability of Default (PD), Exposure at Default (EAD), and Value at Risk (VaR) settings.

Credit VaR Percentile (%):   99.90%

Average Commercial Loans Maturity (Years):   5

Run the PD Analysis from Year   2010   to   2013   for the last   1   periods

Run the EAD Analysis   Monthly   for the last

Date Type in Data File   YYYY-MM-DD

Central Bank Rating: Select the ratings that indicate Default

1   2   3   4   5   Custom

STEP 2: Continue by selecting how to enter your credit data.

Manually enter summary default data

Paste data into a grid to run default analysis

Upload data from text files or Excel files for default analysis

Data is in multiple files

Column   Item

<< Map >>

Delete

Mapped Connections:

STEP 4: Save the Models and Data:

You can save multiple analyses and notes in the profile for future retrieval.

Save Settings Only   Save Settings and Analysis Results

Name:

Manual Default Data Example 1

Notes

Model
Manual Default Data Example 1
Manual Default Data Example 2
Manual Default Data Example 3

Save As   Delete

Edit   Save

View Data Grid

Open Database

<   >

Figure 1.1: Credit Risk Settings

Figure 1.2 illustrates the PEAT utility's ALM-CMOL module for Credit Risk—Economic Regulatory Capital's Results tab. The results are shown in the grid if data files were loaded and preprocessed, and results were computed and presented here (the loading of data files is discussed in connection with Figure 1.1). However, if data are to be manually entered (as previously presented in Figure 1.1), then the grey areas in the data grid are available for manual user input, such as the number of clients for a specific credit or debt category, the number of defaults for said categories historically by period, and the exposure at default values (total amount of debt issued within the total period). One can manually input the number of clients and of credit and loan defaults within specific annual time-period bands. The utility computes the percentage of defaults (number of credit or loan defaults divided by number of clients within the specified time periods), and the average percentage of default is the proxy used for the PD. If users have specific PD rates to use, they can simply enter any number of clients and number of defaults as long as the ratio is what the user wants as the PD input (e.g., a 1% PD means users can enter 100 clients and 1 as the number of defaults). The LGD can be user inputted in the global settings as a percentage (LGD is defined as the percentage of losses of loans and debt that cannot be recovered when they are in default). The EAD is the total loans amount within these time bands. These PD, LGD, and EAD values can also be computed using structural models as is discussed later. *Expected Losses* (EL) is the product of *PD × LGD × EAD*. *Economic Capital* (EC) is based on Basel III/IV and Basel III/IV requirements and is a matter of public record. *Risk Weighted Average* (RWA) is a regulatory requirement per Basel III/IV and Basel III/IV such as *12.5 × EC*. The change in *Capital Adequacy Requirement* (ΔCAR @ 8%) is simply the ratio of the EC to EAD less the 8% holding requirement. In other words, the *Regulatory Capital* (RC) is 8% of EAD.

The results obtained by the model allow for the construction of key risk indicators, comparing basic regulatory capital requirements with these economic capital requirements. Additionally, when coupled with the internal or external rating models (or credit scores), a profile of expected and unexpected losses for each product or asset type can be constructed. This is also the basis for the application of RAROC indicators, and the effective allocation of economic capital, in line with the international standards and local regulatory requirements.

Credit Risk (ERC) Market Risk Asset Liability Management Analytical Models Operational Risk

Global Settings Results

The following summarizes the defaults analysis based on historical data, probabilities of default (PD), Loss Given Default (LGD), Exposure at Default (EAD), Expected Losses (EL), Economic Capital (EC), Risk Weighted Assets (RWA), and Regulatory Capital per Basel requirements, and modeled based on the relevant Credit types.

N	Overdrafts	Number of Clients	Number of Defaults	Total Default Percent	Probability of Default (PD)	Loss Given Default (LGD)	Exposure at Default (EAD)	Expected Losses (EL)	Economic Capital (EC)	Risk Weighted Assets (RWA)	Delta CAR @ 8%	Regulatory Capital	Basel Credit Type
1	2013	1,077	85	7.89%									
2	2012	1,036	95	9.17%	6.47%	75.00%	8,707,946	422,262	749,977	9,374,711	0.61%	696,636	Retail: Revolving Credit
3	2011	1,045	49	4.69%									
4	2010	973	40	4.11%									

N	Discount Documents	Number of Clients	Number of Defaults	Total Default Percent	Probability of Default (PD)	Loss Given Default (LGD)	Exposure at Default (EAD)	Expected Losses (EL)	Economic Capital (EC)	Risk Weighted Assets (RWA)	Delta CAR @ 8%	Regulatory Capital	Basel Credit Type
1	2013	1,321	10	0.76%									
2	2012	1,131	28	2.48%	1.63%	75.00%	25,561,423	313,162	1,868,606	23,357,578	-0.69%	2,044,914	Retail: Other Credit
3	2011	808	9	1.11%									
4	2010	320	7	2.19%									

N	Personal Loans	Number of Clients	Number of Defaults	Total Default Percent	Probability of Default (PD)	Loss Given Default (LGD)	Exposure at Default (EAD)	Expected Losses (EL)	Economic Capital (EC)	Risk Weighted Assets (RWA)	Delta CAR @ 8%	Regulatory Capital	Basel Credit Type
1	2013	96,296	9,822	10.20%									
2	2012	132,106	11,947	9.04%	6.57%	75.00%	664,979,993	32,742,574	60,786,525	759,831,559	1.14%	53,198,399	Retail: Other Credit
3	2011	131,616	4,708	3.58%									
4	2010	82,119	2,825	3.44%									

N	Credit Cards	Number of Clients	Number of Defaults	Total Default Percent	Probability of Default (PD)	Loss Given Default (LGD)	Exposure at Default (EAD)	Expected Losses (EL)	Economic Capital (EC)	Risk Weighted Assets (RWA)	Delta CAR @ 8%	Regulatory Capital	Basel Credit Type
1	2013	13,480	606	4.50%									
2	2012	10,530	614	5.83%	4.12%	75.00%	47,373,537	1,463,899	3,039,216	37,990,198	-1.58%	3,789,883	Retail: Revolving Credit
3	2011	7,680	267	3.48%									
4	2010	3,548	95	2.68%									

N	Other Loans	Number of Clients	Number of Defaults	Total Default Percent	Probability of Default (PD)	Loss Given Default (LGD)	Exposure at Default (EAD)	Expected Losses (EL)	Economic Capital (EC)	Risk Weighted Assets (RWA)	Delta CAR @ 8%	Regulatory Capital	Basel Credit Type
1	2013	2,787	300	10.76%	6.82%	75.00%	1,131,057	57,875	104,004	1,300,046	1.20%	90,485	Retail: Other

Update

Figure 1.2: Economic Regulatory Capital (ERC)

Basel Credit Risk Models and Economic Capital

The CMOL software applies Basel III/IV and Basel III/IV requirements and definitions on regulatory capital. For instance, the Economic Capital is defined as Value at Risk (i.e., the Total Risk Amount) less any Expected Losses. There are 4 categories of equations based on the type of credit and loans: 3 types of Retail Loans plus a category for Corporate Loans.

Retail Loans: Residential Mortgage Exposures

$$Correlation\ (R) = 0.15$$

$Capital\ Requirement\ (K)$

$$= \left[LGD \times \Phi \left(\frac{\phi^{-1}(PD) + \sqrt{R}\phi^{-1}(99.9\%)}{\sqrt{1-R}} \right) - LGD \times PD \right]$$

$Economic\ Capital\ (EC) = EAD \times K$
$$= EAD$$
$$\times \left[LGD \times \Phi \left(\frac{\phi^{-1}(PD) + \sqrt{R}\phi^{-1}(99.9\%)}{\sqrt{1-R}} \right) - LGD \times PD \right]$$

Retail Loans: Qualifying Revolving Retail Exposures

$$Correlation\ (R) = 0.04$$

$Capital\ Requirement\ (K)$

$$= \left[LGD \times \Phi \left(\frac{\phi^{-1}(PD) + \sqrt{R}\phi^{-1}(99.9\%)}{\sqrt{1-R}} \right) - LGD \times PD \right]$$

$Economic\ Capital\ (EC) = EAD \times K$
$$= EAD$$
$$\times \left[LGD \times \Phi \left(\frac{\phi^{-1}(PD) + \sqrt{R}\phi^{-1}(99.9\%)}{\sqrt{1-R}} \right) - LGD \times PD \right]$$

$$Risk\ Weighted\ Assets\ (RWA) = 12.5 \times EC = 12.5 \times EAD \times K$$

Retail Loans: Other Retail Exposures

$$Correlation\ (R) = \frac{0.03 \times (1 - e^{-35 \times PD})}{(1 - e^{-35})} + 0.16 \times \left[1 - \frac{(1 - e^{-35 \times PD})}{(1 - e^{-35})} \right]$$

$Capital\ Requirement\ (K)$

$$= \left[LGD \times \Phi\left(\frac{\phi^{-1}(PD) + \sqrt{R}\phi^{-1}(99.9\%)}{\sqrt{1-R}} \right) - LGD \times PD \right]$$

$Economic\ Capital\ (EC) = EAD \times K$

$$= EAD$$
$$\times \left[LGD \times \Phi\left(\frac{\phi^{-1}(PD) + \sqrt{R}\phi^{-1}(99.9\%)}{\sqrt{1-R}} \right) - LGD \times PD \right]$$

$Risk\ Weighted\ Assets\ (RWA) = 12.5 \times EC = 12.5 \times EAD \times K$

Corporate Loans: Corporate, Sovereign, Bank, and Corporate Loans

$$Correlation\ (R) = \frac{0.12 \times (1 - e^{-50 \times PD})}{(1 - e^{-50})} + 0.24 \times \left[1 - \frac{(1 - e^{-50 \times PD})}{(1 - e^{-50})} \right]$$

$Maturity\ Adjustment\ (B) = [0.11852 - 0.05478 \times \ln(PD)]^2$

$Capital\ Requirement\ (K)$

$$= \left[LGD \times \Phi\left(\frac{\phi^{-1}(PD) + \sqrt{R}\phi^{-1}(99.9\%)}{\sqrt{1-R}} \right) - LGD \times PD \right] \times \left[\frac{1 + (M - 2.5) \times b}{1 - 1.5 \times b} \right]$$

$Economic\ Capital\ (EC) = EAD \times K$

$Economic\ Capital\ (EC)$
$$= EAD$$
$$\times \left[LGD \times \Phi\left(\frac{\phi^{-1}(PD) + \sqrt{R}\phi^{-1}(99.9\%)}{\sqrt{1-R}} \right) - LGD \times PD \right] \times \left[\frac{1 + (M - 2.5) \times B}{1 - 1.5 \times B} \right]$$

$Risk\ Weighted\ Assets\ (RWA) = 12.5 \times EC = 12.5 \times EAD \times K$

$Risk\ Weighted\ Assets\ (RWA) = 12.5 \times EC = 12.5 \times EAD \times K$

$The\ Phi\ function\ \Phi\ is\ the\ CDF\ of\ Normal\ (0,1),$

$and\ \phi^{-1}\ is\ the\ ICDF\ of\ Normal\ (0,1)$

For market risk, as a Pillar I risk, the requirements are similar to those for economic regulatory capital. The particularities of market risk make it, possibly, the one that is easier to model and calculate, and the one that has had more tool development so far. This is explained by the fact that the main input for market risk measurement and modeling is market prices of assets or, more practically, their volatilities. Therefore, there is great public availability of data, as opposed to the other Pillar I risks that do not have daily prices publicly available. As an example, there is no public pricing of a particular group of retail loans issued by a private bank. Yet, modeling tools for both market and credit risk are based on the same approach: utilizing past stylized data to project future behavior under certain assumptions and within a confidence interval. Logically then, market risk has a great bundle of information available and the potential to better test and calibrate models. As presented, market risk models take on a Value at Risk (VAR) approach.

Figure 1.3 illustrates the PEAT utility's ALM-CMOL module for Market Risk where Market Data is entered. Users start by entering the global settings, such as the number of investment assets and currency assets the bank has in its portfolio, that require further analysis; the total number of historical data that will be used for analysis; and various VaR percentiles to run (e.g., 99.00% and 95.00%). In addition, the volatility method of choice (industry standard volatility or Risk Metrics volatility methods) and the date type (mm/dd/yyyy or dd/mm/yyyy) are entered. The amount invested (balance) of each asset and currency is entered and the historical data can be entered, copied and pasted from another data source, or uploaded to the data grid, and the settings as well as the historical data entered can be saved for future retrieval and further analysis in subsequent subtabs.

Credit Risk (ERC) **Market Risk** Asset Liability Management Analytical Models Operational Risk

Market Data Value at Risk Central Bank VaR Result Visuals

Number of Investment Assets:	9
Number of Currency Assets:	2
Number of Rows of Historical Data:	500
Value at Risk VaR Percentile:	99.00%
Value at Risk VaR Percentile:	95.00%

Name: Market Risk Example Model 1
Notes:
Volatility Methodology: Standard Volatility
Date Type: DD/MM/YYYY

New · Save As · Edit · Save · Delete

Saved Dataset
Market Risk Example Model 1
Market Risk Example Model 2

Investment	16,930,566	5,000,000	49,930,731	2,015,397	0	0	0	0	0	421,000	719,080
Dates	Asset 1	Asset 2	Asset 3	Asset 4	Asset 5	Asset 6	Asset 7	Asset 8	Asset 9	Dollar	Euro
19/07/2013	134.92	106.68	77.59		545.00					5.45930	7.17543
22/07/2013	134.67	106.26	77.96		550.00					5.46230	7.20415
23/07/2013	134.03	106.00	78.45		550.00					5.46170	7.22022
24/07/2013	134.41	106.26	79.06		550.00					5.46380	7.20428
25/07/2013	134.90	106.26	79.06		550.00					5.47100	7.25881
26/07/2013	135.13	107.51	78.81		550.00					5.48070	7.28206
29/07/2013	135.18	107.51	79.30		552.00					5.49080	7.28527
30/07/2013	135.13	107.09	79.30		552.00					5.49930	7.29103
31/07/2013	134.03	106.68	78.08		553.50					5.50650	7.32991
01/08/2013	133.72	107.51	78.14		553.50					5.50820	7.28554
02/08/2013	133.72	107.51	79.30		553.50					5.51730	7.32833
05/08/2013	131.83	107.51	76.57		553.50					5.52020	7.32195
06/08/2013	131.70	107.51	76.45		553.50					5.52750	7.35666
07/08/2013	132.08	106.68	75.98		553.50			558.50		5.52850	7.37757
08/08/2013	132.59	106.68	75.86		553.50			558.50		5.53770	7.41584
09/08/2013	132.59	107.51	75.75		553.50			559.50		5.54280	7.39691
12/08/2013	132.46	106.68	75.86		553.50			565.00		5.54930	7.38694
13/08/2013	133.10	107.50	76.45		553.50			565.00		5.56030	7.37410
14/08/2013	133.22	107.50	75.98		562.00			575.00		5.56820	7.37927
15/08/2013	133.98	107.93	76.57		565.00			585.00		5.57480	7.44294

Figure 1.3: Market Risk Data

Figure 1.4 illustrates the computed results for the Market VaR. Based on the data entered in the interface shown as Figure 1.3, the results are computed and presented in two separate grids: the VaR results and asset positions and details. The computations can be triggered to be rerun or Updated, and the results can be exported to an Excel report template if required. The results computed in the first grid are based on user input market data.

For instance, the VaR calculations are simply the *Asset Position × Daily Volatility × Inverse Standard Normal Distribution of VaR Percentile × Square Root of the Horizon in Days.*

In other words, we have:

$$VaR\ X\% = Asset \times Daily\ Volatility \times \sqrt{Days}$$
$$\times Inverse\ Standard\ Normal\ of\ X\%$$

$$VaR_{X\%} = A\sigma\sqrt{D}\Phi^{-1}(x)$$

Therefore, the Gross VaR is simply the summation of all VaR values for all assets and foreign exchange–denominated assets. In comparison, the Internal Historical Simulation VaR uses the same calculation based on the historically simulated time-series of asset values. The historically simulated time-series of asset values is obtained by the *Asset's Investment × Asset Price$_{t-1}$ × Period-Specific Relative Returns − Asset's Current Position.* The Asset's Current Position is simply the *Investment × Asset Price$_t$.* From this simulated time series of asset flows, the $(1 - X\%)$ percentile asset value is the *VaR X%.* Typically, $X\%$ is 99.00% or 95.00% and can be changed as required by the user based on the regional or country-specific regulatory agency's statutes.

This can be stated as:

$$Historical\ Simulation\ (HSS)\ VaR\ X\%$$
$$= (1 - X\%)\ Percentile\ of\ Historically\ Simulated\ Series\ (HSS)$$

$$HSS = Investment \times Price_{t-1} \times Exp(LNRR) - Investment \times Price_t$$

Gross Value at Risk (VaR)

Horizon	VaR 99.00%	VaR 95.00%
1 Day	2,679,921	1,894,849
5 Day	5,992,486	4,237,012
10 Day	8,474,655	5,992,040

	Internal Historical Simulation Value at Risk (VaR) 99.00%			Internal Historical Simulation Value at Risk (VaR) 95.00%		
Horizon	Total Values	Bonds Only	Currency Only	Total Values	Bonds Only	Currency Only
1 Day	1,784,836	1,817,804	55,871	1,352,838	1,348,769	38,157
5 Day	3,991,015	4,064,733	124,932	3,025,037	3,015,939	85,323
10 Day	5,644,147	5,748,400	176,681	4,278,049	4,265,182	120,665

Update

Asset Positions and Details

Asset	Daily Volatility	Current Position	Current Weight	99.00% VaR 1 Day	99.00% VaR 5 Day	99.00% VaR 10 Day	95.00% VaR 1 Day	95.00% VaR 5 Day	95.00% VaR 10 Day
Asset 1	1.06%	26,073,072	30.65%	643,403	1,438,693	2,034,620	454,921	1,017,234	1,438,586
Asset 2	2.61%	3,187,500	3.75%	193,273	432,173	611,184	136,655	305,569	432,140
Asset 3	1.50%	28,710,170	33.75%	999,427	2,234,787	3,160,466	706,649	1,580,115	2,234,620
Asset 4	1.78%	15,720,097	18.48%	652,132	1,458,212	2,062,223	461,093	1,031,035	1,458,103
Asset 5	1.26%	0	0.00%	0	0	0	0	0	0
Asset 6	1.29%	0	0.00%	0	0	0	0	0	0
Asset 7	1.03%	0	0.00%	0	0	0	0	0	0
Asset 8	1.15%	0	0.00%	0	0	0	0	0	0
Asset 9	1.39%	0	0.00%	0	0	0	0	0	0
Dollar	0.68%	3,456,494	4.06%	54,809	122,557	173,322	38,753	86,654	122,548
Euro	0.74%	7,908,463	9.30%	136,876	306,065	432,841	96,779	216,404	306,042

Figure 1.4: Market Value at Risk

Many countries issue regulations for market risk measurement and capital allocation, whereby some standardized models are suggested or even imposed in line with the Basel Standards. We analyze such an example in Figure 1.5, where the regulatory model can be obtained by utilizing the parameters given by the regulator (i.e., volatilities and holding periods for given common assets). The structure of the tool allows for the comparison of regulatory, internal, and stressed scenarios, giving the analysts a large array of results to better interpret risk measurement, capital allocation, and future projections.

Central Bank Market Risk

Figure 1.5 illustrates the Central Bank VaR method and results in computing VaR based on user settings (e.g., the VaR percentile, time horizon of the holding period in days, number of assets to analyze, and the period of the analysis) and the assets' historical data. The VaR computations are based on the same approach as previously described, and the inputs, settings, and results can be saved for future retrieval.

Credit Risk (ERC) **Market Risk** Asset Liability Management Operational Risk

Market Data Value at Risk **Central Bank VaR** Result Visuals

Value at Risk (VaR) %: 99.00%

Time Horizon (Days): 5

Number of Assets: 20

Analysis is for Month/Year:

Name of Dataset: Sample of Central Bank VaR

List of Saved Datasets: Save As

Dataset
Sample of Central Bank VaR

New | Delete

Edit | Save

Asset Type Volatility	T02405 1.0000%	Asset Type Volatility	SX2405 1.0500%	Asset Type Volatility	MU2405 1.1100%	Asset Type Volatility	Asset Type Volatility	Asset Type Volatility	Asset T Volatil
Day	NPV of Position	Value at Risk	NPV of Position	Value at Risk	NPV of Position	Value at Risk	NPV of Position	Value at Risk	Value at
1	11,042.50	575.32	11,000.00	601.76	10,985.00	635.28			
2	11,444.82	596.28	11,115.00	608.05	11,458.00	662.63			
3	11,534.80	600.97	11,534.80	631.02	11,534.80	667.07			
4	11,596.80	604.20	11,596.80	634.41	11,625.00	672.29			
5	11,596.80	604.20	11,596.80	634.41	11,596.80	670.66			
6	11,596.80	604.20	11,596.80	634.41	11,596.80	670.66			
7	11,651.16	607.03	11,651.16	637.38	11,651.16	673.80			
8	11,698.25	609.48	11,698.25	639.96	11,698.25	676.53			
9	11,698.25	609.48	11,698.25	639.96	11,698.25	676.53			
10	16,541.80	861.83	16,541.80	904.93	16,541.80	956.64			
11	17,290.98	900.87	17,290.98	945.91	17,290.98	999.96			
12	17,290.98	900.87	17,290.98	945.91	17,290.98	999.96			
13	17,290.98	900.87	17,290.98	945.91	17,290.98	999.96			
14	17,346.15	903.74	17,346.15	948.93	17,346.15	1,003.15			
15	24,343.58	1,268.31	24,343.58	1,331.73	24,343.58	1,407.82			
16	24,457.51	1,274.25	24,457.51	1,337.96	24,457.51	1,414.41			
17	22,445.01	1,169.39	22,445.01	1,227.86	22,445.01	1,298.03			
18	22,549.57	1,174.84	22,549.57	1,233.58	22,549.57	1,304.07			
19	22,549.57	1,174.84	22,549.57	1,233.58	22,549.57	1,304.07			
20	22,549.57	1,174.84	22,549.57	1,233.58	22,549.57	1,304.07			
21	23,984.37	1,249.59	23,984.37	1,312.07	23,984.37	1,387.05			
22	23,610.71	1,230.13	23,610.71	1,291.63	23,610.71	1,365.44			
23	23,798.73	1,239.92	23,798.73	1,301.92	23,798.73	1,376.31			
24	22,359.26	1,164.93	22,359.26	1,223.17	22,359.26	1,293.07			
25	18,958.36	987.74	18,958.36	1,037.12	18,958.36	1,096.39			

Figure 1.5: Market Central Bank VaR

As with any other Basel-defined risk, key risk indicators or KRIs are constructed based on the inputs and results of the modeling tool and can be duly monitored and reported in line with the IMMM process. Liquidity and interest-rate risk are usually managed together in a function called ALM, short for Asset Liability Management. These two risks are closely intertwined, since liquidity risk monitors the availability of liquid funds to confront disbursement requirements (usually in three time-horizons: immediate and intraday, short-term structure, and long-term structure), while interest-rate risk measures the impact of the difference in maturities, or duration, for assets and liabilities.

Figure 1.6 illustrates the PEAT utility's ALM-CMOL module for Asset Liability Management—Interest Rate Risk's Input Assumptions and general Settings tab. This segment represents the analysis of Asset Liability Management (ALM) computations. ALM is the practice of managing risks that arise due to mismatches between the maturities of assets and liabilities. It is about offering solutions to mitigate or hedge the risks arising from the interaction of assets and liabilities as well as the success in the process of maximizing assets to meet complex liabilities such that it will help increase profitability. The current tab starts by obtaining, as general inputs, the bank's regulatory capital obtained earlier from the credit risk models. In addition, the number of trading days in the calendar year of the analysis (e.g., typically between 250 and 253 days), the local currency's name (e.g., U.S. Dollar or Argentinian Peso), the current period when the analysis is performed and results reported to the regulatory agencies (e.g., January 2015), the number of VaR percentiles to run (e.g., 99.00%), number of scenarios to run and their respective basis point sensitivities (e.g., 100, 200, and 300 basis points, where every 100 basis points represent 1%), and number of foreign currencies in the bank's investment portfolio. As usual, the inputs, settings, and results can be saved for future retrieval. Figure 1.6 further illustrates the PEAT utility's ALM-CMOL module for Asset Liability Management. The tab is specifically for Interest Rate Sensitive Assets and Liabilities data where historical impacts of interest-rate sensitive assets and liabilities, as well as foreign currency–denominated assets and liabilities are entered, copied and pasted, or uploaded from a database. Historical Interest Rate data is uploaded where the rows of periodic historical interest rates of local and foreign currencies can be entered, copied and pasted, or uploaded from a database.

Credit Risk (ERC)   Market Risk   **Asset Liability Management**   Analytical Models   Operational Risk

Interest Rate Risk   Liquidity Risk

Input Assumptions   Gap Analysis   Economic Value of Equity   Net Income Margin

Settings   **Rate Sensitive Assets & Liabilities**   Historical Interest Rates

[Save]

| Time Band | Rate Sensitive Assets & Liabilities | | | |
| | Local Currency | | Foreign Currency 1 | |
	Asset	Liability	Asset	Liability
0	672,157	736,460	360,665	103,854
1	2,468,060	3,142,712	208,843	223,552
2	611,161	601,916	29,513	42,305
3	677,616	168,190	87,424	52,730
4	488,852	74,292	15,585	8,214
5	555,834	121,338	5,258	3,992
6	538,237	77,486	63,228	3,432
7	52,359	176,112	137	97
8	51,593	60,885	2,244	46
9	47,234	47,234	137	85
10	46,616	46,616	137	548
11	42,565	92,751	1,369	1,188
12	52,667	57,777	0	364
13	38,356	38,356	236	78
14	39,077	39,077	0	0
15	35,870	35,870	0	0
16	33,503	33,503	0	0
17	31,235	31,235	0	0
18	28,833	28,833	0	0
19	27,524	27,524	0	0

Figure 1.6: Asset Liability Management—Interest Rate Risk (Asset and Liability Data)

ALM: Net Interest Margin and Economic Value of Equity

The most straightforward way to present ALM structures for liquidity and interest-rate risk management is through the utilization of Gap charts. A Gap chart is simply the listing of all assets and liabilities as affected by interest rate movements or liquidity movements, respectively, ordered on time-defined buckets (i.e., days, weeks, months, or years). Typically, for interest-rate risk there are two main management approaches: a shorter-term structure analysis based on a more accounting-side perspective, usually referred to as the NIM (Net Interest Margin) approach, and a longer-term structure analysis based on a more economic-side perspective, usually referred to as the EVE (Economic Value of Equity) approach. The NIM approach rests on the logic that the natural mismatch between assets and liabilities has an impact on earnings, through the net interest margin, and such impact can be measured through given deltas (variations) in the referential market interest rate. In this case, the impact is measured through the Gap chart, as applied to balance sheet items of the asset and liability sides, respectively. So, on the one hand, a natural NIM approach would deliver a balance sheet impact on earnings, based on the structure and maturity of assets and liabilities, when subjected to a 100-basis point increase in the referential market interest-rate risk. Because the Gap analysis defines which side of the balance sheet (assets or liabilities) the cash flow is on, as well as accounting for each time bucket, analysts can define which sign would apply to earnings should interest rates go up or down. Therefore, the combination of these two tools allows for the establishment of different business and stress scenarios and, hence, the determination of targets and limits on the structure and duration of assets and liabilities. The EVE approach, on the other hand, is a long-term evaluation tool, by which analysts can determine the impact on capital (or equity, defined as assets minus liabilities) of referential market interest-rate valuations, as it affects the net present value and duration of the described balance sheet items. By this approach, the system can calculate the deltas in durations and in net present value of assets, liabilities, and equity, as measured in the Gap charts. Therefore, such variations allow for the construction of scenarios for the different impacts on equity value and duration of changes in the referential market interest rate. These results are then fed into different KRIs for monitoring, defining, and calibrating targets and limits in line with the IMMM risk management structure.

Figure 1.7 illustrates the Gap Analysis results of Interest Rate Risk. The results are shown in different grids for each local and foreign currency. Gap Analysis is, of course, one of the most common ways of measuring liquidity position and represents the foundation for scenario analysis and stress testing, which will be executed in subsequent tabs. The Gap Analysis results are from user inputs in the input assumptions tab. The results are presented for the user again for validation and in a more user-friendly tabular format. The Economic Value of Equity results are based on interest-rate risk computations in previous tabs. The impacts on regulatory capital as denoted by VaR levels on local and foreign currencies are computed, as are the duration gaps and basis point scenarios affecting the cash flows of local and foreign currencies.

Figure 1.8 illustrates the *Net Income Margin* (NIM) Input Assumptions requirements based on interest-rate risk analysis. The highlighted cells in the data grid represent user input requirements for computing the NIM model. The Economic Value of Equity and Gap Analysis calculations previously described are for longer-term interest-rate risk analysis, whereas the NIM approach is for shorter-term (typically 12 months) analysis of liquidity and interest-rate risk effects on assets and liabilities. In the gap analysis and stress testing analysis, we proceed using:

$$Cash\ Flows\ on\ Basis\ Points\ BP$$
$$= -Modified\ Duration \times Asset \times \Delta BP\ in\ \%$$

$$Modified\ Duration = Duration\ Gap \div (1 + Interest\ Rate)$$

$$Duration\ Gap = \sum \frac{PVCF_A}{V_A} \times \frac{Monthly\ Time\ Band}{12}$$
$$- Liability\ Duration \times \frac{NPV_L}{NPV_A}$$

$$Duration\ Gap = Asset\ Duration - Liability\ Duration \times \frac{NPV_L}{NPV_A}$$

$$Duration = \sum_{i=1}^{n} \frac{PVCF_t}{V}\ time$$

$$Modified\ Duration = \frac{Macaulay\ Duration}{\left(1 + \frac{YTM}{\#\ Coupons}\right)}$$

$$Convexity = \frac{d^2p}{di^2} = \frac{\sum_{i=1}^{n} \frac{CF}{(1+i)^t}(t^2 + t)}{(1+i)^2}$$

Credit Risk (ERC)   Market Risk   Asset Liability Management   Analytical Models   Operational Risk

Interest Rate Risk   Liquidity Risk

Input Assumptions   Gap Analysis   Economic Value of Equity   Net Income Margin

Analysis is for the following Month and Year   Jan 2014

Peso	0	1	2	3	4	5	6	7	8	9	10	11
Rate-Sensitive Assets Cash Flows	672,157	2,468,060	611,161	677,616	488,852	555,834	538,237	52,359	51,593	47,234	46,616	42,565
Rate-Sensitive Liabilities Cash Flows	736,460	3,142,712	601,916	168,190	74,292	121,338	77,486	176,112	60,885	47,234	46,616	92,751
Local Currency Gap	-64,303	-674,652	9,245	509,426	414,560	434,496	460,751	-123,753	-9,292	0	0	-50,186
Local Currency Cumulative Gap	-64,303	-738,955	-729,710	-220,284	194,276	628,772	1,089,523	965,770	956,478	956,478	956,478	906,292
Dollar	**0**	**1**	**2**	**3**	**4**	**5**	**6**	**7**	**8**	**9**	**10**	**11**
Rate-Sensitive Assets Cash Flows	360,665	208,843	29,513	87,424	15,585	5,258	63,228	137	2,244	137	137	1,369
Rate-Sensitive Liabilities Cash Flows	103,854	223,552	42,305	52,730	8,214	3,992	3,432	97	46	85	548	1,188
Foreign Currency Gap	256,811	-14,709	-12,792	34,694	7,371	1,266	59,796	40	2,198	52	-411	181
Foreign Currency Cumulative Gap	256,811	242,102	229,310	264,004	271,375	272,641	332,437	332,477	334,675	334,727	334,316	334,497

Figure 1.7: Asset Liability Management—Interest-Rate Risk: Gap Analysis

Credit Risk (ERC) | Market Risk | Asset Liability Management | Analytical Models | Operational Risk

Interest Rate Risk | Liquidity Risk

Input Assumptions | Gap Analysis | Economic Value of Equity | Net Income Margin

Input Assumptions | NIM Results

Local Currency: Show [4] rows of Assets & Liabilities   Foreign Currency (N): Show [4] rows of Assets & Liabilities   Save

Cumulative Cash Flows	Balances	Month 1	Month 2	Month 3	Month 4	Month 5	Month 6	Month 7	Month 8	Month 9	Month 10	Month 11	Month 12	Ending
Interest Income	439,484	541,610	646,274	745,366	839,577	947,322	1,091,682	354,164	431,222	565,146	705,202	872,482	1,015,506	
Financial Expenses	207,291	-243,494	-280,280	-320,207	-340,418	-403,067	455,442	-71,249	-125,699	-197,976	-275,424	-361,920	-448,480	
Net Income	646,775	298,116	365,994	425,159	499,159	1,350,389	1,547,124	282,915	305,523	367,170	429,778	510,562	567,026	
Marginal Cash Flows														
Interest Income	576,022	102,126	104,664	99,092	94,211	107,745	144,360	-737,518	77,058	133,924	140,056	167,280	143,024	
Financial Expenses	-655,771	-450,785	-36,786	-39,927	-20,211	743,485	52,375	-526,691	-54,450	-72,277	-77,448	-86,496	-86,560	
Net Income		-348,659	67,878	59,165	74,000	851,230	196,735	-1,264,209	22,608	61,647	62,608	80,784	56,464	
Net Income Cumulative		-348,659	-280,781	-221,616	-147,616	703,614	900,349	-363,860	-341,252	-279,605	-216,997	-136,213	-79,749	

Peso

Days	30	60	90	120	150	180	210	240	270	300	330	360	
Non-Rate Sensitive Assets	0												
Fixed Rate Assets	5,667,785	2,405,555	440,709	610,453	697,001	589,225	71,235	57,268	49,416	48,946	54,832	55,046	40,584	547,515
Floating Rate Assets (External Indicators)	0												
Floating Rate Assets (Internal Indicators)	0												
Total Assets	5,667,785	2,405,555	440,709	610,453	697,001	589,225	71,235	57,268	49,416	48,946	54,832	55,046	40,584	547,515
Non-Rate Sensitive Liabilities	0												
Fixed Rate Liabilities	4,650,775	3,041,587	385,048	130,104	147,099	58,592	217,110	60,916	4,752	6,305	94,684	60,044	47,534	397,000
Floating Rate Liabilities (External Indicators)	0												
Floating Rate Liabilities (Internal Indicators)	0												
Total Liabilities	4,650,775	3,041,587	385,048	130,104	147,099	58,592	217,110	60,916	4,752	6,305	94,684	60,044	47,534	397,000
Total Contingent Credit Lines													

Dollar

Non-Rate Sensitive Assets	0												

Figure 1.8: Net Income Margin (NIM): Input Assumptions and Model

In NIM calculations, we use:

$$Gap = Asset - Liability + Contingency\ Cash$$

$$\Delta NIM = Change\ in\ Net\ Interest\ Margin$$
$$= Monthly\ Gap \times \Delta\ Basis\ Points$$
$$\times\ \%\ Days\ Left\ to\ Maturity \div 10000$$

$$Total\ NIM = \Sigma\Delta NIM$$

$$Financial\ Margin = Total\ NIM \div Net\ Income$$

Figure 1.9 illustrates the PEAT utility's ALM-CMOL module for Asset Liability Management—Liquidity Risk Input Assumptions tab on the historical monthly balances of interest-rate sensitive assets and liabilities. The typical time horizon is monthly for one year (12 months) where the various assets such as liquid assets (e.g., cash), bonds, and loans are listed, as well as other asset receivables. On the liabilities side, regular short-term deposits and timed deposits are listed, separated by private versus public sectors, as well as other payable liabilities (e.g., interest payments and operations). Adjustments can also be made to account for rounding issues and accounting issues that may affect the asset and liability levels (e.g., contingency cash levels, overnight deposits, etc.). The data grid can be set up with some basic inputs as well as the number of subsegments or rows for each category. As usual, the inputs, settings, and results can be saved for future retrieval.

ROV CREDIT, MARKET, LIQUIDITY RISK - [C:\Users\Dr. Johnathan Mun\Desktop\ROV Credit Market and Liquidity Example.rovxml]

Credit Risk (ERC) Market Risk **Asset Liability Management** Analytical Models Operational Risk

Interest Rate Risk **Liquidity Risk**

Input Assumptions Scenario Analysis Stress Testing Gap Analysis Charts

ASSETS	Balances	Month 1	Month 2	Month 3	Month 4	Month 5	Month 6	Month 7	Month 8	Month 9	Month 10	Month 11	Month 12
Month													
LIQUIDITY	20,292	15,494	0	0	0	0	0	0	0	0	0	0	0
Available	9,839	9,839											
Regulatory	-3,654												
Technical	-1,144												
Notes	1,634	1,634											
Lebac and Nobac	8,968	8,968											
Net Calls	-149	-149											
BONDS	0	204	256	231	304	314	309	306	295	264	247	235	228
Bond Type 1		204	256	231	304	314	309	306	295	264	247	235	228
LOANS	41,294	-764	-1,291	-1,247	-1,332	-1,295	-1,118	-1,720	-1,710	-1,728	-1,724	-1,723	-1,620

LIABILITIES	Balances	Month 1	Month 2	Month 3	Month 4	Month 5	Month 6	Month 7	Month 8	Month 9	Month 10	Month 11	Month 12
Month													
REGULAR DEPOSITS	39,123	-320	491	-764	606	893	469	3,514	-33	492	1,315	1,604	2,690
Public Sector	12,812	110	537	-832	118	494	-1,361	3,559	-121	243	502	889	1,160
Private Sector	26,311	-430	-46	68	488	399	1,830	-45	88	249	813	715	1,530
TIME DEPOSITS	36,182	1,612	1,085	644	394	694	275	1,616	1,261	1,105	1,180	1,141	898
Public Sector	8,911	397	111	57	65	-9	-1	379	222	-2	397	411	324
Private Sector	27,271	1,215	974	587	329	703	276	1,237	1,039	1,107	783	730	574
Interests		34											
Operations		12											
TOTAL LIABILITY CASH FLOWS		1,338	1,576	-120	1,000	1,587	744	5,130	1,228	1,597	2,495	2,745	3,588
Adjustments in Assets & Liabilities		-126	-187	-61	-105	-160	-86	-41	-66	57	72	-105	76
Contingency Cash		-3	-3	-3	-3	-3	-3	0	0	0	0	0	0
Deposits	62,452	76,543	69,339	69,821	69,245	71,166	75,004	74,967	76,543	76,423	77,423	79,011	

Analysis is for Month/Year: Jan 2014
Starting Month/Year: 01/2014
Management Limit: 11.75
Contingency Limit: 10.25
Liquidity Sub-items: 6
Bonds Sub-items: 2
Loans Sub-items: 12
Name of Dataset: Sample Dataset

Save As

List of Saved Datasets:
Dataset
Sample Dataset

New | Delete
Edit | Save

Figure 1.9: Asset Liability Management—Liquidity Risk Model and Assumptions

The Liquidity Risk's Scenario Analysis and Stress Testing settings can be set up to test interest-rate sensitive assets and liabilities. The scenarios to test can be entered as data or percentage changes. Multiple scenarios can be saved for future retrieval and analysis in subsequent tabs as each saved model constitutes a stand-alone scenario to test. Scenario analysis typically tests both fluctuations in assets and liabilities and their impacts on the portfolio's ALM balance, whereas stress testing typically tests the fluctuations on liabilities (e.g., runs on banks, economic downturns where deposits are stressed to the lower limit) where the stressed limits can be entered as values or percentage change from the base case. Multiple stress tests can be saved for future retrieval and analysis in subsequent tabs as each saved model constitutes a stand-alone stress test.

Figure 1.10 illustrates the Liquidity Risk's Gap Analysis results. The data grid shows the results based on all the previously saved scenarios and stress test conditions. The *Gap* is, of course, calculated as the *difference between Monthly Assets and Liabilities, accounting for any Contingency Credit Lines*. The gaps for the multitude of Scenarios and Stress Tests are reruns of the same calculation based on various user inputs on values or percentage changes as described previously in the Scenario Analysis and Stress Testing sections.

ROV CREDIT, MARKET, LIQUIDITY RISK - [C:\Users\Dr. Johnathan Mun\Desktop\ROV Credit Market and Liquidity Example.rovcml]   × ≡

Credit Risk (ERC)   Market Risk   **Asset Liability Management**   Analytical Models   Operational Risk

Interest Rate Risk   **Liquidity Risk**

Input Assumptions   Scenario Analysis   Stress Testing   **Gap Analysis**   Charts

Analysis is for the following Month and Year

GAP ANALYSIS RESULTS	Month 1	Month 2	Month 3	Month 4	Month 5	Month 6	Month 7	Month 8	Month 9	Month 10	Month 11	Month 12
Individual Gap Analysis												
Current Effective Gap	15,785	199	-1,347	-288	442	-538	3,458	-487	-19	858	934	1,952
Scenario 1	22,520	-1,295	881	-185	-1,890	3,067	-317	5,796	657	-2,833	1,879	4,549
Scenario 2	22,520	-1,294	880	-184	-1,891	3,067	-319	5,797	656	-2,832	1,878	4,549
Stress Test 1	574	-6,073	-4,554	-2,266	-1,673	-2,522	-2,215	-2,207	-2,097	-2,107	-2,271	-2,086
Cumulative Gap Analysis												
Current Effective Gap	15,782	15,978	14,628	14,337	14,776	14,235	17,693	17,206	17,187	18,045	18,979	20,931
Scenario 1	22,517	21,219	22,097	21,909	20,016	23,080	22,763	28,558	29,215	26,382	28,261	32,810
Scenario 2	22,517	21,220	22,097	21,910	20,016	23,080	22,761	28,558	29,214	26,382	28,260	32,809
Stress Test 1	571	-5,505	-10,062	-12,332	-14,008	-16,533	-18,749	-20,955	-23,052	-25,159	-27,430	-29,516
Liquidity Indicators Analysis												
Current Effective Gap	25.28	20.88	21.11	20.55	21.36	20.03	23.61	22.98	22.48	23.64	24.54	26.51
Scenario 1	36.06	27.73	31.88	31.40	28.93	32.46	30.37	38.12	38.19	34.54	36.52	41.55
Scenario 2	36.06	27.73	31.88	31.40	28.93	32.46	30.37	38.12	38.19	34.54	36.52	41.55
Stress Test 1	0.92	-7.18	-14.50	-17.64	-20.21	-23.21	-24.97	-27.93	-30.09	-32.90	-35.41	-37.33
Management Limit	11.75	11.75	11.75	11.75	11.75	11.75	11.75	11.75	11.75	11.75	11.75	11.75
Contingency Limit	10.25	10.25	10.25	10.25	10.25	10.25	10.25	10.25	10.25	10.25	10.25	10.25

Figure 1.10: Asset Liability Management—Liquidity Risk: Gap Analysis

Credit and Market Risk Analytical Models

The Analytical Models modules contain models on estimating and valuing PD, EAD, LGD, Volatility, Credit Exposures, Options-based Asset Valuation, Debt Valuation, Credit Conversion Factors (CCF), Loan Equivalence Factors (LEQ), Options Valuation, Hedging Ratios, and multiple other models. In Basel III/IV/III, the regulations specifically state that all Over-the-Counter (OTC) options, options-embedded instruments, and other exotic options need to also be valued and accounted for. This requirement is why CMOL has devoted an entire module to modeling and valuing these exotic nonlinear instruments. The module is divided into four categories depending on their required inputs and structure of the model. In other words, you might see analytical types like Probability of Default or Volatility traversing multiple tabs or analytical segments.

Figure 1.11 illustrates the Analytical Models tab with input assumptions and results. This analytical model segment is divided into Structural, Time-Series, Portfolio, and Analytics models. The current figure shows the Structural models tab where the computed models pertain to credit risk–related model analysis categories such as PD, EAD, LGD, and Volatility calculations. Under each category, specific models can be selected to run. Selected models are briefly described, and users can select the number of model repetitions to run and the decimal precision levels of the results. The data grid in the Computations tab shows the area in which users would enter the relevant inputs into the selected model and the results would be computed. As usual, selected models, inputs, and settings can be saved for future retrieval and analysis.

ROV CREDIT, MARKET, LIQUIDITY RISK - [C:\Users\Dr. Johnathan Mun\Desktop\ROV Credit Market and Liquidity Example.rovcml]

Credit Risk (ERQ)   Market Risk   Asset Liability Management   **Analytical Models**   Operational Risk

Credit (Structural)   Credit (Time Series)   Credit (Portfolio)   Credit (Models)

STEP 1: Select the Analysis Category and the Model to run:

Analysis

Exposure at Default (EAD)
Loss Given Default (LGD)
Probability of Default (PD)
Volatility

Provides various models to compute EAD using the Credit Plus model. Given the total number of credit exposures in a portfolio and the average probability of default, we can compute the expected average number of defaults given a specific percentile and vice versa.

Model

Credit Risk Plus Average Defaults
Credit Risk Plus Percentile Defaults
Retail EAD using Credit Conversion Factor
Retail EAD using Credit LEQ, CCF, EADF

Exposure at Default (EAD) can be computed using three measures: Credit Conversion Factor (CCF), Exposure at Default Factor (EADF), and Loan Equivalence (LEQ), all based on 12-month historical data.

STEP 3: Save the Models and Data:

You can save multiple analyses and notes in the profile for future retrieval.

Name: EAD using LEQ, CCF, EADF

Notes:

Save As

Edit

Save

Delete

Model

EAD using Credit Conversion Factor CCF
Credit Risk Plus Average Defaults Example
EAD using LEQ, CCF, EADF
Loss Given Default (LGD) Example
Probability of Default (Market Comps) Example
Probability of Default (Bond Spreads) Example

Compute

STEP 2: Enter the required inputs:

Show: 3 ⌄ rows and 2 ⌄ decimals for results.

Computations   Charts   Enter numerical inputs only (e.g., $1,000 please enter as 1000 and 99% enter as 0.99 and so forth)

STEP 4: Run the Models:

N	Historical EAD Defaulted Exposure	Historical Committed Credit Limit	Used Credit 12 Months Ago	Current Committed Credit Limit			Current Outstanding Amount	CCF	EAD using CCF	EADF	EAD using EADF	LEQ	EAD using LEQ
					Minimum	24.14%	1,450	24.14%	1,534	57.14%	1,393	22.58%	1,368
					Average	41.71%	1,500	47.15%	2,349	76.86%	2,819	42.66%	2,491
					Maximum	58.07%	1,250	37.50%	1,344	96.00%	5,152	59.79%	4,491
1	1,200	1,750	1,025	1,800	4,000	58.07%	1,534	24.14%	1,690	68.57%	22.58%	1,529
2	3,000	3,500	2,554	3,300		47.15%	2,349	85.71%	3,043	59.79%	2,576
3	1,000	1,750	550	1,500		37.50%	1,344	57.14%	1,393	47.37%	1,368
4	4,800	5,000	4,523	5,200		58.07%	4,697	96.00%	5,152	40.92%	4,491
5											
6											
7											
o											

Figure 1.11: Structural Credit Risk Models

Figure 1.11 illustrates the Structural Analytical Models tab with visual chart results. The results computed are displayed as various visual charts such as bar charts, control charts, Pareto charts, and time-series charts. Figure 1.12 illustrates the Time-Series Analytical Models tab with input assumptions and results. The analysis category and model type is first chosen where a short description explains what the selected model does, and users can then select the number of models to replicate as well as decimal precision settings. Input data and assumptions are entered in the data grid provided (additional inputs can also be entered if required), and the results are computed and shown. As usual, selected models, inputs, and settings can be saved for future retrieval and analysis. Figure 1.13 illustrates the Portfolio Analytical Models tab with input assumptions and results. The analysis category and model type are first chosen where a short description explains what the selected model does, and users can then select the number of models to replicate as well as decimal precision settings. Input data and assumptions are entered in the data grid provided (additional inputs such as a correlation matrix can also be entered if required), and the results are computed and shown.

Additional models are available in the Credit Models tab with input assumptions and results. The analysis category and model type are first chosen and input data and assumptions are entered in the required inputs area (if required, users can Load Example inputs and use these as a basis for building their models), and the results are computed and shown. Scenario tables and charts can be created by entering the From, To, and Step Size parameters, where the computed scenarios will be returned as a data grid and visual chart. As usual, selected models, inputs, and settings can be saved for future retrieval and analysis.

ROV CREDIT, MARKET, LIQUIDITY RISK - [C:\Users\Dr. Johnathan Mun\Desktop\ROV Credit Market and Liquidity Example.rovcml]

Credit Risk (Structural)   Credit (Time Series)   Credit (Portfolio)   Credit (Models)

Credit Risk (ERC)   Market Risk   Asset Liability Management   **Analytical Models**   Operational Risk

STEP 1: Select the Analysis Category and the Model to run:

Analysis
Probability of Default (PD)
Volatility

Model
Historical Volatility
GARCH Forecast Volatility

Computes the annualized volatilities of a market-traded equity or commodity using various methods including implied volatility, historical volatility, and advanced econometric models like the GARCH volatility forecast.

Applies the Generalized Autoregressive Conditional Heteroskedasticity econometric modeling technique to back-fit and forecast a time-series of future volatilities.

STEP 3: Save the Models and Data:

You can save multiple analyses and notes in the profile for future retrieval.

Name: GARCH Volatility Model

Notes:

Model
Sample Historical Volatility
Probability of Default Model on Retail Loans
GARCH Volatility Model

Save As
Edit
Save
Delete

STEP 2: Enter the required inputs:

Show: 150 ⌄ rows by 8 ⌄ variables with 2 ⌄ decimals for results

Computations   Charts

Enter numerical inputs only (e.g. $1.000 please enter as 1000 and 99% enter as 0.99 and so forth).

	Stock Prices	Periodicity	Predictive Base	Forecast Per...	Variance Tar...	P	Q
		252	1	10	0	1	1
1	459.11						
2	460.71						
3	460.34						
4	460.68						
5	460.83						
6	461.68						
7	461.66						
8	461.64						
9	465.97						
10	469.38						
11	470.05						
12	469.72						

STEP 4: Run the Models: Compute

Alpha (ARCH) : 0.000000
Beta (GARCH) : 1.000000
Omega (Intercept) : 0.000000
Log Likelihood : 534.256066
GARCH :
0.000000, 0.000000, 0.080655, 0.080759, 0.080863, 0.080967,
0.081070, 0.081174, 0.081277, 0.081381, 0.081484, 0.081587,
0.081690, 0.081792, 0.081895, 0.081997, 0.082100, 0.082202,
0.082304, 0.082406, 0.082508, 0.082610, 0.082711, 0.082813,
0.082914, 0.083015, 0.083116, 0.083217, 0.083318, 0.083419,
0.083519, 0.083620, 0.083720, 0.083820, 0.083921, 0.084021,
0.084120, 0.084220, 0.084320, 0.084419, 0.084519, 0.084618,
0.084717, 0.084816, 0.084915, 0.085014, 0.085113, 0.085211,
0.085310, 0.085408, 0.085507, 0.085605, 0.085703, 0.085801,
0.085899, 0.085996, 0.086094, 0.086191, 0.086289, 0.086386,
0.086483, 0.086580, 0.086677, 0.086774, 0.086871, 0.086967,
0.087064, 0.087160, 0.087256, 0.087353, 0.087449, 0.087545,
0.087641, 0.087736, 0.087832, 0.087928, 0.088023, 0.088118,
0.088214, 0.088309, 0.088404, 0.088499, 0.088594, 0.088688,
0.088783, 0.088877, 0.088972, 0.089066, 0.089160, 0.089255,

Figure 1.12: Time-Series Credit and Market Models

ROV CREDIT, MARKET, LIQUIDITY RISK - [C:\Users\Dr. Johnnathan Mun\Desktop\ROV Credit Market and Liquidity Example.rovcml]

Credit Risk (ERG)   Market Risk   Asset Liability Management   **Analytical Models**   Operational Risk

Credit (Structural)   Credit (Time Series)   **Credit (Portfolio)**   Credit (Models)

STEP 1: Select the Analysis Category and the Model to run:

Analysis

Bond Related Options, Pricing and Yields
Value at Risk (VaR)

Model
Bond Price (Discrete Discounting)
Bond Price (Continuous Discounting)
Bond Convexity YTM (Continuous Discounting)
Bond Convexity YTM (Discrete Discounting)

Bond Related Options, Pricing and Yields

Returns the debt's first order sensitivity Duration measure using discrete discounting

STEP 2: Enter the required inputs:

Show   10   assets and   4   decimals for results.

Enter numerical inputs only (e.g. $1,000 please enter as 1000 and 99% enter as 0.99 and so forth).

Cash Flows	Interest Rates	Timing
1	100	0.10	1
2	100	0.11	2
3	100	0.105	3
4	100	0.11	4
5	100	0.106	5
6	100	0.108	6
7	100	0.09	7
8	100	0.109	8
9	100	0.11	9
10	1,100	0.115	10

STEP 3: Save the Models and Data:

You can save multiple analyses and notes in the profile for future retrieval.

Name: Bond Duration Discrete Discounting Example

Notes

Save As
Edit
Save
Delete

Model
Bond Price Discrete Discounting Example
Bond Price Continuous Discounting Example
Bond Convexity YTM Continuous Discounting Example
Bond Duration Discrete Discounting Example
Bond Macaulay Duration
Bond Modified Duration

STEP 4: Run the Models:

Correlation Matrix:

	Asset 1	Asset 2	Asset 3	Asset 4	Asset 5
Asset 1					
Asset 2					
Asset 3					
Asset 4					
Asset 5					

Compute

6.5856

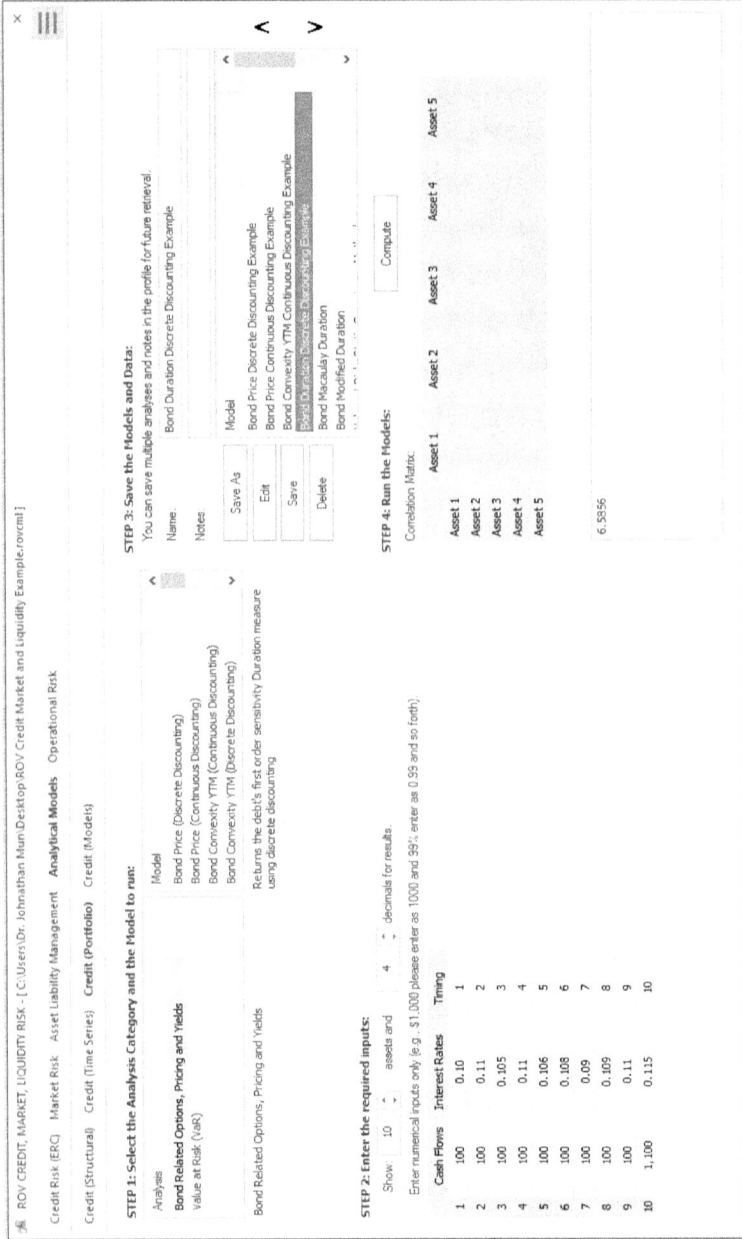

Figure 1.13: Credit Portfolio Models

The case of operational risk is undoubtedly the most difficult to measure and model. The opposite of market risk, by its definition, operational risk data are not only scarce, but biased, unstable, and unchecked in the sense that the most relevant operational risk events do not come identified in the balance sheet of any financial institution. Since the modeling approach is still based on VaR logic, whereby the model utilizes past empirical data to project expected results, modeling operational risk is a very challenging task. As stated, market risk offers daily, publicly audited information to be used and modeled. Conversely, operational risk events are, in most cases, not public, not identified in the general ledger, and, in many instances, not identified at all. But the utmost difficulty comes from the proper definition of operational risk. Even if we managed to go about the impossible task of identifying each and every operational risk event of the past five years, we would still have very incomplete information. The definition of operational risk entails events generated by failures in people, processes, systems, and external events. With market risk, asset prices can either go up or down, or stay unchanged. With operational risk, an unknown event that has never occurred before can take place in the analysis period and materially affect operations even without it being an extreme tail event. So the logic of utilizing similar approaches for such different information availability and behavior requires very careful definitions and assumptions.

With this logic in mind, the Basel Committee has defined that in order to model operational risk properly, banks need to have four sources of operational risk data: internal losses, external losses, business environment and internal control factors, and stressed scenarios. These are known as the four elements of operational risk, and the Basel Committee recommends that they are taken into account when modeling. For smaller banks, and smaller countries, this recommendation poses a definite challenge, because many times these elements are not developed enough, or not present at all. In this light, most banks have resorted to just using internal data to model operational risk. This approach comes with some shortcomings and more assumptions and should be taken as an initial step that considers the later development of the other elements as they become available. The example shown in Figure 1.14 looks at the modeling of internal losses as a simplified approach usually undertaken by smaller institutions. Since operational risk information is scarce and biased, it is necessary to "complete" the loss distributions with randomly generated data. The most common approach for the task is the use of Monte Carlo risk simulations (Figures 1.15, 1.16, and 1.17) that allow for the inclusion of more stable data and for the fitting of the distributions into predefined density functions.

Basel III/IV and Basel III/IV/IV regulations allow for the use of multiple approaches when it comes to computing capital charge on operational risk, defined by the Basel Committee as losses resulting from inadequate or failed internal processes, people, and systems or from external events, which includes legal risk, but excludes any strategic and reputational risks.

- *Basic Indicator Approach* (BIA) uses positive Gross Income of the last 3 years applied to an alpha multiplier.

- *The Standardized Approach* (TSA) uses positive Gross Income of 8 distinct business lines with its own beta risk-weighted coefficients.

- *Alternate Standardized Approach* (ASA) is based on the TSA method and uses Gross Income but applies Total Loans and Advances for the Retail and Commercial business lines, adjusted by a multiplier, prior to using the same TSA beta risk-weighted coefficients.

- *Revised Standardized Approach* (RSA) uses Income and Expenses as proxy variables to obtain the *Business Indicator* required in computing the risk capital charge.

- *Advanced Measurement Approach* (AMA) is open-ended in that individual banks can utilize their own approaches subject to regulatory approval. The typical approach, and the same method used in the ALM-CMOL software application, is to use historical loss data, perform probability distribution-fitting on the frequency and severity of losses, which is then convoluted through Monte Carlo Risk Simulation to obtain probability distributions of future expected losses. The tail event VaR results can be obtained directly from the simulated distributions.

Figure 1.14 illustrates the BIA, TSA, ASA, and RSA methods as prescribed in Basel III/IV/III. The BIA uses total annual gross income for the last 3 years of the bank and multiplies it with an alpha coefficient (15%) to obtain the capital charge. Only positive gross income amounts are used. This is the simplest method and does not require prior regulatory approval. In the TSA method, the bank is divided into 8 business lines (*corporate finance, trading and sales, retail banking, commercial banking, payment and settlement, agency services, asset management,* and *retail brokerage*), each business line's positive total annual gross income values for the last 3 years are used, and each business line has its own beta coefficient multiplier. These beta values are proxies based on industry-wide relationships between operational risk loss experience for each business line and aggregate gross income levels. The total capital charge based on the TSA is simply the sum of the weighted average of these business lines for the last 3 years. The ASA is similar to the TSA except that the retail banking and commercial banking business lines use *total loans and advances* instead of using annual total gross income. These total loans and advances are first multiplied by a 3.50% factor prior to being beta-weighted, averaged, and summed. The ASA is also useful in situations where the bank has extremely high or low net interest margins (NIM), whereby the gross income for the retail and commercial business lines are replaced with an asset-based proxy (total loans and advances multiplied by the 3.50% factor). In addition, within the ASA approach, the 6 business lines can be aggregated into a single business line as long as it is multiplied by the highest beta coefficient (18%), and the 2 remaining loans and advances (retail and commercial business lines) can be aggregated and multiplied by the 15% beta coefficient. In other words, when using the ALM-CMOL software, you can aggregate the 6 business lines and enter it as a single row entry in Corporate Finance, which has an 18% multiplier, and the 2 loans and advances business lines can be aggregated as the Commercial business line, which has a 15% multiplier.

The main issue with BIA, TSA, and ASA methods is that, on average, these methods are undercalibrated, especially for large and complex banks. For instance, these three methods assume that operational risk exposure increases linearly and proportionally with gross income or revenue. This assumption is invalid because certain banks may experience a decline in gross income due to systemic or bank-specific events that may include losses from operational risk events. In such situations, a falling gross income should be commensurate with a higher operational capital requirement, not a lower capital charge. Therefore, the Basel Committee has allowed the inclusion of a revised method, the RSA. Instead of using gross income, the RSA uses both income and expenditures from multiple sources, as shown in Figure 1.14. The RSA uses inputs from an *interest* component (interest income less interest expense), a *services* component (sum of fee income, fee expense, other operating income, and other operating expense), and a *financial* component (sum of the absolute value of net profit and losses on the trading book and the absolute value of net profit and losses on the banking book). The calculation of capital charge is based on the calculation of a *Business Indicator* (BI), where the BI is the sum of the absolute values of these three components (thereby avoiding any counterintuitive results based on negative contributions from any component). The purpose of a BI calculation is to promote simplicity and comparability using a single indicator for operational risk exposure that is sensitive to the bank's business size and business volume, rather than static business line coefficients regardless of the bank's size and volume. Using the computed BI, the risk capital charge is determined from 5 predefined buckets from Basel III/IV/III, increasing in value from 10% to 30%, depending on the size of the BI (ranging from €0 to €30 billion). These Basel predefined buckets are denoted in thousands of Euros, with each bucket having its own weighted beta coefficients. Finally, the risk capital charge is computed based on a marginal incremental or layered approach (rather than a full cliff-effect when banks migrate from one bucket to another) using these buckets.

Figures 1.15, 1.16, and 1.17 illustrate the Operational Risk Loss Distribution analysis when applying the AMA method. Users start at the Loss Data tab where historical loss data can be entered or pasted into the data grid. Variables include losses in the past pertaining to operational risks, segmentation by divisions and departments, business lines, dates of losses, risk categories, and so on. Users then activate the controls to select how the loss data variables are to be segmented (e.g., by risk categories and risk types and business lines), the number of simulation trials to run, and seed values to apply in the simulation if required, all by selecting the relevant variable columns. The distributional fitting routines can also be selected as required. Then the analysis can be run, and distributions fitted to the data. As usual, the model settings and data can be saved for future retrieval.

Credit Risk (ERC)   Market Risk   Asset Liability Management   Analytical Models   Operational Risk

Basel OPRISK (BIA, TSA, ASA, RSA)   Basel OPCAR (AMA)   Loss Distribution Analysis (AMA)

Basel II and Basel III regulations allow for the use of multiple approaches when it comes to computing capital charge on operational risk, (defined as losses resulting from inadequate or failed internal processes, people, and systems or from external events, which includes legal risk, but excludes any strategic and reputational risks). The Basic Indicator Approach (BIA) uses positive Gross Income of the last 3 years applied to an Alpha multiplier. The Standardized Approach (TSA) uses positive Gross Income as well as Total Loans and Advances for the Retail and Commercial business lines adjusted by a multiplier; and the Revised Standardized Approach (RSA) uses Income and Expenses as proxy variables to obtain the Business Indicator used in computing the required capital charge. The other tabs are for the Advanced Measurement Approach (AMA) where using historical loss data, fitted probability distributions on frequency and severity are convoluted through Monte Carlo Risk Simulation to obtain probability distributions of expected losses.

1. Basic Indicator Approach (BIA)

Gross Income Categories	Year 1	Year 2	Year 3	Alpha
Annual Gross Income	75,461,000	55,561,450	89,562,500	15%
Capital Charge (BIA)	11,029,248	15.00%		

2. The Standardized Approach (TSA)

Gross Income Categories	Year 1	Year 2	Year 3	Beta
Corporate Finance	75,561,450	175,561,450	75,561,450	18%
Trading and Sales	55,561,450	85,561,450	85,561,450	18%
Retail Banking	55,561,450	85,561,450	55,561,450	12%
Commercial Banking	55,561,450	55,561,450	255,561,450	15%
Payment and Settlement	95,561,450	95,561,450	95,561,450	18%
Agency Services	55,561,450	55,561,450	55,561,450	15%
Asset Management	55,561,450	95,561,450	55,561,450	12%
Retail Brokerage	55,561,450	45,561,450	55,561,450	12%
Capital Charge (TSA)	101,273,740	15.47%		

3. Alternate Standardized Approach (ASA)

	Year 1	Year 2	Year 3	Beta
Gross Income, Loans & Advances	75,561,450	175,561,450	75,561,450	18%
Corporate Finance	55,561,450	85,561,450	85,561,450	18%
Trading and Sales	85,561,450	85,561,450	85,561,450	12%
Total Retail Loans & Advances	155,561,450	285,561,450	355,561,450	15%
Total Commercial Loans & Advances	411,561,450	655,561,450	755,561,450	15%
Payment and Settlement	95,561,450	95,561,450	95,561,450	18%
Agency Services	55,561,450	55,561,450	55,561,450	15%
Asset Management	55,561,450	95,561,450	55,561,450	12%
Retail Brokerage	55,561,450	45,561,450	55,561,450	12%
Loans & Advances Multiplier	0.035			
Capital Charge (ASA)	79,377,204	15.96%		

4. Revised Standardized Approach (RSA)

Enter values below in thousands of Euro ('000 Euro) as Basel II/III categories are in '000 Euro.

Interest Income	Net Profit & Loss on Trading Book	51,250
50,000	Net Profit & Loss on Banking Book	92,550
Interest Expense		
5,254	Enter the name of the currency type (e.g., Euro...	Euro
Fee Income		
6,750	Business Indicator (BI)	213,891
Fee Expense		
8,195	Capital Charge (RSA)	61,574
Other Operating Income		
9,255	Effective OPRISK Capital %	28.79%
Other Operating Expense		
1,145		

BI Categories (in '000 Euro)	100	1000	3000	30000	30000
BI Ranges (in '000 Euro)	0-100	100-1000	1000-3000	3000-30000	Over 30000
Beta Coefficient	10%	13%	17%	22%	30%

Name:

Saved Model

Sample III - BIA, TSA, ASA, RSA

Sample I - BIA, TSA, ASA, RSA
Sample II - BIA, TSA, ASA, RSA
Sample III - BIA, TSA, ASA, RSA

Notes:

| Save As |
| Edit |
| Save |
| Delete |

New

<   >

Figure 1.14: Basel III/IV/III BIA, TSA, ASA, RSA Methods

Credit Risk (ERC)   Market Risk   Asset Liability Management   Analytical Models   **Operational Risk**

Basel OPRISK (BIA, TSA, ASA, RSA)   Basel OPCAR (AMA)   **Loss Distribution Analysis (AMA)**

Loss Data & Fitting (AMA)   Fitted Loss Distribution (AMA)   Simulated Losses (AMA)

Internal Losses Data   Show   1,000   Rows   Show   50   Variables

Variables	VAR 1	VAR 2	VAR 3	VAR 4	VAR 5	VAR 6	VAR 7	VAR 8	VAR 9	VAR 10
Name	Risk Type	Biz Unit	Losses	Date Index						
1	XYZ	California	5.7182	7						
2	XYZ	California	2.3474	8						
3	ABC	California	12.5851	5						
4	MNO	California	29.5335	5						
5	XYZ	New York	21.4308	1						
6	MNO	New York	11.3403	8						
7	XYZ	California	8.7417	1						
8	ABC	New York	57.5989	5						
9	ABC	California	2.1354	3						
10	MNO	New York	20.5699	6						
11	MNO	New York	0.5811	5						
12	MNO	New York	5.7012	2						
13	XYZ	California	7.7165	8						
14	XYZ	California	91.6430	5						
15	MNO	California	22.9218	5						
16	XYZ	California	21.2777	1						
17	MNO	California	6.6460	6						
18	XYZ	New York	19.1082	2						
19	MNO	California	24.3649	7						
20	XYZ	California	24.1996	8						
21	MNO	California	59.8262	1						
22	ABC	New York	1.9608	8						
23	MNO	California	3.5087	1						
24	MNO	New York	9.6244	5						

Loss Data is in Variable:
VAR 3: Losses
☑ Fit Positive Losses Only
☑ Segment Risk Category by:
VAR 1: Risk Type
☑ Segment Business Lines by:
VAR 2: Biz Unit
○ Data is within one analysis period
◉ Data is from multiple periods:
Period Identifier: VAR 4: Date Index

Simulation Trials: 10,000
☐ Apply Seed Value: 123
Kolmogorov-Smirnov
Run Distribution Fitting

Save the data if desired:
Name: Bank Loss Data
Save As

List of Saved Analyses

Analysis
Bank Loss Data
Sample

New   Delete
Edit   Save

Figure 1.15: Operational Risk Data in Advanced Measurement Approach (AMA)

Figure 1.16 illustrates the Operational Risk—Fitted Loss Distribution subtab. Users start by selecting the fitting segments for setting the various risk category and business line segments, and, based on the selected segment, the fitted distributions and their p-values are listed and ranked according to the highest p-value to the lowest p-value, indicating the best to the worst statistical fit to the various probability distributions. The empirical data and fitted theoretical distributions are shown graphically, and the statistical moments are shown for the actual data versus the theoretically fitted distribution's moments. After deciding on which distributions to use, users can then run the simulations.

Credit Risk (ERC)   Market Risk   Asset (Liability Management   Analytical Models   **Operational Risk**

Basel OPRISK (BIA, TSA, ASA, RSA)   Basel OPCAR (AMA)   **Loss Distribution Analysis (AMA)**

Loss Data & Fitting (AMA)   **Fitted Loss Distribution (AMA)**   Simulated Losses (AMA)

Start by selecting the segment to view the fitted results:

FITTED HISTORICAL FREQUENCY DATA

Default fitted to Poisson Distribution with:

◉ Auto Fit Poisson   ○ Manual Override (Poisson's Mean)   21.1250

Risk Segment & Business Line

XYZ and California
XYZ and New York
ABC and California
ABC and New York
MNO and California
MNO and New York
All XYZ
All ABC
All MNO
All California
All New York

The Poisson distribution describes the number of times an event occurs in a given interval, such as the number of telephone calls per minute or the number of errors per page in a document. The number of possible occurrences in any interval is unlimited, the occurrences are independent. The number of occurrences in one interval does not affect the number of occurrences in other intervals, and the average number of occurrences must remain the same from interval to interval. Rate or Lambda is the only distributional parameter.

The Weibull distribution describes data resulting from life and fatigue tests. It is commonly used to describe failure time in reliability studies as well as the breaking strengths of materials in reliability and quality control tests. Weibull distributions are also used to represent various physical quantities, such as wind speed. The Weibull distribution is a family of distributions that can assume the properties of several other distributions. For example, depending on the shape parameter you define, the Weibull distribution can be used to model the exponential and Rayleigh distributions, among others.

FITTED HISTORICAL SEVERITY DATA

Selected distribution's parameters:

Alpha 1.0931   Beta 26.6214

Top 10 Distributions	P-Value
◉ Weibull	0.9996
○ Exponential	0.9130
○ Gamma	0.7941
○ Exponential2	0.5661
○ LognormalArithmetic	0.1771
○ GumbelMax	0.0620
○ Logistic	0.0093
○ PearsonV	0.0052
○ Cauchy	0.0052
○ Normal	0.0017

Save

	Actual	Theoretical
Mean	26.2461	24.7739
Median	17.6624	18.3228
Stdev	27.3333	22.6877
Skew	2.6665	1.7503
Kurtosis	11.0695	4.4529
1%	0.2770	0.3811
5%	1.9679	1.6927
95%	75.5239	69.9048
99%	115.5710	103.5949

◉ Run Simulations on All Segments
○ Run Simulation on Selected Segment

Run Simulation

Chart   Control

Historical Empirical Distribution vs. Theoretical Fitted Distributions

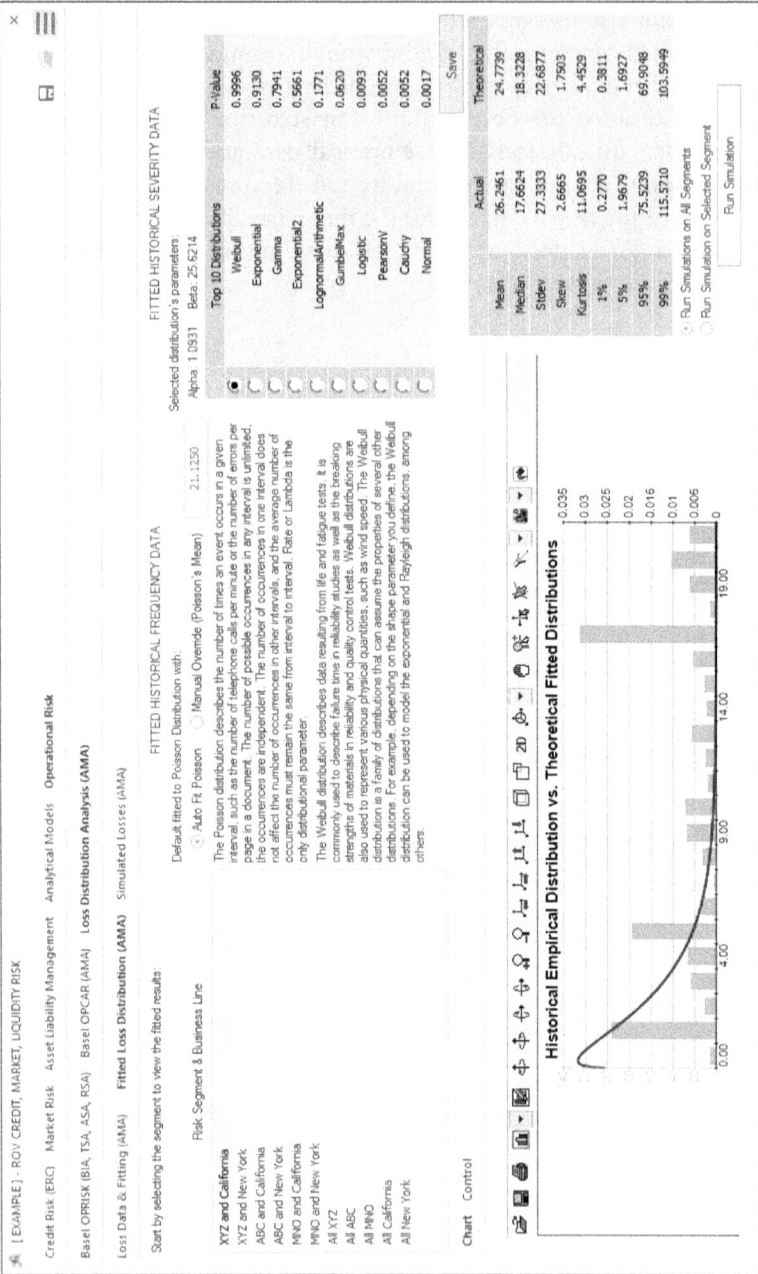

Figure 1.16: Fitted Distributions on Operational Risk Data

Figure 1.17 illustrates the Operational Risk—Risk Simulated Losses subtab using convolution of frequency and severity of historical losses, where, depending on which risk segment and business line was selected, the relevant probability distribution results from the Monte Carlo risk simulations are displayed, including the simulated results on Frequency, Severity, and the multiplication between frequency and severity, termed Expected Loss Distribution, as well as the Extreme Value Distribution of Losses (this is where the extreme losses in the dataset are fitted to the extreme value distributions—see the examples in the following chapters for details on extreme value distributions and their mathematical models). Each of the distributional charts has its own confidence and percentile inputs where users can select one-tail (right-tail or left-tail) or two-tail confidence intervals and enter the percentiles to obtain the confidence values (e.g., user can enter right-tail 99.90% percentile to receive the VaR confidence value of the worst-case losses on the left tail's 0.10%).

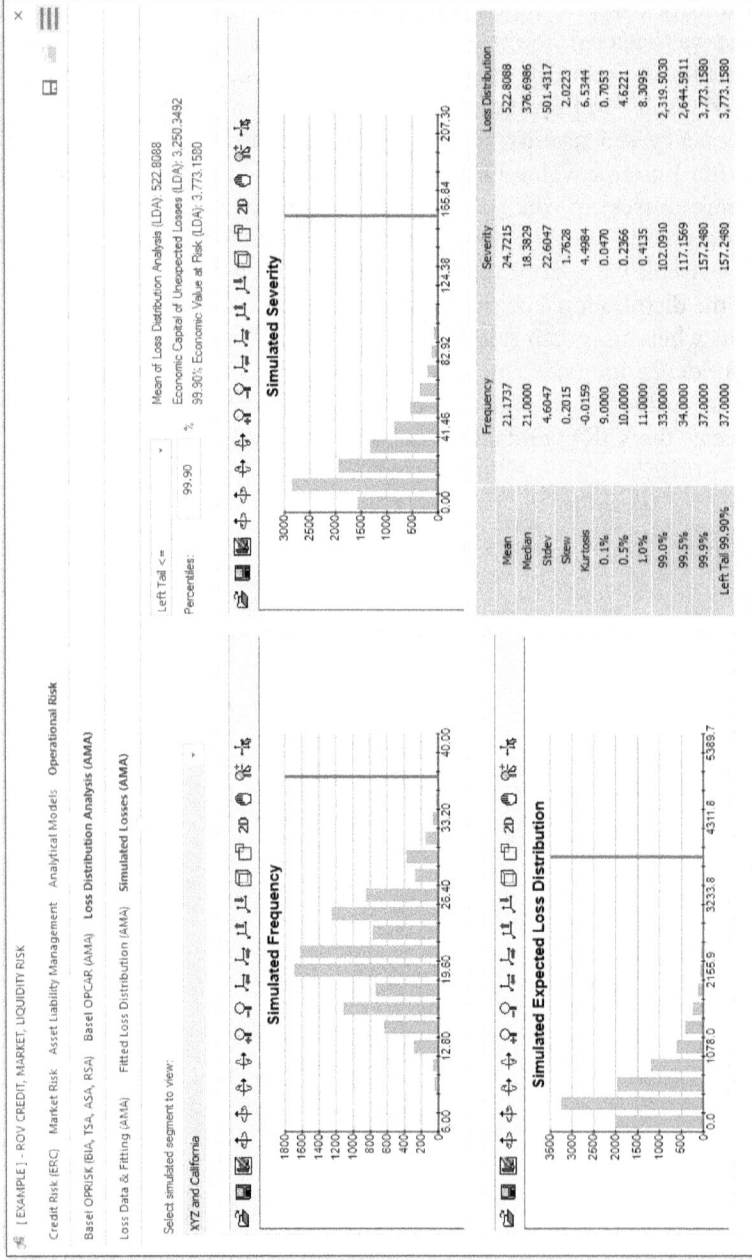

Figure 1.17: Monte Carlo Risk Simulated Operational Losses

Figure 1.18 shows the computations of Basel III/IV/III's OPCAR (Operational Capital at Risk) model where the probability distribution of risk event Frequency is multiplied by the probability distribution of Severity of operational losses, the approach where Frequency × Severity is termed the Single Loss Approximation (SLA) model. The SLA is computed using convolution methods of combining multiple probability distributions. SLA using convolution methods is complex and very difficult to compute and the results are only approximations, and valid only at the extreme tails of the distribution (e.g., 99.9%). However, Monte Carlo Risk Simulation provides a simpler and more powerful alternative when convoluting and multiplying two distributions of random variables to obtain the combined distribution. Clearly the challenge is setting the relevant distributional input parameters. This is where the data-fitting and percentile-fitting tools come in handy, as will be explained later.

Figure 1.19 shows the convolution simulation results where the distribution of loss frequency, severity, and expected losses are shown. The resulting Expected Losses (EL), Unexpected Losses (UL), and Total Operational Capital at Risk (OPCAR) are also computed and shown. EL is, of course, the mean value of the simulated results, OPCAR is the tail-end 99.90th percentile, and UL is the difference between OPCAR and EL.

Figure 1.20 shows the loss severity data fitting using historical loss data. Users can paste historical loss data, select the required fitting routines (Kolmogorov–Smirnov, Akaike Criterion, Bayes Information Criterion, Anderson–Darling, Kuiper's Statistic, etc.), and run the data fitting routines. When in doubt, use the Kolmogorov–Smirnov routine. The best-fitting distributions, p-values, and their parameters will be listed, and the same interpretation applies as previously explained.

Figure 1.21 shows the loss severity percentile fitting instead, which is particularly helpful when there are no historical loss data and where there only exist high-level management assumptions of the probabilities certain events occur. In other words, by entering a few percentiles (%) and their corresponding values, one can obtain the entire distribution's parameters.

Credit Risk (ERC)   Market Risk   Asset Liability Management   Analytical Models   **Operational Risk**

Basel OPRISK (BIA, TSA, ASA, RSA)   **Basel OPCAR (AMA)**   Loss Distribution Analysis (AMA)

Loss Severity Fitting   **Frequency and Severity Assumptions**   Convoluted Simulation Results

Simulated Compound-Convolution Single Loss Approximation (SLA) models are shown for computing Expected Losses (EL), Unexpected Losses (UL), and Operational Capital at Risk (OPCAR) in the Basel II/III Advanced Measurement Approach (AMA). All inputs must be Lambda > 1, Alpha > 1, Beta > 1, Mu > 0, Sigma > 0, Location > 0, 0% < Probability < 100%, Location and Rate (Rho) can be any value. Use the Loss Severity data and percentile fitting tab to identify the best fitting distribution and calibrate the relevant distributional input parameters. Start by entering the following two global inputs for the Poisson Distribution's Average Frequency and Operational Value at Risk %, and then proceed to enter the relevant inputs for the distribution you have selected to run the OPCAR results.

☐ Run Convolution Models (this make take a few extra minutes)   Convolute and Simulate

Poisson (Frequency Distribution)

Probability (Operational Value at Risk)	99.90%
Poisson Average Frequency (Lambda)	30.00

Number of Simulation Trials	10,000
Simulation Seed Value	123

Compound Poisson-Logistic

Alpha (Median)	1.50
Beta (Scale)	2.50
Expected Losses (EL)	
Unexpected Losses (UL)	
Operational Capital at Risk (OPCAR)	

Compound Poisson-Gumbel Max

Alpha (Mode)	1.50
Beta (Scale)	2.50
Expected Losses (EL)	
Unexpected Losses (UL)	
Operational Capital at Risk (OPCAR)	

Compound Poisson-Exponential

Mean Rate (Rho)	0.01

Compound Poisson-Log Logistic

Alpha (Median)	1.50
Beta (Scale)	2.50
Expected Losses (EL)	
Unexpected Losses (UL)	
Simulated OPCAR	

Compound Poisson-Pareto

Alpha (Shape)	1.50
Beta (Min)	2.50
Expected Losses (EL)	
Unexpected Losses (UL)	
Simulated OPCAR	

Compound Poisson-Frechet

Alpha (Shape)	1.50
Beta (Scale)	2.50
Expected Losses (EL)	
Unexpected Losses (UL)	
Simulated OPCAR	

Compound Poisson-Lognormal

Mean (Mu) (Arithmetic)	1.50
Stdev (Sigma) (Arithmetic)	2.50
Expected Losses (EL)	
Unexpected Losses (UL)	
Simulated OPCAR	

Compound Poisson-Weibull

Alpha (Shape)	1.50
Beta (Scale)	2.50
Expected Losses (EL)	
Unexpected Losses (UL)	
Simulated OPCAR	

Compound Poisson-Gamma

Alpha (Shape)	1.50
Beta (Scale)	2.50
Expected Losses (EL)	
Unexpected Losses (UL)	
Simulated OPCAR	

Compound Poisson-Lognormal (Log)

Mean (Mu) (Log)	1.50
Stdev (Sigma) (Log)	2.50
Expected Losses (EL)	
Unexpected Losses (UL)	
Simulated OPCAR	

Name: Model 1 - Simulation Only

Saved Model

Model 1 - Simulation Only
Model 2 - Convolution 99.9%
Model 3 - Convolution 90%

New
Delete
Save
Edit
Save As

Figure 1.18: Basel OPCAR Frequency and Severity Assumptions

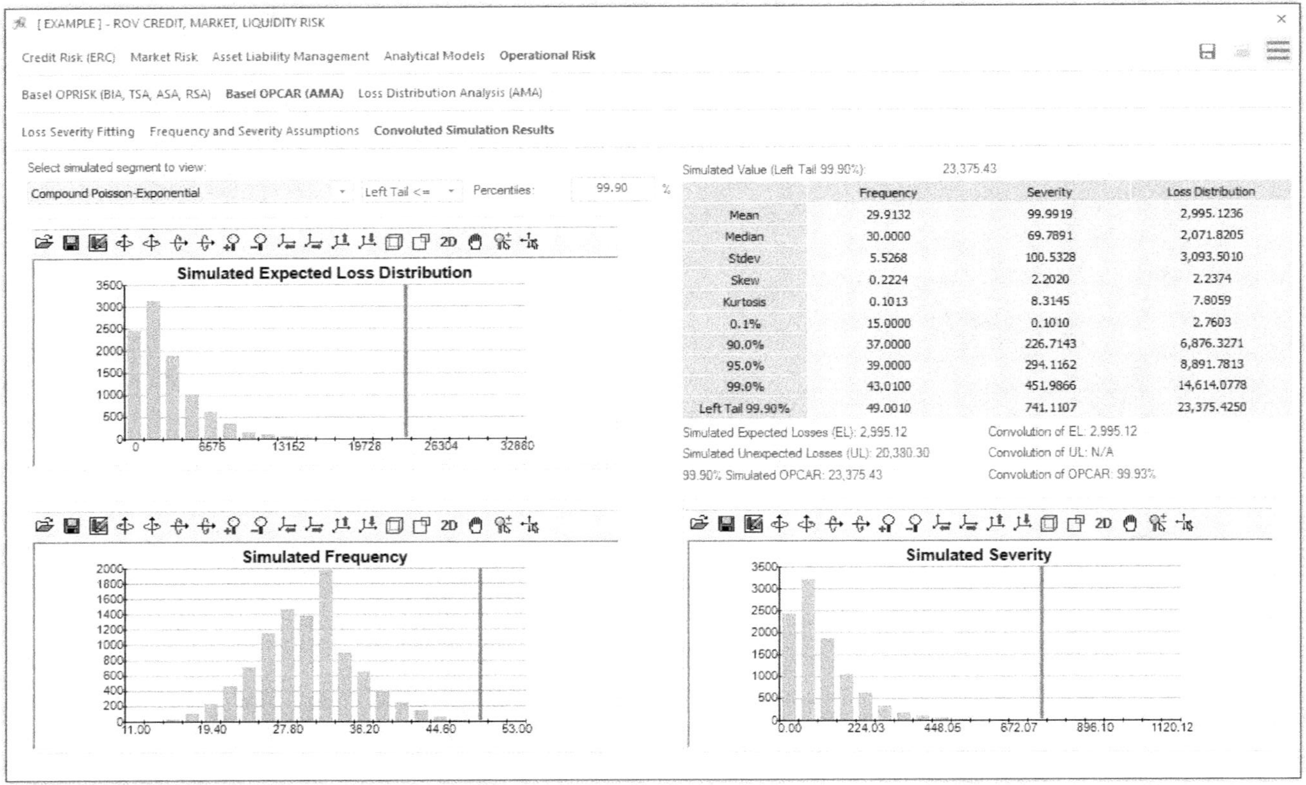

Credit Risk (ERC)   Market Risk   Asset Liability Management   Analytical Models   **Operational Risk**

Basel OPRISK (BIA, TSA, ASA, RSA)   **Basel OPCAR (AMA)**   Loss Distribution Analysis (AMA)

Loss Severity Fitting   Frequency and Severity Assumptions   **Convoluted Simulation Results**

Select simulated segment to view:

Compound Poisson-Exponential   Left Tail <=   ▾   Percentiles: 99.90

Simulated Expected Loss Distribution

Simulated Value (Left Tail 99.90%)   23,375.43

	Frequency	Severity	Loss Distribution
Mean	29.9132	99.9919	2,995.1236
Median	30.0000	69.7891	2,071.8205
Stdev	5.5268	100.5328	3,093.5010
Skew	0.2224	2.2020	2.2374
Kurtosis	0.1013	8.3145	7.8059
0.1%	15.0000	0.1010	2.7603
90.0%	37.0000	226.7143	6,876.3271
95.0%	39.0000	294.1162	8,891.7813
99.0%	43.0100	451.9866	14,614.0778
Left Tail 99.90%	49.0010	741.1107	23,375.4250

Simulated Expected Losses (EL): 2,995.12   Convolution of EL: 2,995.12
Simulated Unexpected Losses (UL): 20,380.30   Convolution of UL: N/A
99.90% Simulated OPCAR: 23,375.43   Convolution of OPCAR: 99.93%

Simulated Frequency

11.00   19.40   27.80   38.20   44.60   53.00

Simulated Severity

0.00   224.03   448.05   672.07   896.10   1120.12

Figure 1.19: Basel OPCAR Convoluted Simulation Results

These modeling tools allow smaller banks to have a first approach at more advanced operational risk management techniques. The use of internal models allows for a better calibration of regulatory capital that knowingly overestimated for operational risk. The use of different scenarios providing various results can allow smaller banks to have a much more efficient capital allocation for operational risk that, being a Pillar I risk, tends to be quite expensive in terms of capital, and quite dangerous at the same time if capital was severely underestimated. Together with the traditional operational risk management tools, such as self-assessment and KRIs, these basic models allow for a proper IMMM risk management structure, aligned with the latest international standards.

[EXAMPLE] - ROV CREDIT, MARKET, LIQUIDITY RISK

Credit Risk (ERC) Market Risk Asset Liability Management Analytical Models **Operational Risk**

Basel OPRISK (BIA, TSA, ASA, RSA) **Basel OPCAR (AMA)** Loss Distribution Analysis (AMA)

Loss Severity Fitting Frequency and Severity Assumptions Convoluted Simulation Results

◉ Use historical loss data and distributional fitting
○ Use subject matter estimates and percentile fitting

Internal Losses Data Show | 1,000 | Rows Show | 5 | Variables
COUNT: VAR1 250; VAR2 250

Name	VAR 1 Dept 1	VAR 2 Dept 2	VAR 3	VAR 4	VAR 5
1	2.121	0.599			
2	2.908	3.242			
3	3.598	1.713			
4	2.514	5.061			
5	1.430	2.547			
6	0.850	1.083			
7	2.391	6.897			
8	3.696	2.605			
9	2.253	2.425			
10	3.788	2.839			
11	5.425	0.532			
12	1.745	1.535			
13	4.223	0.814			
14	4.201	1.282			
15	4.360	4.198			
16	3.221	2.919			
17	3.767	0.143			
18	6.562	3.479			
19	4.578	0.402			
20	3.073	2.054			
21	2.215	7.390			
22	3.733	1.551			

Kolmogorov-Smirnov
Show Fitting Results for VAR 2

FITTED HISTORICAL SEVERITY DATA

Selected distribution's parameters
Alpha 1.5467 Beta 1.1239

Top 10 Distributions	P-Value
Gamma	0.9312
Weibull	0.6304
GumbelMax	0.6217
PearsonVI	0.4360
Laplace	0.0224
Rayleigh	0.0210
TDist2	0.0193
Normal	0.0150
PearsonV	0.0054
Cauchy	0.0049

	Actual	Theoretical
Mean	2.1980	2.1879
Median	1.7705	1.8268
Stdev	1.5717	1.5681
Skew	1.1846	1.4334
Kurtosis	1.3401	3.0821
1%	0.1174	0.1539
5%	0.3818	0.3756
95%	5.1429	5.2343
99%	7.3537	7.3490

Run Distribution Fitting

You can paste historical loss data in the grid for each risk type, select the distributional fitting method, and run the fitting routine. The best fitting distributions are listed with the highest p-values. Select the distribution you wish to use to see the actual versus theoretical moments. Save the data as required and paste the fitted distributional parameters back to the assumptions tab.

Paste Fitted Parameters to Frequency and Severity Assumptions tab

Save the data if desired.

Name: Historical Loss Severity

List of Saved Analyses: Save As

Analysis
Historical Loss Severity
Subject Matter Expert Percentile

New Delete
Edit Save

< >

Figure 1.20: Basel OPCAR Loss Severity Data Fitting

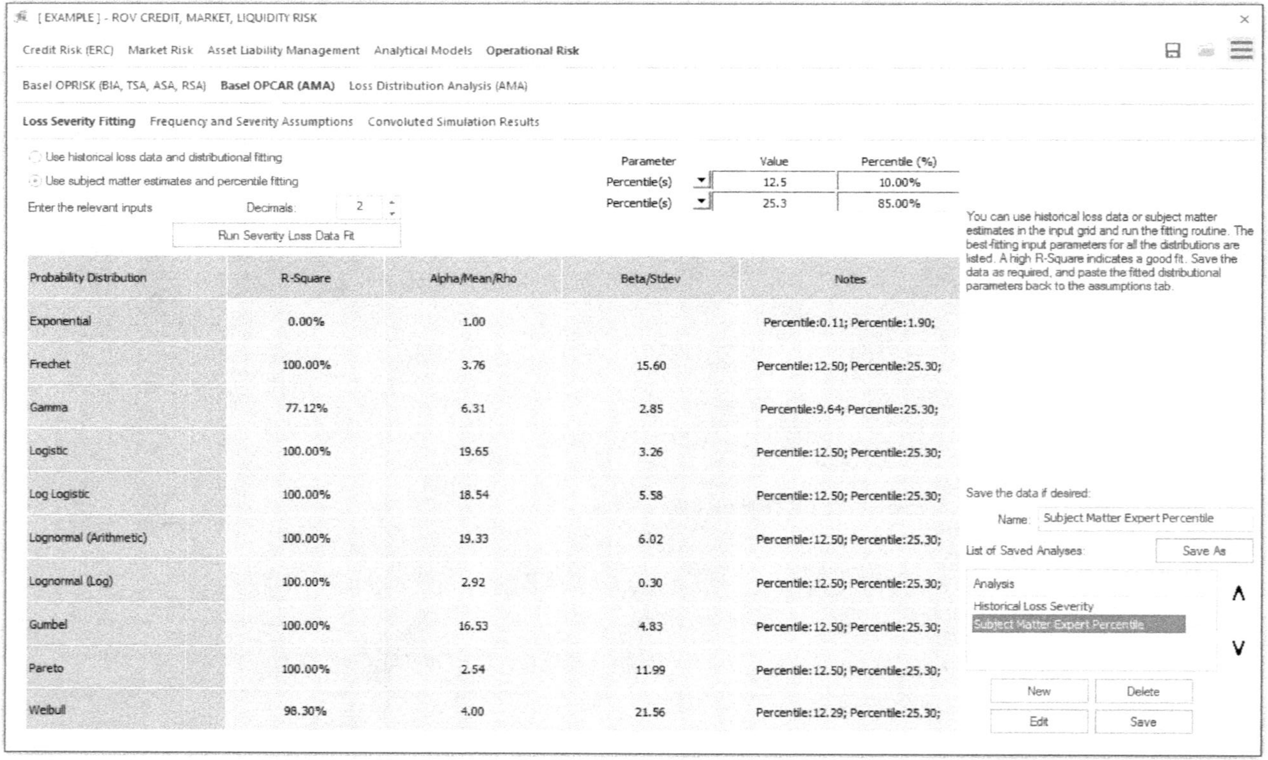

Figure 1.21: Basel OPCAR Loss Severity Percentile

ANALYTICAL MODELS

With the new Basel III/IV/IV and IV Accords, internationally active banks are now required to compute their own risk capital requirements using the internal ratings–based (IRB) approach. Not only is adequate risk capital analysis important as a compliance obligation, it provides banks with the ability to optimize their capital through the ability to compute and allocate risks, carry out performance measurements, execute strategic decisions, increase competitiveness, and enhance profitability. This chapter discusses the various *scientific risk management* approaches required to implement an IRB method, as well as the step-by-step models and methodologies in implementing and valuing economic capital, Value at Risk (VaR), probability of default, and loss given default, the key ingredients required in an IRB approach, through the use of advanced analytics such as Monte Carlo and historical risk simulation, portfolio optimization, stochastic forecasting, and options analysis. This chapter shows the use of Risk Simulator and the Modeling Toolkit software in computing and calibrating these critical input parameters. Instead of dwelling on theory or revamping what has already been written many times over, this chapter focuses solely on the practical modeling applications of the key ingredients to the Basel III/IV and III Accords.

To follow along the analyses in this chapter, we assume that the reader already has *Risk Simulator*, *Real Options SLS*, and the *ROV Modeling Toolkit* installed, and are somewhat familiar with the basic functions of each software program. If not, please refer to www.realoptionsvaluation.com (click on the Downloads link) and watch the getting started videos, read some of the getting started case studies, or to install the latest trial versions of these software programs and their extended licenses. You can download and install the demo version of Modeling Toolkit from the ROV website.

Probability of Default

Probability of default measures the degree of likelihood that the borrower of a loan or debt (the obligor) will be unable to make the necessary scheduled repayments on the debt, thereby defaulting on the debt. Should the obligor be unable to pay, the debt is in default, and the lenders of the debt have legal avenues to attempt a recovery of the debt, or at least partial repayment of the entire debt. The higher the default probability a lender estimates a borrower to have, the higher the interest rate the lender will charge the borrower as compensation for bearing the higher default risk.

Probability of default models are categorized as *structural* or *empirical*. Structural models look at a borrower's ability to pay based on market data such as equity prices, market and book values of asset and liabilities, as well as the volatility of these variables, and, hence, are used predominantly to estimate the probability of default of *companies* and *countries*, most applicable within the areas of commercial and industrial banking. In contrast, empirical models or credit scoring models are used to quantitatively determine the probability that a loan or loan holder will default, where the loan holder is an individual, by looking at historical portfolios of loans held, where individual characteristics are assessed (e.g., age, educational level, debt to income ratio, and so forth), making this second approach more applicable to the retail banking sector.

Structural Models of Probability of Default

Probability of default models differ from regular credit scoring models in several ways. First of all, credit scoring models are usually applied to smaller credits—individuals or small businesses—whereas default models are applied to larger credits—corporations or countries. Credit scoring models are largely statistical, regressing instances of default against various risk indicators, such as an obligor's income, home renter or owner status, years at a job, educational level, debt to income ratio, and so forth, something that will be shown later in this case. Structural default models, in contrast, directly model the default process, and are typically calibrated to market variables, such as the obligor's stock price, asset value, book value of debt, or the credit spread on its bonds. Default models have many applications within financial institutions. They are used to support credit analysis and for finding the probability that a firm will default, to value counterparty credit risk limits, or to apply financial engineering techniques in developing credit derivatives or other credit instruments.

The example illustrated next uses the Merton probability of default model. This model is used to solve the probability of default of a publicly traded company with equity and debt holdings, and accounting for its volatilities in the market (Figure 2.1). This model is currently used by KMV and Moody's to perform credit risk analysis. This approach assumes that the book value of an asset and asset volatility are unknown and solved in the model, and that the company is relatively stable, and the growth rate of the company's assets are stable over time (e.g., not in startup mode). The model uses several simultaneous equations in options valuation theory coupled with optimization to obtain the implied underlying asset's market value and volatility of the asset in order to compute the probability of default and distance to default for the firm.

Illustrative Example: Structural Probability of Default Models on Public Firms

It is assumed that at this point, the reader is well versed in running simulations and optimizations in Risk Simulator. The example model used is the *Probability of Default – External Options Model* and can be accessed through *Modeling Toolkit | Prob of Default | External Options Model (Public Company)*.

To run this model (Figure 2.1), enter in the required inputs such as the market value of equity (obtained from market data on the firm's capitalization, that is, stock price times number of shares outstanding), equity volatility (computed in the Volatility or LPVA worksheets in the model), book value of debt and liabilities (the firm's book value of all debt and liabilities), the risk-free rate (the prevailing country's risk-free interest rate for the same maturity as the debt), and the debt maturity (the debt maturity to be analyzed, or enter 1 for the annual default probability). The comparable option parameters are shown in cells G18 to G23. All these comparable inputs are computed except for Asset Value (the market value of asset) and the Volatility of Asset. You will need to input some rough estimates as a starting point so that the analysis can be run. The rule of thumb is to set the volatility of the asset in G22 to be one fifth to half of the volatility of equity computed in G10, and the market value of asset (G19) to be approximately the sum of the market value of equity and book value of liabilities and debt (G9 and G11).

Then, an optimization needs to be run in Risk Simulator in order to obtain the desired outputs. To do this, set Asset Value and Volatility of Asset as the decision variables (make them continuous variables with a lower limit of 1% for volatility and $1 for asset, as both these inputs can only take on positive values). Set cell G29 as the objective to minimize as this is the absolute error value. Finally, the constraint is such that cell H33, the implied volatility in the default model is set to exactly equal the numerical value of the equity volatility in cell G10. Run a static optimization using Risk Simulator.

If the model has a solution, the absolute error value in cell G29 will revert to zero (Figure 2.2). From here, the probability of default (measured in percent) and distance to default (measured in standard deviations) are computed in cells G39 and G41.

Then, using the resulting probability of default, the relevant credit spread required can be determined using the *Credit Analysis – Credit Premium* model or some other credit spread tables (such as using the *Internal Credit Risk Rating* model).

The results indicate that the company has a probability of default at 0.87% with 2.37 standard deviations to default, indicating good creditworthiness (Figure 2.2).

Illustrative Example: Structural Probability of Default Models on Private Firms

In addition, several other structural models exist for computing the probability of default of a firm. Specific models are used depending on the need and availability of data. In the previous example, the firm is a publicly traded firm, with stock prices and equity volatility that can be readily obtained from the market. In this next example, we assume that the firm is privately held, meaning that there would be no market equity data available. It essentially computes the probability of default or the point of default for the company when its liabilities exceed its assets, given the asset's growth rates and volatility over time (Figure 2.3). It is recommended that before using this model, the previous model on external publicly traded companies is first reviewed. Similar methodological parallels exist between these two models, whereby this example builds upon the knowledge and expertise of the previous example. In Figure 2.3, the example firm with an asset value of $12M and a book value of debt at $10M with significant growth rates of its internal assets and low volatility returns a 0.67% probability of default. In addition, instead of relying on the valuation of the firm, external market benchmarks can be used if such data are available. In Figure 2.4, we see that additional input assumptions such as the market fluctuation (market returns and volatility) and relationship (correlation between the market benchmark and the company's assets) are required. The model used is the *Probability of Default – Merton Market Options Model* accessible from *Modeling Toolkit | Prob of Default | Merton Market Options Model (Industry Comparable)*.

DEFAULT PROBABILITY (EXTERNAL MARKET APPROACH)

This model is used to solve the probability of default of a publicly traded company with equity and debt holdings, and accounting for its volatilities in the market. This model is currently used by KMV and Moody's to perform credit risk analysis. This approach assumes that the book value of asset and asset volatility are unknown and solved.

STEP ONE:

Available market and corporate data stating that we have:

Market Value Equity	$3,000	(in millions)
Market Equity Volatility	46.62%	(annualized)
Book Value Liabilities and Debt	$10,000	(in millions)
Risk-free Spot Rate	5.00%	
Maturity of Debt	1.00	

Inputs in the real options model:

	Solved	Starting	Optimized
Call Value	$2.491		
Asset Value*	$12,000	$12,000	$12,509
Strike Value	$10,000	Using Modeling Toolkit Functions	
Maturity	1		
Volatility of Asset*	10.00%	10.00%	11.26%
Risk-free Rate	5.0%	Using Modeling Toolkit Functions	

Optimization parameters:

Call value:	$3,000
Computed value:	$2,491
Minimize Absolute Difference:	$509

Optimization Constraints:

Set value	39.65%	to be exactly	46.62%
Set Lower Bounds for Asset Value and Volatility of Asset at $1 and 1%			

STEP TWO:

Default Probability is computed using the Risk Simulator Distribution Analysis tool on:

Default Probability:	1.1507%	This is the computed probability of def
Distance to Default:	2.2732	This is the computed distance to defac
Computed Expected Recovery Rate:	96.33%	
Computed Market Value of Debt:	9509.11	

Figure 2.1: Probability of Default Model for External Public Firms

DEFAULT PROBABILITY (EXTERNAL MARKET APPROACH)

This model is used to solve the probability of default of a publicly traded company with equity and debt holdings and accounting for its volatilities in the market. This model is currently used by KMV and Moody's to perform credit risk analysis. This approach assumes that the book value of asset and asset volatility are unknown and solved

Real Options Valuation
www.realoptionsvaluation.com

STEP ONE:

Available market and corporate data stating that we have

Market Value Equity	$3,000	(in millions)
Market Equity Volatility	46.62%	(annualized)
Book Value Liabilities and Debt	$10,000	(in millions)
Risk-free Spot Rate	5.00%	
Maturity of Debt	1.00	

This value is obtained from market data on the firm's capitalization
This value is computed in the Volatility or LPVA worksheets
This is the firm's book value of debt and liabilities
This is the prevailing risk-free interest rate for the same maturity
This is the expected annualized cumulative growth rate of the firm's assets
This is the debt maturity or enter 1 for the annual default probability
*** Usually this is set as the risk-free rate for a risk-neutral analysis

Inputs in the real options model:

	Solved	Starting	Optimized	
Call Value	$3,000	$3,000		This is the value of the option and should be set to the equity value using o
Asset Value*	$12,509	$12,000	$12,509	This is the value to be solved* and is hence set as a decision variable in R
Strike Value	$10,000	$10,000		This is set as the book value of debt
Maturity	1			For simplicity, we set this as 1 year to obtain the 1-year default probability
Volatility of Asset*	11.26%	10.00%	11.26%	This is the value to be solved* and is hence set as a decision variable in R
Risk-free Rate	5.0%			This is the corresponding risk-free rate for the maturity of the option being

Using Modeling Toolkit Functions
Using Modeling Toolkit Functions

Optimization parameters:

Call value	$3,000	This is the target result
Computed value	$3,000	This is the computed result
Minimize Absolute Difference:	$0	Objective to Minimize (we minimize the error function to solve the simultan

Optimization Constraints
Set value   46.64%   to be exactly   46.62%   which is the equity volatility
Set Lower Bounds for Asset Value and Volatility of Asset at $1 and 1% (so they do not go negative)

STEP TWO:

Default Probability is computed using the Risk Simulator Distribution Analysis tool on:

Default Probability:	0.8736%	This is the computed probability of default
Distance to Default:	2.3766	This is the computed distance to default in standard deviations
Computed Expected Recovery Rate:	96.33%	
Computed Market Value of Debt:	9509.11	

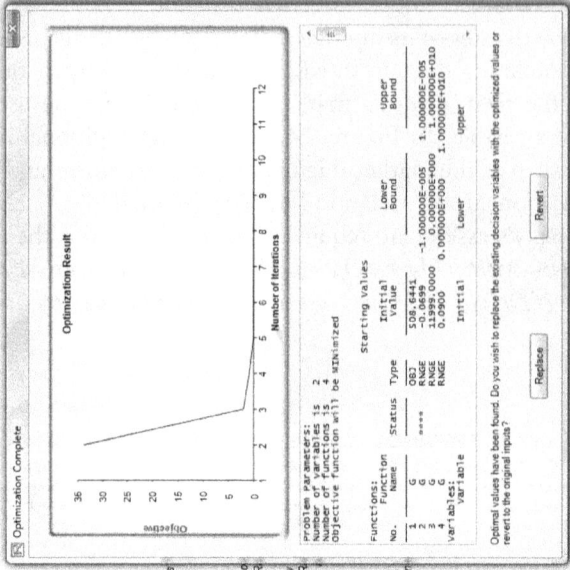

Optimization Complete

Optimization Result

Objective (y-axis: 36, 30, 25, 20, 16, 10, 5)
Number of Iterations (x-axis: 2, 3, 4, 5, 6, 7, 8, 9, 10, 11, 12)

Problem Parameters:
Number of variables is   2
Number of functions is   4
Objective function will be MINImized

Functions:

No.	Function Name	Status	Type	Initial Value
1	G	*****	OBJ	$08.6441
2	G		RNGE	-0.0699
3	G		RNGE	11999.0000

Variables:

variable			Initial	Lower	Upper

Starting Values

	Initial Value	Lower Bound	Upper Bound
	$08.6441		
	-0.0699	-1.0000000E-005	1.0000000E-005
	11999.0000	0.0000000E+000	1.0000000E+010
	0.0900	0.0000000E+000	1.0000000E+010

Optimal values have been found. Do you wish to replace the existing decision variables with the optimized values or revert to the original inputs?

Replace   Revert

Figure 2.2: Optimized Model Results Showing Probability of Default

CREDIT RISK DEFAULT PROBABILITY (OPTIONS APPROACH)

VALUING DEFAULT PROBABILITY AND DISTANCE TO DEFAULT BASED ON OPTIONS MODELING OF INTERNAL DEBT

This is the options approach to computing the probability of default and distance to default of a company assuming that the book values of asset and debt are known, as are the asset volatilities and anticipated annual growth rates. If the book value of assets or volatility of assets are not known and the company is publicly traded, use the External Markets model instead. This model assumes these inputs are known or the company is privately held and not traded.

Input Assumptions

Asset Book Value	$12.0000
Debt Book Value	$10.0000
Maturity	1.0000
Risk-free Rate	7.00%
Volatility of Asset	10.00%

Probability of Default   0.6695%
Distance to Default   2.4732

Function: B2ProbabilityDefaultMertonII (Asset Value, Strike, Maturity, Riskfree, Asset Volatility)
Function: B2ProbabilityDefaultMertonDefaultDistance(Asset Value, Strike, Maturity, Asset Volatility, Riskfree Rate)

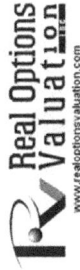

Figure 2.3: Probability of Default of a Privately Held Company

MERTON MODEL OF DEBT DEFAULT PROBABILITY

VALUING THE PROBABILITY OF DEFAULT BASED ON MARKET RELATIONSHIPS

This models the probability of default for both public and private companies using an index or set of comparables (the market), assuming that the company's asset and debt book values are known, as well as the asset's annualized volatility. Based on this volatility and the correlation of the company's assets to the market, we can determine the probability of default.

Input Assumptions

Asset Value	$100.0000
Debt Value	$50.0000
Time to Maturity	1.00
Risk-free Rate	5.00%
Volatility of Asset	20.00%
Market Volatility	10.00%
Market Return	8.00%
Correlation	0.00

Probability of Default   0.0150%

Function: B2ProbabilityDefaultMertonI (Asset, Debt, Maturity, Riskfree, Asset Volatility, Market Volatility, Market Return, Correlation)

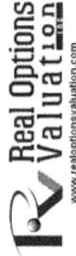

Credit Risk (ERC)   Market Risk   Asset Liability Management   **Analytical Models**   Operational Risk   Key Risk Indicator (KRI)

Credit (Structural)   Credit (Time Series)   Credit (Portfolio)   Credit (Models)

STEP 1: Select the Analysis Category and the Model to run:

Analysis	Model
Exposure at Default (EAD)	**PD using Market Comparables**
Loss Given Default (LGD)	PD using Bond Yields and Spreads
Probability of Default (PD)	
Volatility	

Probability of default measures the degree of likelihood that the borrower of a loan or debt (the obligor) will be unable to make the necessary scheduled repayments on the debt.

Given the annualized spot risk-free yields over time, the corresponding corporate bond yields (both are zero coupon bonds), and the expected recovery rate upon default, we can compute the cumulative default probability, the default probability in a particular year, and the hazard rates for each year.

STEP 2: Enter the required inputs:

Show   3 ⌄   rows and   6 ⌄   decimals for results

Computations   Charts

Enter numerical inputs only (e.g. $1,000 please enter as 1000 and 99% enter as 0.99 and so forth).

STEP 3: Save the Models and Data:

You can save multiple analyses and notes in the profile for future retrieval.

Name: _____   Probability of Default (Market Comps) Example

Notes:

	Model
Save As	EAD using Credit Conversion Factor CCF
Edit	Credit Risk Plus Average Defaults Example
	EAD using LEQ, CCF, EADF
Save	Loss Given Default (LGD) Example
	Probability of Default (Market Comps) Exa...
Delete	Probability of Default (Bond Spreads) Exa...
	Implied Volatility from a Call Option

STEP 4: Run the Models: [Compute]

N	Probability Of Default	Name	Asset Value	Book Value of Li...	Risk-Free Rate	Maturity	Asset Volatility	Market Equity V...	Market Return	Correlation
1	0.001150	Company 1	100,000	50,000	0.05	1	0.20	0.10	0.08	0
2	0.147610	Company 2	15,000	13,000	0.05	3	0.15	0.25	0.12	0.1
3	0.009802	Company 3	20,000	10,000	0.02	1	0.30	0.45	0.14	0.4

Figure 2.4: Default Probability of a Privately Held Entity Calibrated to Market Fluctuations

As mentioned previously, empirical models of probability of default are used to compute an individual's default probability, applicable within the retail banking arena, where empirical or actual historical or comparable data exists on past credit defaults. The dataset in Figure 2.5 represents a sample of several thousand previous loans and credit or debt issues. The data shows whether each loan had defaulted or not (0 for no default, and 1 for default), as well as the specifics of each loan applicant's age, education level (1–3 indicating high school, university, or graduate professional education), years with current employer, and so forth. The idea is to model these empirical data to see which variables affect the default behavior of individuals, using Risk Simulator's *Maximum Likelihood Estimation* (MLE) tool. The resulting model will help the bank or credit issuer compute the expected probability of default of an individual credit holder of having specific characteristics.

Illustrative Example: Applying Empirical Models of Probability of Default

The example file is *Probability of Default – Empirical* and can be accessed through *Modeling Toolkit | Prob of Default | Empirical (Individuals)*. To run the analysis, select the dataset (include the headers) and make sure that the data have the same length for all variables, without any missing or invalid data points. Then, using Risk Simulator, click on *Risk Simulator | Forecasting | Maximum Likelihood Models*. A sample set of results is provided in the MLE worksheet, complete with detailed instructions on how to compute the expected probability of default of an individual.

The MLE approach applies a modified binary multivariate logistic analysis to model dependent variables to determine the expected probability of success of belonging to a certain group. For instance, given a set of independent variables (e.g., age, income, education level of credit card or mortgage loan holders), we can model the probability of default using MLE. A typical regression model is invalid because the errors are heteroskedastic and non-normal, and the resulting estimated probability forecast will sometimes be above 1 or below 0. MLE analysis handles these problems using an iterative optimization routine. The computed results show the coefficients of the estimated MLE intercept and slopes.[1]

The coefficients estimated are actually the logarithmic odds ratios and cannot be interpreted directly as probabilities. A quick but simple computation is first required. The approach is simple. To estimate the probability of success of belonging to a certain group (e.g., predicting if a debt holder will default given the amount of debt he or she holds), simply compute the estimated Y value using the MLE coefficients. Figure 2.6 illustrates an individual with 8 years at a current employer and current address, a low 3% debt to income ratio, and $2,000 in credit card debt has a log-odds ratio of -3.1549. Then, the inverse antilog of the odds ratio is obtained by computing:

$$\frac{exp(\ estimated\ Y)}{1 + exp(\ estimated\ Y)} = \frac{exp(-\ 3.1549)}{1 + exp(-\ 3.1549)} = 0.0409$$

So, such a person has a 4.09% chance of defaulting on the new debt. Using this probability of default, you can then use the *Credit Analysis – Credit Premium* model to determine the additional credit spread to charge this person given this default level and the customized cash flows anticipated from this debt holder.

---

[1] For instance, the coefficients are estimates of the true population β values in the following equation: $Y = \beta_0 + \beta_1 X_1 + \beta_2 X_2 + ... + \beta_n X_n$. The standard error measures how accurate the predicted coefficients are, and the Z-statistics are the ratios of each predicted coefficient to its standard error. The Z-statistic is used in hypothesis testing, where we set the null hypothesis (H_o) such that the real mean of the coefficient is equal to zero, and the alternate hypothesis (H_a) such that the real mean of the coefficient is not equal to zero. The Z-test is very important as it calculates if each of the coefficients is statistically significant in the presence of the other regressors. This means that the Z-test statistically verifies whether a regressor or independent variable should remain in the model or should be dropped. That is, the smaller the p-value, the more significant the coefficient. The usual significant levels for the p-value are 0.01, 0.05, and 0.10, corresponding to the 99%, 95%, and 90% confidence levels.

PROBABILITY OF DEFAULT (EMPIRICAL METHOD USING MAXIMUM LIKELIHOOD MODELS ON HISTORICAL DATA)

Real Options Valuation
www.realoptionsvaluation.com

The data here represents a sample of several hundred previous loans, credit, or debt issues. The data show whether each loan had defaulted or not, as well as the specifics of each loan applicant's age, education level (1-3 indicating high school, university, or graduate professional education), years with current employer and so forth. The idea is to model these empirical data to see which variables affect the default behavior of individuals, using Risk Simulator's Maximum Likelihood Models. The resulting model will help the bank or credit issuer compute the expected probability of default of an individual credit holder of having specific characteristics.

To run the analysis, select the data on the left or any other data set (include the headers) and make sure that the data have the same length for all variables, without any missing or invalid data. Then, click on Risk Simulator | Forecasting | Maximum Likelihood Models. A sample set of results are provided in the MLE worksheet, complete with detailed instructions on how to compute the expected probability of default of an individual.

Defaulted	Age	Education Level	Years with Current Employer	Years at Current Address	Household Income (Thousands $)	Debt to Income Ratio (%)	Credit Card Debt (Thousands $)	Other Debt (Thousands $)
1	41	3	17	12	176	9.3	11.36	5.01
0	27	1	10	6	31	17.3	1.36	4
0	40	1	15	14	55	5.5	0.86	2.17
0	41	1	15	14	120	2.9	2.66	0.82
1	24	2	2	0	28	17.3	1.79	3.06
0	41	2	5	5	25	10.2	0.39	2.16
0	39	1	20	9	67	30.6	3.83	16.67
0	43	1	12	11	38	3.6	0.13	1.24
1	24	1	3	4	19	24.4	1.36	3.28
0	36	1	0	13	25	19.7	2.78	2.15
0	27	1	0	1	16	1.7	0.18	0.09
0	25	1	4	0	23	5.2	0.25	0.94
0	52	1	24	14	64	10	3.93	2.47
0	37	1	6	9	29	16.3	1.72	3.01
0	48	1	22	15	100	9.1	3.7	5.4
1	36	2	9	6	49	8.6	0.82	3.4
1	36	2	13	6	41	16.4	2.92	3.81
0	43	1	23	19	72	7.6	1.18	4.29
0	39	1	6	9	61	5.7	0.56	2.91
0	41	3	0	21	26	1.7	0.1	0.34
0	39	1	22	3	52	3.2	1.15	0.51
0	47	1	17	21	43	5.6	0.59	1.82
0	28	1	3	6	26	10	0.43	2.17
0	29	1	8	6	27	9.8	0.4	2.24
1	21	2	1	2	16	18	0.24	2.64
0	25	4	0	2	32	17.6	2.14	3.49
0	45	2	9	26	69	6.7	0.71	3.92
0	43	1	25	21	64	16.7	0.95	9.74

Figure 2.5: Empirical Analysis of Probability of Default

MLE Results

Log Likelihood Value   -200.507

Variable	Coefficients	Standard Error	Z-Statistic	p-Value	Sample Inputs
Age	-1.7003	0.7512	-2.2634	0.0236	
Education Level	0.0279	0.0205	1.3588	0.1742	
Years with Current Employer	0.0728	0.1447	0.5028	0.6151	8.000
Years at Current Address	-0.2528	0.0391	-6.4644	0.0000	8.000
Household Income (Thousands)	-0.0952	0.0271	-3.5064	0.0005	
Debt to Income Ratio (%)	0.0009	0.0125	0.0754	0.9399	
Credit Card Debt (Thousands $)	0.0750	0.0396	1.8934	0.0583	3.000
Other Debt (Thousands $)	0.5521	0.1324	4.1697	0.0000	2.000
	0.0461	0.1005	0.4592	0.6461	

Log Odds	-3.1549
Ratio	
Default	
Probability	**4.09%**

Figure 2.6: MLE Results

As shown previously, probability of default is a key parameter for computing credit risk of a portfolio. In fact, the Basel III/IV and III Accords require the probability of default as well as other key parameters such as the loss given default (LGD) and exposure at default (EAD), be reported as well. The reason is that a bank's expected loss is equivalent to:

Expected Losses = (Probability of Default)
× (Loss Given Default) × (Exposure at Default)
or simply: EL = PD × LGD × EAD

PD and LGD are both percentages, whereas EAD is a value. As we have shown how to compute PD in the previous section, we will now revert to some estimations of LGD. There are again several methods used to estimate LGD. The first is through a simple empirical approach where we set *LGD = 1 – Recovery Rate*. That is, whatever is not recovered at default is the loss at default, computed as the charge off (net of recovery) divided by the outstanding balance:

$$LGD = 1 - Recovery\ Rate$$

or

$$LGD = \frac{Charge\ Offs\ (Net\ of\ Recovery)}{Outstanding\ Balance\ at\ Default}$$

Therefore, if market data or historical information is available, LGD can be segmented by various market conditions, types of obligor, and other pertinent segmentations (use Risk Simulator's segmentation tool to perform this). LGD can then be readily read off a chart.

A second approach to estimate LGD is more attractive in that if the bank has available information, it can attempt to run some econometric models to create the best-fitting model under an ordinary least squares approach. By using this approach, a single model can be determined and calibrated, and this same model can be applied under various conditions, and no data mining is required. However, in most econometric models, a normal transformation will have to be performed first. Suppose the bank has some historical LGD data (Figure 2.7), then the best-fitting distribution can be found using Risk Simulator by first selecting the historical data, and then clicking on *Risk Simulator | Analytical Tools | Distributional Fitting (Single Variable)* to perform the fitting routine. The example's result is a beta distribution for the thousands of LGD values. The p-value can also be evaluated for the goodness-of-fit of the theoretical distribution (i.e., the higher the p-value, the better the distributional fit; so in this example, the historical LGD fits a beta distribution 81% of the time, indicating a good fit).

Past LGD   Normalized

Past LGD	Normalized
49.69%	28.54%
25.76%	18.27%
14.61%	11.84%
26.91%	18.83%
18.47%	14.33%
21.29%	15.95%
26.00%	18.39%
11.84%	9.76%
51.85%	29.41%
19.35%	14.84%
24.74%	17.76%
15.68%	12.57%
14.35%	11.66%
21.36%	15.98%
35.31%	22.65%
50.71%	28.95%
28.58%	19.63%
5.96%	3.77%
3.84%	0.38%
21.70%	16.17%
71.28%	37.64%
23.49%	17.12%
20.25%	15.36%
44.01%	26.26%
31.27%	20.87%
40.86%	24.98%
26.54%	18.65%
25.29%	18.04%
28.51%	19.60%
55.40%	30.84%
31.57%	21.00%
16.30%	12.98%
24.37%	17.57%
8.46%	6.70%
77.08%	40.52%

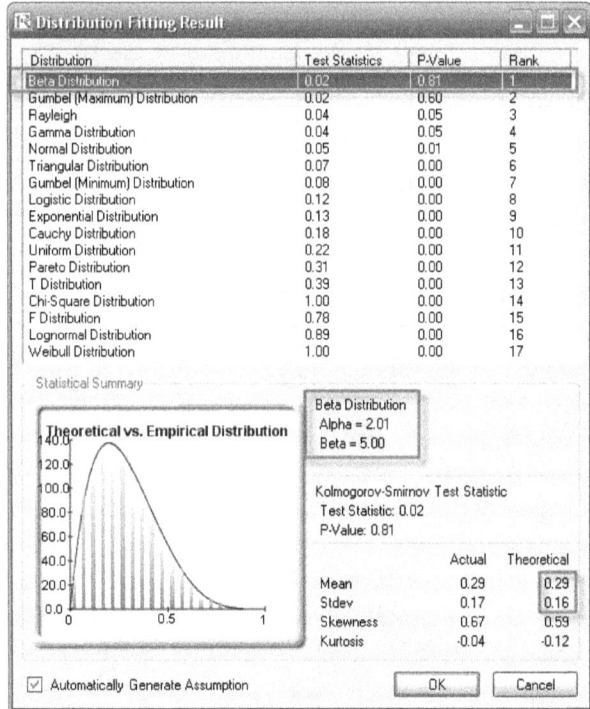

Distribution Fitting Result

Distribution	Test Statistics	P-Value	Rank
Beta Distribution	0.02	0.81	1
Gumbel (Maximum) Distribution	0.02	0.60	2
Rayleigh	0.04	0.05	3
Gamma Distribution	0.04	0.05	4
Normal Distribution	0.05	0.01	5
Triangular Distribution	0.07	0.00	6
Gumbel (Minimum) Distribution	0.08	0.00	7
Logistic Distribution	0.12	0.00	8
Exponential Distribution	0.13	0.00	9
Cauchy Distribution	0.18	0.00	10
Uniform Distribution	0.22	0.00	11
Pareto Distribution	0.31	0.00	12
T Distribution	0.39	0.00	13
Chi-Square Distribution	1.00	0.00	14
F Distribution	0.78	0.00	15
Lognormal Distribution	0.89	0.00	16
Weibull Distribution	1.00	0.00	17

Statistical Summary

Theoretical vs. Empirical Distribution

Beta Distribution
Alpha = 2.01
Beta = 5.00

Kolmogorov-Smirnov Test Statistic
Test Statistic: 0.02
P-Value: 0.81

	Actual	Theoretical
Mean	0.29	0.29
Stdev	0.17	0.16
Skewness	0.67	0.59
Kurtosis	-0.04	-0.12

☑ Automatically Generate Assumption   OK   Cancel

Figure 2.7: Fitting Historical LGD Data

Next, using the Distribution Analysis tool in Risk Simulator, obtain the theoretical mean and standard deviation of the fitted distribution (Figure 2.8). Then, transform the LGD variable using the *MTNormalTransform* function in the Modeling Toolkit software. For instance, the value 49.69% will be transformed and normalized to 28.54% (Figure 2.7). Using this newly transformed dataset, you can now run some nonlinear econometric models to determine LGD.

The following is a partial list of independent variables that might be significant for a bank, in terms of determining and forecasting the LGD value:

- Debt to capital ratio
- Profit margin
- Revenue
- Current assets to current liabilities
- Risk rating at default and one year before default
- Industry
- Authorized balance at default
- Collateral value
- Facility type
- Tightness of covenant
- Seniority of debt
- Operating income to sales ratio (and other efficiency ratios)
- Total asset, total net worth, total liabilities

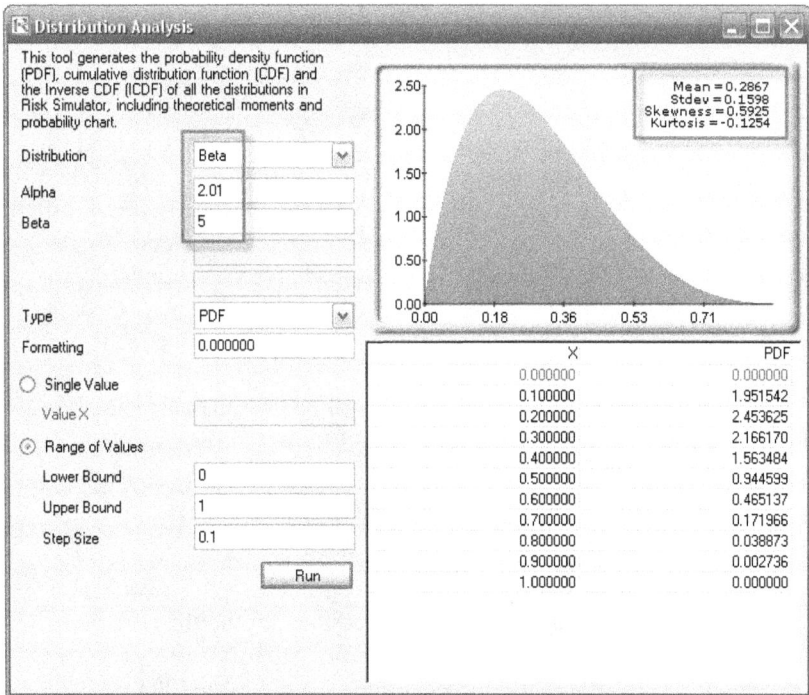

Figure 2.8: Distributional Analysis Tool

Economic Capital and Value at Risk

Economic capital is critical to a bank as it links a bank's earnings and returns to risks that are specific to a business line or business opportunity. In addition, these economic capital measurements can be aggregated into a portfolio of holdings. Value at Risk or (VaR) is used in trying to understand how the entire organization is affected by the various risks of each holding as aggregated into a portfolio, after accounting for their cross-correlations among various holdings. VaR measures the maximum possible loss given some predefined probability level (e.g., 99.90%) over some holding period or time horizon (e.g., 10 days). The selected probability or confidence interval is typically a decision made by senior management at the bank and reflects the board's risk appetite. Stated another way, we can define the probability level as the bank's desired probability of surviving per year. In addition, the holding period is usually chosen such that it coincides with the time period it takes to liquidate a loss position.

VaR can be computed several ways. Two main families of approaches exist: structural closed-form models and Monte Carlo risk simulation approaches. We will showcase both methods in this case, starting with the structural models.

The second and much more powerful approach is the use of Monte Carlo risk simulation. Instead of simply correlating individual business lines or assets in the structural models, entire probability distributions can be correlated using more advanced mathematical copulas and simulation algorithms in Monte Carlo simulation methods by using Risk Simulator. In addition, tens to hundreds of thousands of scenarios can be generated using simulation, providing a very powerful stress-testing mechanism for valuing VaR. In addition, distributional fitting methods are applied to reduce the thousands of data points into their appropriate probability distributions, allowing their modeling to be handled with greater ease.

Illustrative Example: Structural VaR Models

The first VaR example model shown is the *Value at Risk – Static Covariance Method,* accessible through *Modeling Toolkit | Value at Risk | Static Covariance Method.* This model is used to compute the portfolio's VaR at a given percentile for a specific holding period, after accounting for the cross-correlation effects between the assets (Figure 2.9). The daily volatility is the annualized volatility divided by the square root of trading days per year. Typically, positive correlations tend to carry a higher VaR compared to zero correlation asset mixes, whereas negative correlations reduce the total risk of the portfolio through the diversification effect (Figure 2.10). The approach used is a portfolio VaR with correlated inputs, where the portfolio has multiple asset holdings with different amounts and volatilities. Each asset is also correlated to each other. The covariance or correlation structural model is used to compute the VaR given a holding period or horizon and percentile value (typically 10 days at 99% confidence). Of course, the example only illustrates a few assets or business lines or credit lines for simplicity's sake. Nonetheless, using the functions in the Modeling Toolkit, many more lines, assets, or businesses can be modeled (the function MTVaRCorrelationMethod is used in this example).

VALUE AT RISK (VARIANCE-COVARIANCE METHOD)

Asset Allocation	Amount	Daily Volatility
Asset A	$1,000,000.00	1.20%
Asset B	$2,000,000.00	2.00%
Asset C	$3,000,000.00	1.89%
Asset D	$4,000,000.00	3.25%
Asset E	$5,000,000.00	4.20%

Correlation Matrix	Asset A	Asset B	Asset C	Asset D	Asset E
Asset A	1.0000	0.1000	0.1000	0.1000	0.1000
Asset B	0.1000	1.0000	0.1000	0.1000	0.1000
Asset C	0.1000	0.1000	1.0000	0.1000	0.1000
Asset D	0.1000	0.1000	0.1000	1.0000	0.1000
Asset E	0.1000	0.1000	0.1000	0.1000	1.0000

Horizon (Days)	10
Percentile	99.00%

Value at Risk (Daily)	$655,915.30
Value at Risk (Horizon)	$2,074,186.30

Daily Value at Risk (Positive Correlations)	$2,074,186.30
Daily Value at Risk (Zero Correlations)	$1,889,345.26
Daily Value at Risk (Negative Correlations)	$1,684,340.28

Figure 2.9: Computing Value at Risk with Structural Covariance (continues)

Credit Risk (ERC)   Market Risk   Asset Liability Management   **Analytical Models**   Operational Risk   Key Risk Indicator (KRI)

Credit (Structural)   Credit (Time Series)   **Credit (Portfolio)**   Credit (Models)

STEP 1: Select the Analysis Category and the Model to run:

Analysis	Model
Bond Related Options, Pricing and Yields	**Static Covariance Method**
Value at Risk (VaR)	Value at Risk (Options)
	Portfolio Returns
	Portfolio Risk

Value at Risk (VaR) is worst case scenario X percentile (confidence level) losses or exposure of a portfolio or assets for a specific number of holding days.

This model is used to compute the portfolio's Value at Risk at a given percentile for a specific holding period, after accounting for the volatility and cross-correlation effects between the assets.

STEP 2: Enter the required inputs:

Show   5 ⌃⌄   assets and   5 ⌃⌄   decimals for results

Enter numerical inputs only (e.g. $1,000 please enter as 1000 and 99% enter as 0.99 and so forth).

	Amounts	Daily Volatility	Holding Days	Percentile
1	1,000,000.00	0.0120	10	0.99
2	2,000,000.00	0.0200		
3	3,000,000.00	0.0189		
4	4,000,000.00	0.0325		
5	5,000,000.00	0.0420		

STEP 3: Save the Models and Data:

You can save multiple analyses and notes in the profile for future retrieval.

Name.   Value at Risk: Static Covariance Method

Notes:

Save As		Model
Edit		Bond Price Discrete Discounting Example
		Bond Price Continuous Discounting Example
Save		Bond Convexity YTM Continuous Discountin...
		Bond Duration Discrete Discounting Example
Delete		Bond Macaulay Duration
		Bond Modified Duration
		Value at Risk: Static Covariance Method

STEP 4: Run the Models:

Correlation Matrix

	Asset 1	Asset 2	Asset 3	Asset 4	Asset 5
Asset 1	1.0000	0.1000	0.1000	0.1000	0.1000
Asset 2	0.1000	1.0000	0.1000	0.1000	0.1000
Asset 3	0.1000	0.1000	1.0000	0.1000	0.1000
Asset 4	0.1000	0.1000	0.1000	1.0000	0.1000
Asset 5	0.1000	0.1000	0.1000	0.1000	1.0000

Compute

Value at Risk (Daily) :
655915.232829;

Value at Risk (Horizon) :
2074186.087740;

Figure 2.9: Computing Value at Risk with Structural Covariance

Correlation Matrix	Asset A	Asset B	Asset C	Asset D	Asset E
Asset A	1.0000	0.1000	0.1000	0.1000	0.1000
Asset B	0.1000	1.0000	0.1000	0.1000	0.1000
Asset C	0.1000	0.1000	1.0000	0.1000	0.1000
Asset D	0.1000	0.1000	0.1000	1.0000	0.1000
Asset E	0.1000	0.1000	0.1000	0.1000	1.0000

Correlation Matrix	Asset A	Asset B	Asset C	Asset D	Asset E
Asset A	1.0000	0.0000	0.0000	0.0000	0.0000
Asset B	0.0000	1.0000	0.0000	0.0000	0.0000
Asset C	0.0000	0.0000	1.0000	0.0000	0.0000
Asset D	0.0000	0.0000	0.0000	1.0000	0.0000
Asset E	0.0000	0.0000	0.0000	0.0000	1.0000

Correlation Matrix	Asset A	Asset B	Asset C	Asset D	Asset E
Asset A	1.0000	-0.1000	-0.1000	-0.1000	-0.1000
Asset B	-0.1000	1.0000	-0.1000	-0.1000	-0.1000
Asset C	-0.1000	-0.1000	1.0000	-0.1000	-0.1000
Asset D	-0.1000	-0.1000	-0.1000	1.0000	-0.1000
Asset E	-0.1000	-0.1000	-0.1000	-0.1000	1.0000

Figure 2.10: Different Correlation Levels

Illustrative Example: VaR Models using Monte Carlo Risk Simulation

The model used is Value at Risk – Portfolio Operational and Capital Adequacy and is accessible through *Modeling Toolkit | Value at Risk | Portfolio Operational and Capital Adequacy*. This model shows how operational risk and credit risk parameters are fitted to statistical distributions and their resulting distributions are modeled in a portfolio of liabilities to determine the Value at Risk (e.g., 99.50th percentile certainty) for the capital requirement under Basel III/IV and III requirements. It is assumed that the historical data of the operational risk impacts (Historical Data worksheet) are obtained through econometric modeling of the Key Risk Indicators.

The *Distributional Fitting Report* worksheet is a result of running a distributional fitting routine in Risk Simulator to obtain the appropriate distribution for the operational risk parameter. Using the resulting distributional parameters, we model each liability's capital requirements within an entire portfolio. Correlations can also be inputted if required, between pairs of liabilities or business units. The resulting Monte Carlo simulation results show the Value at Risk or VaR capital requirements.

Note that an appropriate empirically based historical VaR cannot be obtained if distributional fitting and risk-based simulations were not first run. Only by running simulations will the VaR be obtained. To perform distributional fitting, follow the steps below:

1. In the Historical Data worksheet (Figure 2.11), select the data area (cells C5:L104) and click on *Risk Simulator | Analytical Tools | Distributional Fitting (Single Variable)*.

2. Browse through the fitted distributions and select the best-fitting distribution (in this case, the exponential distribution with a particularly high p-value fit, as shown in Figure 2.12) and click *OK*.

3. You may now set the assumptions on the *Operational Risk Factors* with the exponential distribution (fitted results show *Lambda* = 1) in the Credit Risk worksheet. Note that the assumptions have already been set for you in advance. You may set them by going to cell *F27* and clicking on *Risk Simulator | Set Input Assumption*, selecting *Exponential* distribution and entering *1* for the *Lambda* value, and clicking *OK*. Continue this process for the remaining cells in column F or simply perform a *Risk Simulator Copy* and *Risk Simulator Paste* on the remaining cells:

    a. Note that since the cells in column F have assumptions set, you will first have to clear them if you wish to reset and copy/paste parameters. You can do so by first selecting cells *F28:F126* and clicking on the *Remove Parameter* icon or select *Risk Simulator | Remove Parameter*.

    b. Then select cell F27, click on the Risk Simulator Copy icon or select *Risk Simulator | Copy Parameter*, and then select cells F28:F126 and click on the Risk Simulator Paste icon or select *Risk Simulator | Paste Parameter*.

4. Next, additional assumptions can be set such as the probability of default using the Bernoulli distribution (column H) and *Loss Given Default* (column J). Repeat the procedure in Step 3 if you wish to reset the assumptions.

5. Run the simulation by clicking on the *Run* icon or clicking on *Risk Simulator | Run Simulation*.

6. Obtain the Value at Risk by going to the forecast chart once the simulation is done running and selecting *Left-Tail* and typing in *99.50*. Hit *Tab* on the keyboard to enter the confidence value and obtain the VaR of $25,959 (Figure 2.13).

Basel II - Credit Risk and Capital Requirement (Portfolio-Based)

This model applies the Basel II requirements on capital adequacy and modeling the operational risk of probability of default on 100 loans as well as the loss given default. These values are fitted based on the bank's historical loss data (Historical Data and Distributional Fitting Report sheets) using Risk Simulator. Then, the relevant historical simulation assumptions are set in this model (Credit Risk sheet) and a Monte Carlo risk-based simulation was run in Risk Simulator to determine the expected capital required and 99.50% Value at Risk (VaR). A simulation has to be run in order to determine the VaR.

Market Factor	2.000	Rating level	P (Default) - Long term
		1	0.5%
		2	1.0%
Weighting:		3	1.5%
Macro	50%	4	2.0%
Micro	50%	5	2.5%
		6	3.0%
Correlation	100%	7	5.0%

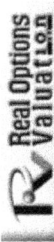

	Static	Stochastic with Risk-Simulation
Expected Value of Total Capital	$11,734.54	$11,112.81
VaR 99.50% of Total Capital	$30,888.34	$25,959.60

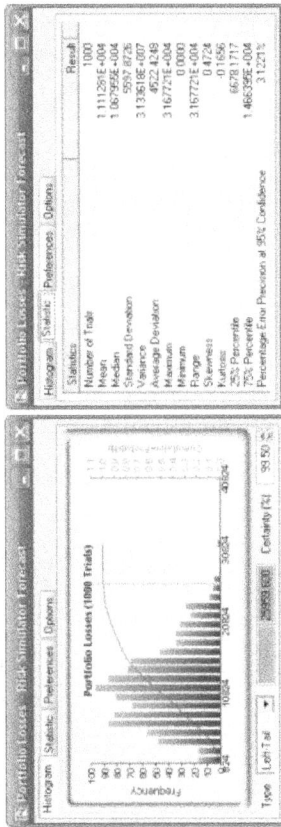

Without running historical simulations, the 99.50% VaR cannot be obtained directly. The only recourse is to apply a theoretical distributional analysis using the fitted distributions' empirical parameters and estimating the theoretical cumulative density function value at 99.50%, and computing the relevant theoretical confidence level. This approach is at best an overestimation of the required capital (thereby requiring too much capital) and at worst, wrong.

							Loss Given Default (LGD%)		Losses	
Bank loan	Size of loan	Rating grade	P (Default) - Long term	Operational Risk Factor	P (Default) - Now	Default?	Static	Stochastic	Static	Stochastic
1	$ 13,274.73	5	2.5%	2.000	5.00%	0	30.0%	30.0%	$ 199.12	$ -
2	$ 14,215.77	6	3.0%	2.000	6.00%	0	30.0%	30.0%	$ 255.88	$ -
3	$ 9,003.59	1	0.5%	2.000	1.00%	0	30.0%	30.0%	$ 27.01	$ -
4	$ 1,324.27	3	1.5%	2.000	3.00%	0	30.0%	30.0%	$ 11.92	$ -
5	$ 11,203.14	1	0.5%	2.000	1.00%	0	30.0%	30.0%	$ 33.61	$ -
6	$ 5,480.61	4	2.0%	2.000	4.00%	0	30.0%	30.0%	$ 65.77	$ -
7	$ 9,853.12	5	2.5%	2.000	5.00%	0	30.0%	30.0%	$ 147.80	$ -
8	$ 12,356.22	3	1.5%	2.000	3.00%	0	30.0%	30.0%	$ 111.21	$ -
9	$ 8,255.80	4	2.0%	2.000	4.00%	0	30.0%	30.0%	$ 99.07	$ -
10	$ 1,662.99	2	1.0%	2.000	2.00%	0	30.0%	30.0%	$ 9.98	$ -
11	$ 7,175.82	3	1.5%	2.000	3.00%	0	30.0%	30.0%	$ 64.58	$ -

Sum	$11,734.54	$ -
	Static 99.50%	$ 30,888.34

Figure 2.11: Sample Historical Bank Loans

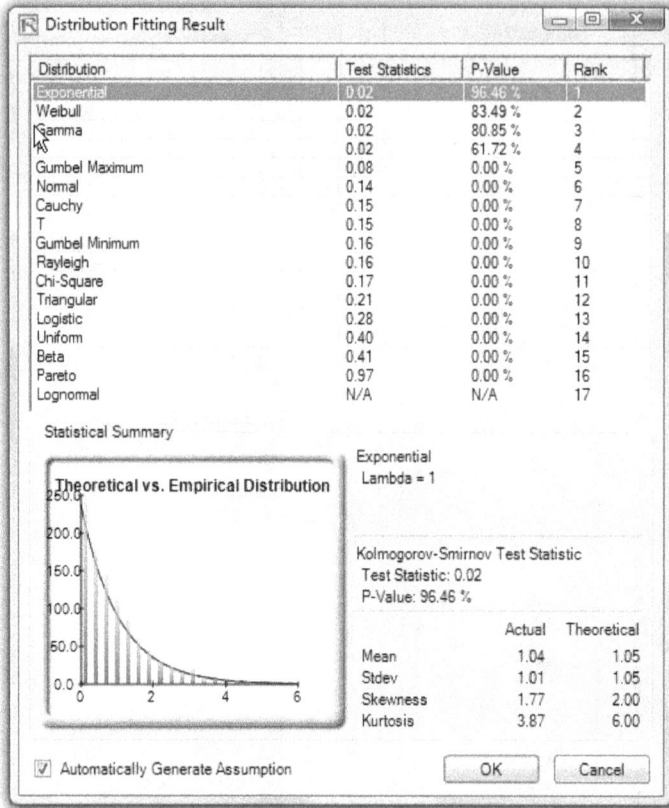

Distribution	Test Statistics	P-Value	Rank
Exponential	0.02	96.46 %	1
Weibull	0.02	83.49 %	2
Gamma	0.02	80.85 %	3
	0.02	61.72 %	4
Gumbel Maximum	0.08	0.00 %	5
Normal	0.14	0.00 %	6
Cauchy	0.15	0.00 %	7
T	0.15	0.00 %	8
Gumbel Minimum	0.16	0.00 %	9
Rayleigh	0.16	0.00 %	10
Chi-Square	0.17	0.00 %	11
Triangular	0.21	0.00 %	12
Logistic	0.28	0.00 %	13
Uniform	0.40	0.00 %	14
Beta	0.41	0.00 %	15
Pareto	0.97	0.00 %	16
Lognormal	N/A	N/A	17

Statistical Summary

Theoretical vs. Empirical Distribution

Exponential
Lambda = 1

Kolmogorov-Smirnov Test Statistic
Test Statistic: 0.02
P-Value: 96.46 %

	Actual	Theoretical
Mean	1.04	1.05
Stdev	1.01	1.05
Skewness	1.77	2.00
Kurtosis	3.87	6.00

Figure 2.12: Data Fitting Results

Another example of VaR computation is shown next, where the model Value at Risk – Right Tail Capital Requirements is used and available through *Modeling Toolkit | Value at Risk | Right Tail Capital Requirements*. This model shows the capital requirements per Basel III/IV and III requirements (99.95th percentile capital adequacy based on a specific holding period's Value at Risk). Without running risk-based historical and Monte Carlo simulation using Risk Simulator, the required capital is $37.01M (Figure 2.14) as compared to only $14.00M required using a correlated simulation (Figure 2.15). This is due to the cross-correlations between assets and business lines and can only be modeled using Risk Simulator. This lower VaR is preferred as banks can now be required to hold less capital and can reinvest the remaining capital in various profitable ventures, thereby generating higher profits.

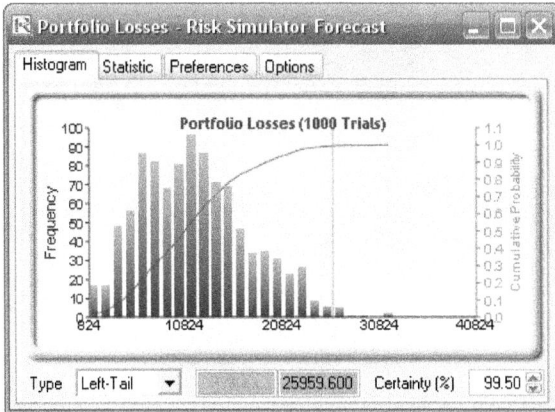

Portfolio Losses - Risk Simulator Forecast

Histogram | Statistic | Preferences | Options

Portfolio Losses (1000 Trials)

Type Left-Tail ▼   25959.600   Certainty [%]   99.50

Portfolio Losses - Risk Simulator Forecast

Histogram | Statistic | Preferences | Options

Statistics	Result
Number of Trials	1000
Mean	1.111281E+004
Median	1.067955E+004
Standard Deviation	5597.8726
Variance	3.133618E+007
Average Deviation	4522.4248
Maximum	3.167721E+004
Minimum	0.0000
Range	3.167721E+004
Skewness	0.4724
Kurtosis	-0.1656
25% Percentile	6678.1717
75% Percentile	1.466395E+004
Percentage Error Precision at 95% Confidence	3.1221%

Figure 2.13: Simulated Forecast Results and the
99.50% Value at Risk Value

TAIL VALUE AT RISK MODEL (BASEL II REQUIREMENT)

Line of Business	Mean Required Capital	99.95th Percentile	Capital Required	Allocation Weights	Minimum Allowed	Maximum Allowed	
Business 1	$10.50	$36.52	$26.01	10.00%	5.00%	15.00%	3.48
Business 2	$11.12	$47.52	$36.39	10.00%	5.00%	15.00%	4.27
Business 3	$11.77	$48.99	$37.22	10.00%	5.00%	15.00%	4.16
Business 4	$10.77	$37.34	$26.56	10.00%	5.00%	15.00%	3.47
Business 5	$13.49	$49.52	$36.03	10.00%	5.00%	15.00%	3.67
Business 6	$14.24	$55.59	$41.35	10.00%	5.00%	15.00%	3.91
Business 7	$15.60	$60.24	$44.64	10.00%	5.00%	15.00%	3.86
Business 8	$14.95	$64.69	$49.74	10.00%	5.00%	15.00%	4.33
Business 9	$14.15	$61.02	$46.87	10.00%	5.00%	15.00%	4.31
Business 10	$10.08	$35.37	$25.29	10.00%	5.00%	15.00%	3.51
Portfolio Total	$12.67	$49.68	$37.01	100.00%			
Total Capital Required			$14.00				

Correlation Matrix

	1	2	3	4	5	6	7	8	9	10
1										
2	-0.20									
3	-0.13	0.35								
4	-0.05	0.01	0.00							
5	0.23	0.50	0.15	0.00						
6	0.00	0.00	-0.15	0.00	0.03					
7	0.25	0.00	-0.26	0.01	0.10	-0.10				
8	0.36	-0.25	-0.60	-0.30	0.00	0.00	-0.15			
9	-0.01	-0.20	0.16	0.04	-0.01	0.01	0.00	0.00		

Figure 2.14: Right-tail VaR Model

1. To run the model, click on *Risk Simulator | Run Simulation* (if you had other models open, make sure you first click on *Risk Simulator | Change Simulation | Profile*, and select the *Tail VaR* profile before starting).

2. When simulation is complete, select *Left-Tail* in the forecast chart and enter in *99.95* in the *Certainty* box and hit *TAB* on the keyboard to obtain the value of $14.00M Value at Risk for this correlated simulation.

3. Note that the assumptions have already been set for you in advance in the model in cells *C6:C15*. However, you may set them again by going to cell *C6* and clicking on *Risk Simulator | Set Input Assumption*, selecting your distribution of choice or using the default *Normal Distribution* or performing a distributional fitting on historical data, and click *OK*. Continue this process for the remaining cells in column C. You may also decide to first *Remove Parameters* of these cells in column C and setting your own distributions. Further, correlations can be set manually when assumptions are set (Figure 2.16) or by going to *Analytical Tools | Edit Correlations* (Figure 2.17) after all the assumptions are set.

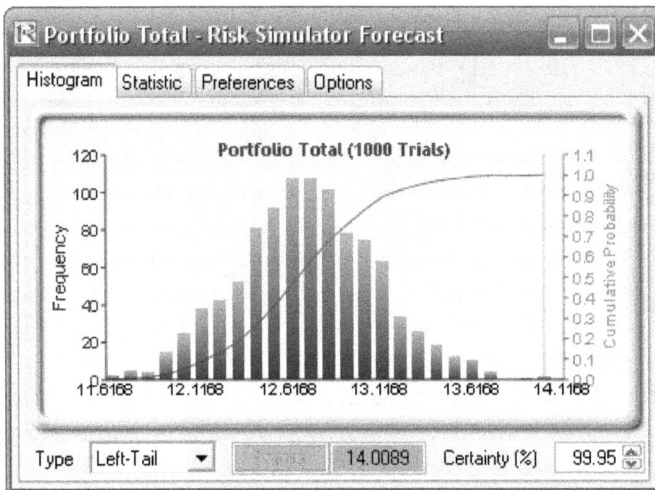

Figure 2.15: Simulated Results of the Portfolio VaR

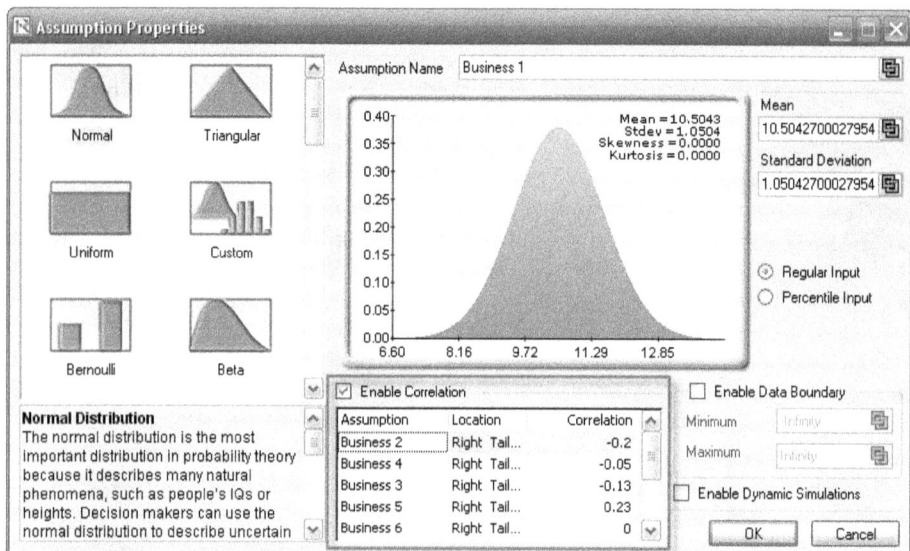

Figure 2.16: Setting Correlations One at a Time

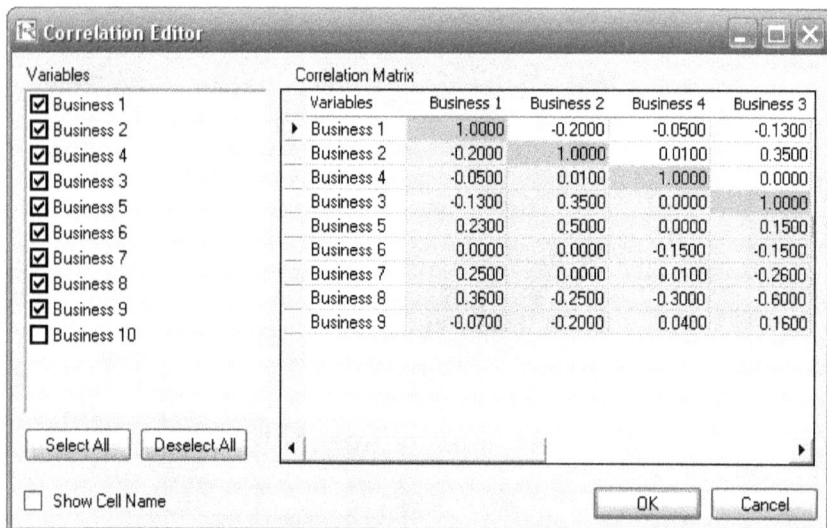

Figure 2.17: Setting Correlations Using the Correlation Matrix Routine

If risk simulation was not run, the VaR or economic capital required would have been $37M, as opposed to only $14M. And all cross-correlations between business lines have been modeled, as are stress and scenario tests, as well as thousands and thousands of possible iterations having been run. Individual risks are now aggregated into a cumulative portfolio level VaR.

Efficient Portfolio Allocation and Economic Capital VaR

As a side note, by performing portfolio optimization, a portfolio's VaR can actually be reduced. We start by first introducing the concept of stochastic portfolio optimization through an illustrative hands-on example. Then, using this portfolio optimization technique, we apply it to four business lines or assets to compute the VaR or an unoptimized versus an optimized portfolio of assets, and see the difference in computed VaR. You will note that at the end, the optimized portfolio bears less risk and has a lower required economic capital.

Illustrative Example: Portfolio Optimization and the Effects on Portfolio VaR

Now that we understand the concepts of optimized portfolios, let us see what the effects are on computed economic capital through the use of a correlated portfolio VaR. This model uses Monte Carlo simulation and optimization routines in Risk Simulator to minimize the VaR of a portfolio of assets (Figure 2.18). The file used is *Value at Risk – Optimized and Simulated Portfolio VaR* that is accessible via *Modeling Toolkit | Value at Risk | Optimized and Simulated Portfolio VaR*. In this example model, we intentionally used only 4 asset classes to illustrate the effects of an optimized portfolio, whereas in real life, we can extend this to cover a multitude of asset classes and business lines. In addition, we now illustrate the use of a left-tail VaR, as opposed to a right-tail VaR, but the concepts are similar.

First, simulation is used to determine the 90% left-tail VaR (this means that there is a 10% chance that losses will exceed this VaR for a specified holding period). With an equal allocation of 25% across the 4 asset classes, the VaR is determined using simulation (Figure 2.19). The annualized returns are uncertain and, hence, simulated. The VaR is then read off the forecast chart. Then, optimization is run to find the best portfolio subject to the 100% allocation across the 4 projects that will maximize the portfolio's bang-for-the-buck (returns to risk ratio). The resulting optimized portfolio is then simulated once again and the new VaR is obtained (Figure 2.20). The VaR of this optimized portfolio is a lot less than the not optimized portfolio. That is, the expected loss is $35.8M instead of $42.2M, which means that the bank will have a lower required economic capital if the portfolio of holdings is first optimized.

VALUE AT RISK WITH ASSET ALLOCATION OPTIMIZATION MODEL

Asset Class Description	Annualized Returns	Volatility Risk	Allocation Weights	Required Minimum Allocation	Required Maximum Allocation
S&P 500	7.10%	9.80%	10.00%	10.00%	40.00%
Small Cap	9.51%	14.35%	27.30%	10.00%	40.00%
High Yield	15.90%	22.50%	22.70%	10.00%	40.00%
Govt Bonds	4.50%	7.25%	40.00%	10.00%	40.00%
		Total Weight:	100.00%		

Correlation Matrix	S&P 500	Small Cap	High Yield	Govt Bonds
S&P 500	1.0000	0.7400	0.6500	0.5500
Small Cap	0.7400	1.0000	0.4200	0.3100
High Yield	0.6500	0.4200	1.0000	0.2300
Govt Bonds	0.5500	0.3100	0.2300	1.0000

Covariance Matrix	S&P 500	Small Cap	High Yield	Govt Bonds
S&P 500	0.0096	0.0104	0.0143	0.0039
Small Cap	0.0104	0.0206	0.0136	0.0032
High Yield	0.0143	0.0136	0.0506	0.0038
Govt Bonds	0.0039	0.0032	0.0038	0.0053

Starting Value	$1,000,000.00
Term (Years)	5.00

Annualized Return	8.72%	Profit/Loss	$87,151.94
Portfolio Risk	9.84%	Return to Risk Ratio	88.59%
Ending Value	$1,087,151.94		

Specifications of the optimization model:

Objective:	Maximize Return to Risk Ratio (E28)
Decision Variables:	Allocation Weights (E6:E9)
Restrictions on Decision Variables:	Minimum and Maximum Required (F6:G9)
Constraints:	Portfolio Total Allocation Weights 100% (E10 is set to 100%)

Figure 2.18: Computing Value at Risk (VaR) with Simulation

Profit/Loss - Risk Simulator Forecast

Histogram | Statistic | Preferences | Options

Profit/Loss (1000 Trials)

Stochastic VaR
(25% Allocation)

Type | Left-Tail ▼ | -42157.016 | Certainty (%) | 10.00

Profit/Loss - Risk Simulator Forecast

Histogram | Statistic | Preferences | Options

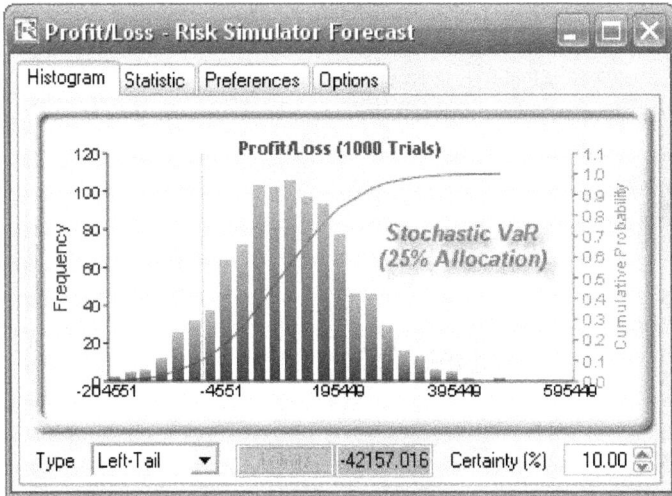

Statistics	Result
Number of Trials	1000
Mean	9.343691E+004
Median	9.273733E+004
Standard Deviation	1.068285E+005
Variance	1.141234E+010
Coefficient of Variation	1.1433
Maximum	4.699904E+005
Minimum	-222557.3169
Range	6.925477E+005
Skewness	0.0611
Kurtosis	0.1405
25% Percentile	2.533585E+004
75% Percentile	1.625164E+005
Percentage Error Precision at 95% Confidence	7.0863%

Figure 2.19: Unoptimized Value at Risk

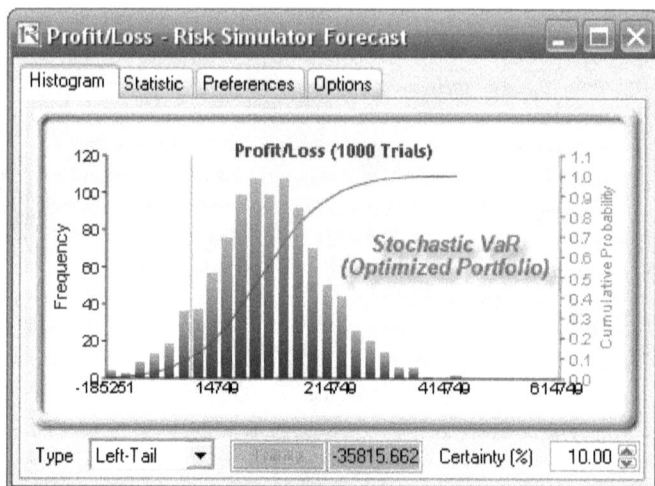

Profit/Loss - Risk Simulator Forecast

Histogram | Statistic | Preferences | Options

Profit/Loss (1000 Trials)

Stochastic VaR (Optimized Portfolio)

Type: Left-Tail | -35815.662 | Certainty (%): 10.00

Profit/Loss - Risk Simulator Forecast

Histogram | Statistic | Preferences | Options

Statistics	Result
Number of Trials	1000
Mean	8.808004E+004
Median	8.492705E+004
Standard Deviation	9.800709E+004
Variance	9.605389E+009
Coefficient of Variation	1.1127
Maximum	4.316936E+005
Minimum	-201719.8899
Range	6.334135E+005
Skewness	0.0540
Kurtosis	0.1536
25% Percentile	2.502848E+004
75% Percentile	1.493300E+005
Percentage Error Precision at 95% Confidence	6.8965%

Figure 2.20: Optimal Portfolio's Value at Risk through Optimization and Simulation

File Name: Risk Analysis – Interest Rate Risk

Location: *Modeling Toolkit | Risk Analysis | Interest Rate Risk*

Brief Description: Applies duration and convexity measures to account for a bond's sensitivity and how interest rate shifts can affect the new bond price, and how this new bond price can be approximated using these sensitivity measures

Requirements: Modeling Toolkit, Risk Simulator

Modeling Toolkit Functions Used: *MTBondPriceDiscrete, MTModifiedDuration, MTConvexityDiscrete*

Banks selling fixed income products and vehicles need to understand interest-rate risks. This model uses duration and convexity to show how fixed income products react under various market conditions. To compare the effects of interest rate and credit risks on fixed income investments, this model uses modified duration and convexity (discrete discounting) to analyze the effects of a change in interest rates on the value of a bond or debt (Figure 2.21).

Duration and convexity are sensitivity measures that describe exposure to parallel shifts in the spot interest rate yield curve, applicable to individual fixed income instruments or entire fixed income portfolios. These sensitivities cannot warn of exposure to more complex movements in the spot curve, including tilts and bends, only parallel shifts. The idea behind duration is simple. Suppose a portfolio has a duration measure of 2.5 years. This means that the portfolio's value will decline about 2.5% for each 1% increase in interest rates—or rise about 2.5% for each 1% decrease in interest rates. Typically, a bond's duration will be positive but exotic instruments such as mortgage-backed securities may have negative durations, or portfolios that short fixed income instruments or pay fixed for floating on an interest rate swap. Inverse floaters tend to have large positive durations. Their values change significantly for small changes in rates. Highly leveraged fixed income portfolios tend to have very large (positive or negative) durations.

In contrast, convexity summarizes the second-most significant piece of information, or the nonlinear curvature of the yield curve, whereas duration measures the linear or first-approximation sensitivity. Duration and convexity have traditionally been used as tools for immunization or asset-liability management. To avoid exposure to parallel spot curve shifts, an organization (such as an insurance company or defined benefit pension plan) with significant fixed income exposures might perform duration matching by structuring its assets so that their duration matches the duration of its liabilities so the two offset each other. Even more effective (but less frequently practical) is duration-convexity matching, in which assets are structured so that durations and convexities match.

INTEREST RATE RISK

Face Value	$100.00
Coupon Rate	5.50%
Maturity	30.00
Current Interest Rate	5.50%
Interest Rate Shift	0.25%

Original Bond Price	$100.00	
Modified Duration	14.5337	
Convexity	321.0265	
	Duration and Convexity	**Using New Rates**
New Price After Shift	$96.47	$96.46
Price Change After Shift	-3.53%	-3.54%

Cash Flow	Interest Rates	Year	Shifted Interest Rates
$5.50	5.50%	1	5.75%
$5.50	5.50%	2	5.75%
$5.50	5.50%	3	5.75%
$5.50	5.50%	4	5.75%
$5.50	5.50%	5	5.75%
$5.50	5.50%	6	5.75%
$5.50	5.50%	7	5.75%
$5.50	5.50%	8	5.75%
$5.50	5.50%	9	5.75%
$5.50	5.50%	10	5.75%

Figure 2.21: Interest Rate Risk

File Name: Risk Analysis – Delta Gamma Hedge

Location: *Modeling Toolkit | Risk Analysis | Delta Gamma Hedge*

Brief Description: Sets up a delta-gamma riskless and costless hedge in determining the number of call options to sell and buy, number of common stocks to buy, and the borrowing amount required to set up a perfect arbitrage-free hedge

Requirements: Modeling Toolkit

Modeling Toolkit Functions Used: *MTDeltaGammaHedgeCallSold, MTDeltaGammaHedgeSharesBought, MTDeltaGammaHedgeMoneyBorrowed*

The Delta-Gamma hedge (Figure 2.22) provides a hedge against larger changes in the asset value. This is done by buying some equity shares and a call option, which are funded by borrowing some amount of money and selling a call option at a different strike price. The net amount is a zero-sum game, making this hedge completely effective in generating a zero delta and zero gamma for the portfolio, just like in a delta hedge, where the total portfolio's delta is zero (e.g., to offset a positive delta of some underlying assets, call options are sold to generate sufficient negative delta to completely offset the existing deltas to generate a zero delta portfolio). The problem of delta neutral portfolios is that secondary changes, that is, larger shocks, are not hedged. Delta-gamma hedged portfolios, on the contrary, hedge both delta and gamma risk, making it a much more expensive hedge to generate. The typical problem with such a hedging vehicle is that in larger quantities, buying and selling additional options or underlying assets may change the market value and prices of the same instruments used to perform the hedge. Therefore, typically, a dynamic hedge, or continuously changing hedge portfolios, might be required.

DELTA-GAMMA HEDGE

Asset	$100.00
Strike for Call Sold	$95.00
Strike for Call Bought	$100.00
Maturity for Call Sold	0.50
Maturity for Call Bought	0.75
Riskfree	8.00%
Volatility	20.00%
DividendRate	3.00%

Sell Calls	**$9.7258**
Shares to Buy	**($6.9058)**
Buy Calls	**($9.1991)**
Borrow This Amount	**$6.3791**
Delta-Gamma-Neutral Position Sum	**$0.0000**

Figure 2.22: Delta-Gamma Hedging (Continues)

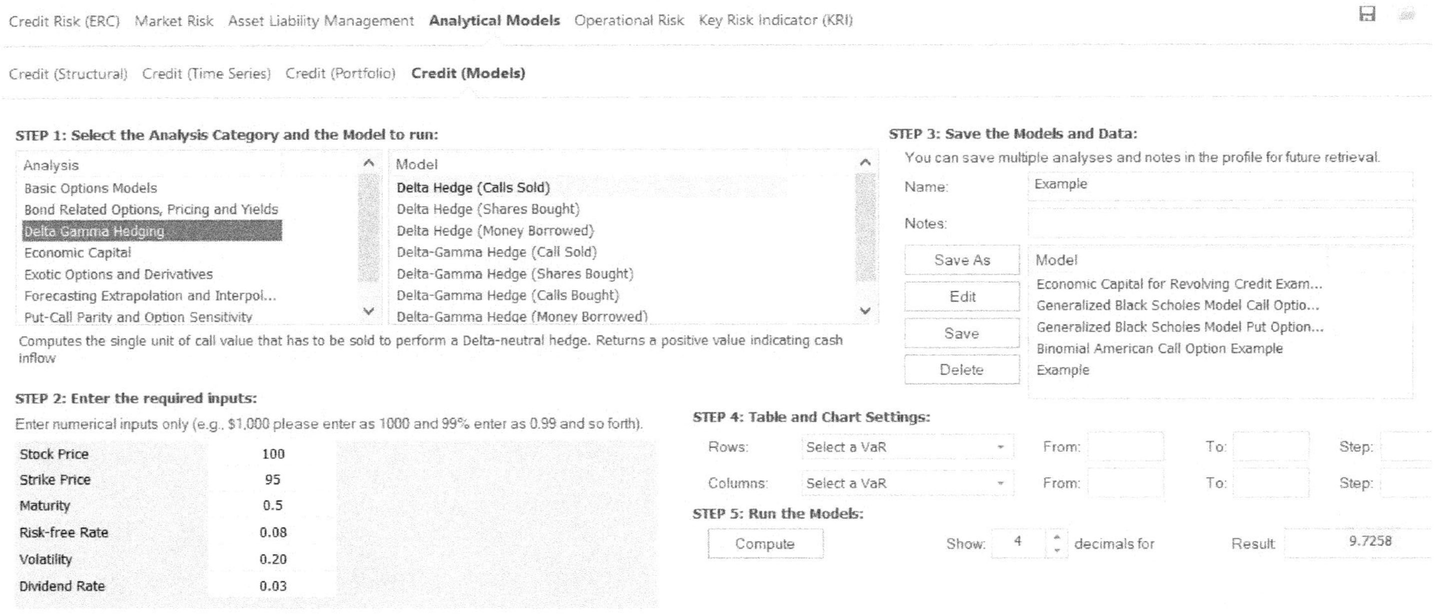

Credit Risk (ERC)   Market Risk   Asset Liability Management   **Analytical Models**   Operational Risk   Key Risk Indicator (KRI)

Credit (Structural)   Credit (Time Series)   Credit (Portfolio)   **Credit (Models)**

STEP 1: Select the Analysis Category and the Model to run:

Analysis	Model
Basic Options Models	**Delta Hedge (Calls Sold)**
Bond Related Options, Pricing and Yields	Delta Hedge (Shares Bought)
Delta-Gamma Hedging	Delta Hedge (Money Borrowed)
Economic Capital	Delta-Gamma Hedge (Call Sold)
Exotic Options and Derivatives	Delta-Gamma Hedge (Shares Bought)
Forecasting Extrapolation and Interpol...	Delta-Gamma Hedge (Calls Bought)
Put-Call Parity and Option Sensitivity	Delta-Gamma Hedge (Money Borrowed)

Computes the single unit of call value that has to be sold to perform a Delta-neutral hedge. Returns a positive value indicating cash inflow

STEP 2: Enter the required inputs:

Enter numerical inputs only (e.g. $1,000 please enter as 1000 and 99% enter as 0.99 and so forth).

Stock Price	100
Strike Price	95
Maturity	0.5
Risk-Free Rate	0.08
Volatility	0.20
Dividend Rate	0.03

STEP 3: Save the Models and Data:

You can save multiple analyses and notes in the profile for future retrieval.

Name: Example

Notes:

Save As

Edit

Save

Delete

Model
Economic Capital for Revolving Credit Exam...
Generalized Black Scholes Model Call Optio...
Generalized Black Scholes Model Put Option...
Binomial American Call Option Example

Example

STEP 4: Table and Chart Settings:

Rows: Select a VaR

Columns: Select a VaR

STEP 5: Run the Models:

Compute

From: To: Step:

From: To: Step:

Show: 4   decimals for   Result   9.7258

Figure 2.22: Delta-Gamma Hedging

Illustrative Example: Risk Hedging – Delta Hedging

File Name: Risk Analysis – Delta Hedge

Location: *Modeling Toolkit | Risk Analysis | Delta Hedge*

Brief Description: Sets up a delta riskless and costless hedge in determining the number of call options to sell, number of common stocks to buy, and the borrowing amount required to set up a costless hedge

Requirements: Modeling Toolkit

Modeling Toolkit Functions Used: *MTDeltaHedgeCallSold, MTDeltaHedgeSharesBought, MTDeltaHedgeMoneyBorrowed*

The Delta hedge (Figure 2.23) provides a hedge against small changes in the asset value by buying some equity shares of the asset and financing it through selling a call option and borrowing some money. The net should be a zero-sum game to provide a hedge where the portfolio's delta is zero. For instance, an investor computes the portfolio delta of some underlying asset and offsets this delta through buying or selling some additional instruments such that the new instruments will offset the delta of the existing underlying assets. Typically, say an investor holds some stocks or commodity like gold in the long position, creating a positive delta for the asset. To offset this, he or she sells some calls to generate negative delta, such that the amount of the call options sold on the gold is sufficient to offset the delta in the portfolio.

DELTA HEDGE

Asset	$100.00
Strike	$95.00
Maturity	0.50
Riskfree	8.00%
Volatility	20.00%
DividendRate	3.00%
Sell 1 Call	**$9.7258**
Shares to Buy	($71.8275)
Borrow This Amount	**$62.1018**
Delta-Neutral Position Sum	**$0.0000**

Figure 2.23: Delta Hedging (continues)

Credit Risk (ERC) Market Risk Asset Liability Management **Analytical Models** Operational Risk Key Risk Indicator (KRI)

Credit (Structural) Credit (Time Series) Credit (Portfolio) **Credit (Models)**

STEP 1: Select the Analysis Category and the Model to run:

Analysis	Model
Basic Options Models	Delta Hedge (Calls Sold)
Bond Related Options, Pricing and Yields	Delta Hedge (Shares Bought)
Delta Gamma Hedging	**Delta Hedge (Money Borrowed)**
Economic Capital	Delta-Gamma Hedge (Call Sold)
Exotic Options and Derivatives	Delta-Gamma Hedge (Shares Bought)
Forecasting Extrapolation and Interpol...	Delta-Gamma Hedge (Calls Bought)
Put-Call Parity and Option Sensitivity	Delta-Gamma Hedge (Money Borrowed)

Computes the amount of money that has to be borrowed to perform a Delta-neutral hedge. Returns a positive value indicating cash inflow

STEP 2: Enter the required inputs:

Enter numerical inputs only (e.g. $1,000 please enter as 1000 and 99% enter as 0.99 and so forth).

Stock Price	100
Strike Price	95
Maturity	0.5
Risk-free Rate	0.08
Volatility	0.20
Dividend Rate	0.03

STEP 3: Save the Models and Data:

You can save multiple analyses and notes in the profile for future retrieval.

Name: Example

Notes:

Save As		
	Model	
Edit	Economic Capital for Revolving Credit Exam...	
	Generalized Black Scholes Model Call Optio...	
Save	Generalized Black Scholes Model Put Option...	
	Binomial American Call Option Example	
Delete	Example	

STEP 4: Table and Chart Settings:

Rows:	Select a VaR	•	From:	To:	Step
Columns:	Select a VaR	•	From:	To:	Step

STEP 5: Run the Models:

Compute

Show 4 ⏷ decimals for   Result   62.1018

Figure 2.23: Delta Hedging

File Name: Risk Hedging – Effects of Fixed versus Floating Rates

Location: *Modeling Toolkit | Risk Hedging | Effects of Fixed vs Floating*

Brief Description: Sets up various levels of hedging to determine the impact on earnings per share

Requirements: Modeling Toolkit

This model illustrates the impact to financial earnings and earnings before interest and taxes (EBIT) on a hedged versus unhedged position (Figure 2.24). The hedge is done through an interest rate swap payment. Various scenarios of swaps (different combinations of fixed rate versus floating rate debt are tested and modeled) can be generated in this model to determine the impact to earnings per share (EPS) and other financial metrics. The foreign exchange cash-flow hedge model (shown next) goes into more detail on the hedging aspects of foreign exchange through the use of risk simulation.

IMPACTS OF FIXED VERSUS FLOATING RATE INTEREST PAYMENTS

Assumptions

EBIT	$3,000,000
Shares Outstanding	$500,000
Tax Rate	40.00%
Total Debt	$8,000,000
Fixed Interest Rate	7.00%
LIBOR	6.00%
10-Year Swap Rate	5.00%

		Scenarios		
Initial Debt Structure (before swap)	Current	1	2	3
% of Total Debt in Fixed-rate Debt	50.00%	50.00%	50.00%	50.00%
% of Total Debt in Floating-rate Debt	50.00%	50.00%	50.00%	50.00%
Desired Debt Structure (after swap)				
% of Total Debt in Fixed-rate Debt	50.00%	30.00%	100.00%	0.00%
% of Total Debt in Floating-rate Debt	50.00%	70.00%	0.00%	100.00%
Change in Interest Rates	0.00%	1.00%	0.50%	0.10%
Financials				
Fixed-rate Debt	7.00%	7.00%	7.00%	7.00%
Floating-rate Debt	8.00%	9.00%	8.50%	8.10%
EBIT	3,000,000	3,000,000	3,000,000	3,000,000
Interest Expense	(600,000)	(672,000)	(560,000)	(648,000)
Net Income before Taxes	2,400,000	2,328,000	2,440,000	2,352,000
Earnings	1,440,000	1,396,800	1,464,000	1,411,200
EPS	2.8800	2.7936	2.9280	2.8224
Change in Interest Expense		72,000	(40,000)	48,000
Change in Earnings		(43,200)	24,000	(28,800)

Figure 2.24: Impacts of an Unhedged Versus Hedged Position

File Name: Risk Hedging – Foreign Exchange Cash Flow Model

Location: *Modeling Toolkit | Risk Hedging | Foreign Exchange Cash Flow Model*

Brief Description: This model illustrates how to use Risk Simulator for simulating foreign exchange rates to determine if the value of a hedged fixed exchange rate or floating unhedged rate is worth more

Requirements: Modeling Toolkit, Risk Simulator

This is a cash flow model used to illustrate the effects of hedging foreign exchange rates (Figure 2.25). The tornado sensitivity analysis illustrates that foreign exchange rate, or forex, has the highest effects on the profitability of the project (shown in the Excel model). Suppose for the moment that the project undertaken is in a foreign country (FC) and the values obtained are denominated in FC currency, and the parent company is in the United States (U.S.) and requires that the net revenues be repatriated back to the U.S. The question we try to ask here is what is the appropriate forex rate to hedge at and the appropriate costs for that particular rate? Banks will be able to provide your firm with the appropriate pricing structure for various exchange forward rates but by using the model here, we can determine the added value of the hedge and, hence, can decide if the value added exceeds the cost to obtain the hedge. This model is already preset for you to run a simulation on.

The *Forex Data* worksheet shows historical exchange rates between the FC and U.S. Dollar. Using these values, we can create a *custom* distribution (we simply used the rounded values in our illustration), which is already preset in this example model.

However, should you wish to replicate creating the simulation model, you can follow the steps below:

1. Start a new profile (*Risk Simulator | New Profile*) and give it an appropriate name.

2. Go to the *Forex Data* worksheet and select the data in cells *K6:K490* and click on *Edit | Copy* or *Ctrl + C*.

3. Select an empty cell (e.g., cell *K4*) and click on *Risk Simulator | Set Input Assumption* and select *Custom Distribution*.

4. Click on *Paste* to paste the data into the custom distribution, then *Update Chart* to view the results on the chart. Then, *File | Save* and save the newly created distribution to your hard drive. Close the set assumption dialog.

5. Go to the *Model* worksheet and select the *Forex* cell (*J9*) and click on *Risk Simulator | Set Input Assumption*, and choose *Custom*, then click on *Open* a distribution and select the previously saved custom distribution.

6. You may continue to set assumptions across the entire model, and set the *NPV* cell (*G6*) as a forecast (*Risk Simulator | Set Output Forecast*).

7. *RUN* the simulation with the custom distribution to denote an unhedged position. You can then rerun the simulation but this time, delete the custom distribution (use the *Delete Simulation Parameter* icon and not Excel's delete function nor hitting the keyboard's delete key) and enter in the relevant hedged exchange rate, indicating a fixed rate. You may create a report after each simulation to compare the results.

From the sample analysis, we see the following:

	Mean ($'000)	Stdev ($'000)	% Confidence ($'000)	CV (%)
Unhedged	2292.82	157.94	2021 to 2550	6.89%
Hedged at 0.85	2408.81	132.63	2199 to 2618	5.51%
Hedged at 0.83	2352.13	129.51	2147 to 2556	5.51%
Hedged at 0.80	2267.12	124.83	2069 to 2463	5.51%

From this table, several things are evident:

- The higher the hedged exchange rate is, the more profitable the project (e.g., 0.85 USD/FC is worth more than 0.80 USD/FC).

- The relative risk ratio, computed as the coefficient of variation (CV, or the standard deviation divided by the mean) is the same regardless of the exchange rate, as long as it is hedged.

- The CV is lower for hedged positions than unhedged positions, indicating that the relative risk is reduced by hedging.

- It seems that the exchange rate hedge should be above 0.80, such that the hedged position is more profitable than the unhedged.

- In comparing a hedged versus unhedged position, we can determine the amount of money the hedging is worth, for instance, going with a 0.85 USD/FC means that, on average, the hedge is worth $115,990,000 (computed as $2,408.81 – $2,292.82 denominated in thousands). This means that as long as the cost of the hedge is less than this amount, it is a good idea to pursue the hedge.

Cash Flow Model

Base Year	2006	Sum PV Net Benefits: FC 3,809.62
Start Year	2006	Sum PV Investments: FC 1,389.08
Discount Rate	15.00%	Net Present Value: FC 2,420.54
Private-Risk Discount Rate	5.00%	Internal Rate of Return: 54.64%
Terminal Period Growth Rate	2.00%	Return on Investment: 174.25%
Tax Rate	40.00%	Profitability Index: 2.74

Forex Rate (USD/FC)   0.85000

	2006	2007	2008	2009	2010	2011	2012	2013	2014	2015
Prod A Price	FC 10.00	FC 10.50	FC 11.00	FC 11.50	FC 12.00	FC 12.00	FC 12.00	FC 12.00	FC 12.00	FC 12.00
Prod B Price	FC 12.25	FC 12.50	FC 12.75	FC 13.00	FC 13.25	FC 13.25	FC 13.25	FC 13.25	FC 13.25	FC 13.25
Prod C Price	FC 15.15	FC 15.30	FC 15.45	FC 15.60	FC 15.75	FC 15.75	FC 15.75	FC 15.75	FC 15.75	FC 15.75
Prod A Quantity	50	50	50	50	50	50	50	50	50	50
Prod B Quantity	35	35	35	35	35	35	35	35	35	35
Prod C Quantity	20	20	20	20	20	20	20	20	20	20
Total Revenues (Local Currency)	FC 1,231.75	FC 1,268.50	FC 1,305.25	FC 1,342.00	FC 1,378.75	FC 1,378.75	FC 1,378.75	FC 1,378.75	FC 1,378.75	FC 1,378.75
Direct Cost of Goods Sold	FC 184.76	FC 190.28	FC 195.79	FC 201.30	FC 206.81	FC 206.81	FC 206.81	FC 206.81	FC 206.81	FC 206.81
Gross Profit	**FC 1,046.99**	**FC 1,078.23**	**FC 1,109.46**	**FC 1,140.70**	**FC 1,171.94**	**FC 1,171.94**	**FC 1,171.94**	**FC 1,171.94**	**FC 1,171.94**	**FC 1,171.94**
Operating Expenses	FC 157.50	FC 157.50	FC 157.50	FC 157.50	FC 157.50	FC 157.50	FC 157.50	FC 157.50	FC 157.50	FC 157.50
Sales, General and Admin. Costs	FC 15.75	FC 15.75	FC 15.75	FC 15.75	FC 15.75	FC 15.75	FC 15.75	FC 15.75	FC 15.75	FC 15.75
Operating Income (EBITDA)	**FC 873.74**	**FC 904.98**	**FC 936.21**	**FC 967.45**	**FC 998.69**	**FC 998.69**	**FC 998.69**	**FC 998.69**	**FC 998.69**	**FC 998.69**
Depreciation	FC 10.00	FC 10.00	FC 10.00	FC 10.00	FC 10.00	FC 10.00	FC 10.00	FC 10.00	FC 10.00	FC 10.00
Amortization	FC 3.00	FC 3.00	FC 3.00	FC 3.00	FC 3.00	FC 3.00	FC 3.00	FC 3.00	FC 3.00	FC 3.00
EBIT	**FC 860.74**	**FC 891.98**	**FC 923.21**	**FC 954.45**	**FC 985.69**	**FC 985.69**	**FC 985.69**	**FC 985.69**	**FC 985.69**	**FC 985.69**
Interest	FC 2.00	FC 2.00	FC 2.00	FC 2.00	FC 2.00	FC 3.00	FC 4.00	FC 5.00	FC 6.00	FC 7.00
EBT	**FC 858.74**	**FC 889.98**	**FC 921.21**	**FC 952.45**	**FC 983.69**	**FC 982.69**	**FC 981.69**	**FC 980.69**	**FC 979.69**	**FC 978.69**
Taxes	FC 343.50	FC 355.99	FC 368.49	FC 380.98	FC 393.48	FC 393.08	FC 392.68	FC 392.28	FC 391.88	FC 391.48
Net Income	**FC 515.24**	**FC 533.99**	**FC 552.73**	**FC 571.47**	**FC 590.21**	**FC 589.61**	**FC 589.01**	**FC 588.41**	**FC 587.81**	**FC 587.21**
Depreciation/Amort	FC 13.00	FC 13.00	FC 13.00	FC 13.00	FC 13.00	FC 13.00	FC 13.00	FC 13.00	FC 13.00	FC 13.00
Net Working Capital	FC 0.00	FC 0.00	FC 0.00	FC 0.00	FC 0.00	FC 0.00	FC 0.00	FC 0.00	FC 0.00	FC 0.00
Capital Expenditures	FC 0.00	FC 0.00	FC 0.00	FC 0.00	FC 0.00	FC 0.00	FC 0.00	FC 0.00	FC 0.00	FC 0.00
Free Cash Flow	**FC 528.24**	**FC 546.99**	**FC 565.73**	**FC 584.47**	**FC 603.21**	**FC 602.61**	**FC 602.01**	**FC 601.41**	**FC 600.81**	**FC 4,709.36**
Investments	FC 500.00		FC 1,500.00							
Net Free Cash Flow	**-FC 1,105.97**	**FC 546.99**	**FC 565.73**	**FC 584.47**	**FC 603.21**	**FC 602.61**	**FC 602.01**	**FC 601.41**	**FC 600.81**	**FC 4,709.36**

Figure 2.25: Hedging Foreign Exchange Risk Cash Flow Model

File Name: Risk Hedging – Hedging Foreign Exchange Exposure

Brief Description: This model illustrates how to use Risk Simulator for simulating foreign exchange rates to determine the value of a hedged currency option position

Requirements: Modeling Toolkit, Risk Simulator

This model is used to simulate possible foreign exchange spot and future prices and the effects on the cash flow statement of a company under a freely floating exchange rate versus using currency options to hedge the foreign exchange exposure (Figure 2.26).

Figure 2.27 shows the effects of the Value at Risk (VaR) of a hedged versus unhedged position. Clearly, the right-tailed VaR of the loss distribution is higher without the currency options hedge. Figure 2.27 shows that there is a lower risk, lower risk to returns ratio, higher returns, and less swing in the outcomes of a currency hedged position than an exposed position, with Figure 2.28 showing the simulated forecast statistics of the loss distribution. Finally, Figure 2.29 shows the hedging effectiveness, that is, how often the hedge is in the money and become usable.

Hedging Foreign Exchange Exposure with Currency Options

Months	Jan	Feb	Mar	April	May	June	July
FX Spot Rate (HKD/USD)	7.80	7.40	7.60	7.30	7.10	7.20	7.40
FX Strike Rate (HKD/USD)	7.80	7.80	7.80	7.80	7.80	7.80	7.80
Maturity (Years)	0.5833	0.5000	0.4167	0.3333	0.2500	0.1667	0.0833
Risk Free Rate US	6.08%	6.08%	6.08%	6.08%	6.08%	6.08%	6.08%
Risk Free Rate HK	5.06%	5.06%	5.06%	5.06%	5.06%	5.06%	5.06%
Volatility	15.00%	15.00%	15.00%	15.00%	15.00%	15.00%	15.00%
Quantity of Options Hedge Position	10,000,000	10,000,000	10,000,000	10,000,000	10,000,000	10,000,000	10,000,000
Currency Put Option Value (HKD/USD)	0.3229	0.5191	0.3795	0.5533	0.7012	0.6034	0.4102
Market Value of Hedge	3,229,135	5,191,009	3,794,813	5,532,845	7,012,229	6,034,435	4,102,320
Intrinsic Value	0	4,000,000	2,000,000	5,000,000	7,000,000	6,000,000	4,000,000
Time Value	3,229,135	1,191,009	1,794,813	532,845	12,229	34,435	102,320

FINANCIAL STATEMENTS IMPACTS - MARK TO MARKET

Balance Sheet (in 000's)	Jan	Feb	Mar	April	May	June	July
Option Contract	3,229,135	5,191,009	3,794,813	5,532,845	7,012,229	6,034,435	4,102,320
Other Comp Income (SE)		4,000,000	2,000,000	5,000,000	7,000,000	6,000,000	4,000,000

Income Statement (in 000's)	Jan	Feb	Mar	April	May	June	July
Hedge Effectiveness gain or loss per period		(2,038,126)	603,805	(1,261,969)	(520,615)	22,206	67,884
Hedge Effectiveness sum of all periods							(3,126,816)
Market Cost of Hedge (Current Period)							3,229,135
Income from Option Exercise							4,000,000
Net Valuation of Hedging							770,865
Income from Hedging							74,770,865
Income from No Hedge							74,000,000
Loss Distribution from Hedging							3,229,135
Loss Distribution from No Hedge							4,000,000

Figure 2.26: Hedging Currency Exposures with Currency Options

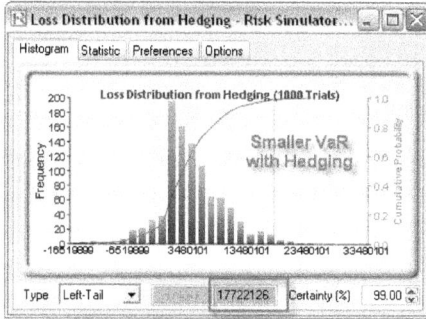

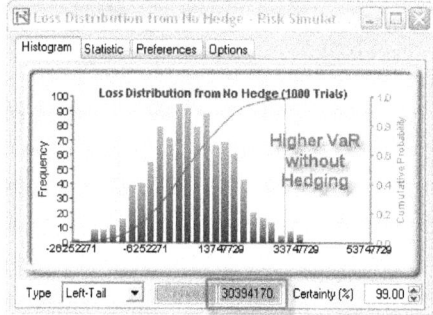

Figure 2.27: Values at Risk (VaR) of Hedged Versus Unhedged Positions

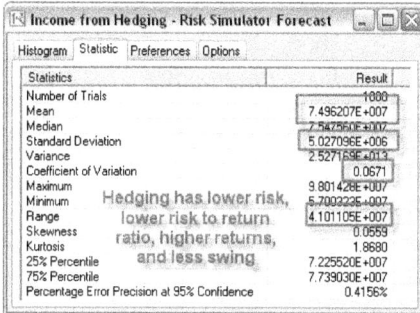

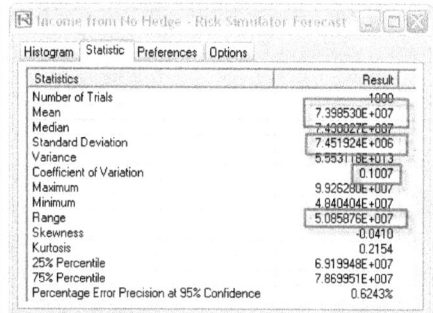

Figure 2.28: Forecast Statistics of the Loss Distribution

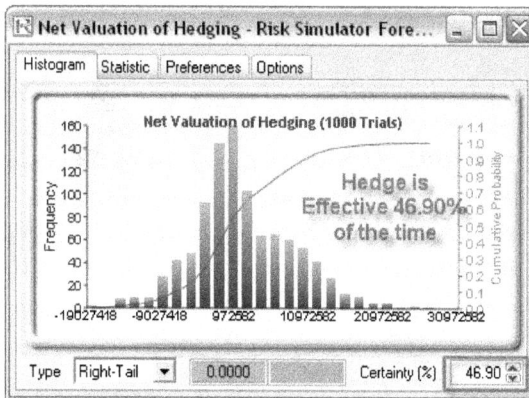

Figure 2.29: Hedging Effectiveness

Illustrative Example: Volatility – Implied Volatility

File Name: Volatility – Implied Volatility

Location: *Modeling Toolkit | Volatility | Implied Volatility*

Brief Description: This model computes the implied volatilities using an internal optimization routine, given the values of a call or put option, as well as all their required inputs

Requirements: Modeling Toolkit, Risk Simulator

Modeling Toolkit Functions Used: *MTImpliedVolatilityCall, MTImpliedVolatilityPut*

This implied volatility computation is based on an internal iterative optimization, which means that it will work under typical conditions (without extreme volatility values, i.e., too small or too large). It is always good modeling technique to recheck the imputed volatility using an options model to make sure the answers coincide with each other before adding more sophistication to the model. That is, given all the inputs in an option analysis as well as the option value, the volatility can be imputed (Figure 2.30).

IMPLIED VOLATILITY FUNCTION

Asset	$100.00
Strike	$95.00
Maturity	0.50
Riskfree	8.00%
Volatility	25.00%
DividendRate	3.00%
Call Option	$10.9126
Put Option	$3.6764
Implied Volatility Calculation	
Call Option	25.00%
Put Option	25.00%

Figure 2.30 Getting the Implied Volatility from Options (continues)

Credit (Structural)   Credit (Time Series)   Credit (Portfolio)   Credit (Models)

STEP 1: Select the Analysis Category and the Model to run:

Analysis

Exposure at Default (EAD)
Loss Given Default (LGD)
Probability of Default (PD)
Volatility

Model

Implied Volatility Call
Implied Volatility put

Computes the annualized volatilities of a market-traded equity or commodity using various methods including implied volatility, historical volatility, and advanced econometric models like the GARCH volatility forecast.

The implied volatility computation is based on an internal iterative optimization, which means it will work under typical conditions (without extreme volatility values, i.e., too small or too large). It is always good modeling technique to recheck the imputed volatility using an options model to make sure the answers are valid before adding more sophistication to the model.

STEP 2: Enter the required inputs:

Show: 5   rows and   4   decimals for results.

Computations   Charts

Enter numerical inputs only (e.g. $1,000 please enter as 1000 and 99% enter as 0.99 and so forth).

STEP 3: Save the Models and Data:

You can save multiple analyses and notes in the profile for future retrieval

Name: Implied Volatility from a Call Option

Notes:

Save As

Edit

Save

Delete

Model

EAD using Credit Conversion Factor CCF
Credit Risk Plus Average Defaults Example
EAD using LEQ, CCF, EADF
Loss Given Default (LGD) Example
Probability of Default (Market Comps) Exa...
Probability of Default (Bond Spreads) Exa...
Implied Volatility from a Call Option

Compute

STEP 4: Run the Models:

N	Call Option	Name	Asset	Strike	Maturity	Risk-Free Rate	Dividend	Call Option Value
1	0.2500	Call Option 1	100	95	0.5	0.08	0.03	10.9126
2	0.0403	Call Option 2	100	105	2	0.05	0	5.55
3	0.3210	Call Option 3	120	100	1	0.05	0	29.55
4	0.3129	Call Option 4	120	100	2	0.05	0.02	33.00
5	0.2400	Call Option 5	130	110	3	0.05	0.03	32.15

Figure 2.30 Getting the Implied Volatility from Options

File Name: Volatility – Volatility Computations

Location: *Modeling Toolkit | Volatility | Volatility Computations*

Brief Description: This model uses Risk Simulator to apply Monte Carlo simulation in order to compute a project's volatility measure

Requirements: Modeling Toolkit, Risk Simulator

There are several ways to estimate the volatility used in the option models. The most common and valid approaches are:

Logarithmic Cash Flow Returns Approach or Logarithmic Stock Price Returns Approach: This method is used mainly for computing the volatility of liquid and tradable assets such as stocks in financial options; however, it is sometimes used for other traded assets such as price of oil and price of electricity. The drawback is that discounted cash flow models with only a few cash flows will generally overstate the volatility and this method cannot be used when negative cash flows occur. This means that this volatility approach is only applicable for financial instruments and not for real options analysis. The benefits include its computational ease, transparency, and modeling flexibility of the method. In addition, no simulation is required to obtain a volatility estimate. The approach is simply to take the annualized standard deviation of the logarithmic relative returns of the time-series data as the proxy for volatility. The Modeling Toolkit function *MTVolatility* is used to compute this volatility, where the time series of stock prices is arranged in time series (can be chronological or reverse chronological). See the **Log Cash Flow Returns** example model under the Volatility section of Modeling Toolkit for details.

Exponentially Weighted Moving Average (EWMA) Models: This approach is similar to the previous logarithmic cash flow returns approach, using the *MTVolatility* function, to compute the annualized standard deviation of the natural logarithms of relative stock returns. The difference here is that the most recent value will have a higher weight than values farther in the past. A *lambda* or weight variable is required (typically, industry standards set this at 0.94), where the most recent volatility is weighted at this lambda value, and the period before that is (1 – lambda), and so forth. See the **EWMA** example model under the Volatility section of Modeling Toolkit for details.

Logarithmic Present Value Returns Approach: This approach is used mainly when computing the volatility of assets with cash flows. A typical application is in real options. The drawback of this method is that simulation is required to obtain a single volatility and is not applicable for highly traded liquid assets such as stock prices. The benefits include the ability to accommodate certain negative cash flows and to apply more rigorous analysis than the logarithmic cash flow returns approach, providing a more accurate and conservative estimate of volatility when assets are analyzed. In addition, within, say, a cash flow model, multiple simulation assumptions can be set up (we can insert any types of risks and uncertainties such as related assumptions, correlated distributions and nonrelated inputs, multiple stochastic processes, and so forth), and we allow the model to distill all the interacting risks and uncertainties in these simulated assumptions and obtain the single value volatility, which represents the integrated risk of the project. See the **Log Asset Returns** example model under the Volatility section of Modeling Toolkit for details.

Management Assumptions and Guesses: This approach is used for both financial options and real options. The drawbacks are that the volatility estimates are very unreliable and are only subjective best guesses. The benefit of this approach is its simplicity—this method is very easy to explain to management the concept of volatility, both in execution and interpretation. That is, most people understand what probability is, but have a hard time understanding what volatility is. Using this approach, we can impute one from the other. See the **Probability to Volatility** example model under the Volatility section of Modeling Toolkit for details.

Generalized Autoregressive Conditional Heteroskedasticity (GARCH) Models: These models are used mainly for computing the volatility of liquid and tradable assets such as stocks in financial options. They are sometimes used for other traded assets such as price of oil and price of electricity. The drawbacks are that a lot of data is required, advanced econometric modeling expertise is required, and this approach is highly susceptible to user manipulation. The benefit is that rigorous statistical analysis is performed to find the best-fitting volatility curve, providing different volatility estimates over time. The EWMA model is a simple weighting model whereas the GARCH model is a more advanced analytical and econometric model that requires advanced algorithms such as generalized method of moments to obtain the volatilities.

File Name: Yield Curve – CIR Model

Location: *Modeling Toolkit | Yield Curve | CIR Model*

Brief Description: This is the CIR model for estimating and modeling the term structure of interest rates and yield curve approximation assuming the interest rates are mean reverting

Requirements: Modeling Toolkit, Risk Simulator

Modeling Toolkit Function Used: *MTCIRBondYield*

The yield curve is the time-series relationship between interest rates and the time to maturity of the debt. The more formal mathematical description of this relationship is called the term structure of interest rates. The yield curve can take on various shapes. The normal yield curve means that yields rise as maturity lengthens and the yield curve is positively sloped, reflecting investor expectations for the economy to grow in the future (and, hence, an expectation that inflation rates will rise in the future). An inverted yield curve occurs when the opposite happens, where the long-term yields fall below short-term yields, and long-term investors will settle for lower yields now if they think the economy will slow or even decline in the future, indicative of a worsening economic situation in the future (and, hence, an expectation that inflation will remain low in the future). Another potential situation is a flat yield curve, signaling uncertainty in the economy. The yield curve can also be humped or show a smile or a frown. The yield curve over time can change in shape through a twist or bend, a parallel shift, or a movement on one end versus another.

As the yield curve is related to inflation rates as discussed above, and central banks in most countries have the ability to control monetary policy to target inflation rates, inflation rates are mean reverting in nature. This also implies that interest rates are mean reverting, as well as stochastically changing over time.

This section shows the Cox–Ingersoll–Ross (CIR) model that is used to compute the term structure of interest rates and yield curve (Figure 2.31). The CIR model assumes a mean-reverting stochastic interest rate. The rate of reversion and long-run mean rates can be determined using Risk Simulator's statistical analysis tool. If the long-run rate is higher than the current short rate, the yield curve is upward sloping, and vice versa.

CIR MODEL
YIELD CURVE CONSTRUCTION

Input Assumptions

Time to Maturity of the Bond or Debt (Years)	1.00
Riskfree Rate (Short Rate)	3.00%
Long-run Mean Rate	8.00%
Annualized Volatility of Interest Rate	6.00%
Market Price of Interest Rate Risk	0.00%
Rate of Mean Reversion	25.00%

Yield of Zero Coupon Bond   **3.5744%**

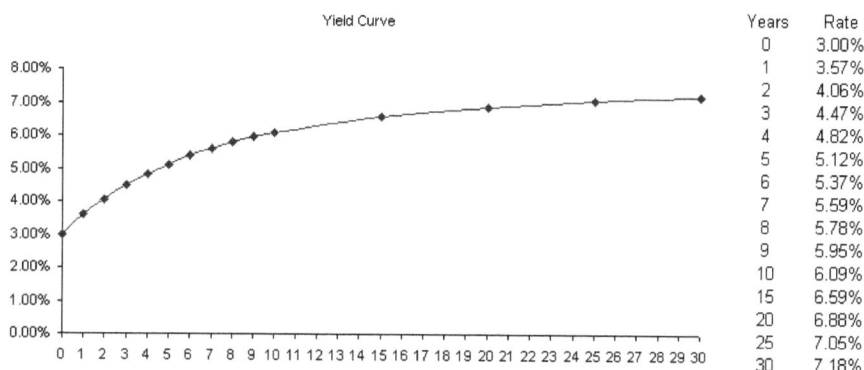

Years	Rate
0	3.00%
1	3.57%
2	4.06%
3	4.47%
4	4.82%
5	5.12%
6	5.37%
7	5.59%
8	5.78%
9	5.95%
10	6.09%
15	6.59%
20	6.88%
25	7.05%
30	7.18%

Figure 2.31: CIR Model

Illustrative Example: Yield Curve – Curve Interpolation BIM Model

File Name: Yield Curve – Curve Interpolation BIM

Location: *Modeling Toolkit | Yield Curve | Curve Interpolation BIM*

Brief Description: This is the BIM model for estimating and modeling the term structure of interest rates and yield curve approximation using curve interpolation methods

Requirements: Modeling Toolkit, Risk Simulator

Modeling Toolkit Function Used: *MTYieldCurveBIM*

A number of alternative methods exist for estimating the term structure of interest rates and the yield curve. Some are fully specified stochastic term structure models while others are simply interpolation models. The former are models such as the CIR and Vasicek models (illustrated in other sections in this book), while the latter are interpolation models such as the Bliss or Nelson approach. This section looks at the Bliss interpolation model (Figure 2.32) for generating the term structure of interest rates and yield curve estimation. This model requires several input parameters whereby their estimations require some econometric modeling techniques to calibrate their values. The Bliss approach is a modification of the Nelson–Siegel method by adding an additional generalized parameter. Virtually any yield curve shape can be interpolated using these models, which are widely used at banks around the world.

YIELD CURVE - INTERPOLATION MODEL

Beta 0	0.0500
Beta 1	0.1000
Beta 2	0.1000
Lambda 1	0.2000
Lambda 2	0.2000

Time	Rate
1	8.91%
2	7.00%
3	6.33%
4	6.00%
5	5.80%
6	5.67%
7	5.57%
8	5.50%
9	5.44%
10	5.40%
11	5.36%
12	5.33%
13	5.31%
14	5.29%
15	5.27%
16	5.25%
17	5.24%
18	5.22%
19	5.21%
20	5.20%
21	5.19%
22	5.18%
23	5.17%
24	5.17%
25	5.16%
26	5.15%
27	5.15%
28	5.14%
29	5.14%
30	5.13%

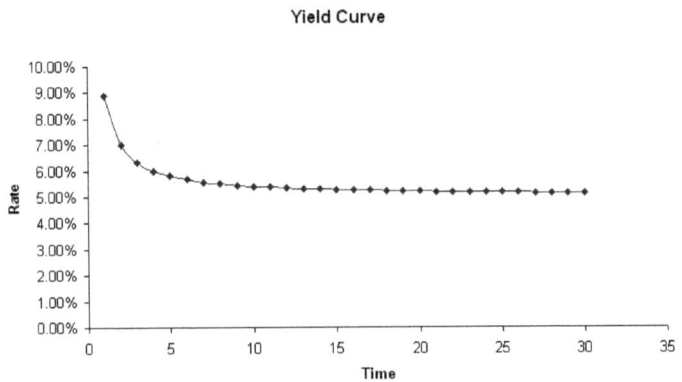

Figure 2.32: BIM Model (Continues)

Credit Risk (ERC)   Market Risk   Asset Liability Management   **Analytical Models**   Operational Risk   Key Risk Indicator (KRI)

Credit (Structural)   Credit (Time Series)   Credit (Portfolio)   **Credit (Models)**

STEP 1: Select the Analysis Category and the Model to run:

Analysis	Model
Bond Related Options, Pricing and Yields	**Yield Curve (Bliss)**
Delta Gamma Hedging	Yield Curve (Nelson-Siegel)
Economic Capital	
Exotic Options and Derivatives	
Forecasting Extrapolation and Interpol...	
Put-Call Parity and Option Sensitivity	

Returns the Yield Curve at various points in time using the Bliss model

STEP 2: Enter the required inputs:

Enter numerical inputs only (e.g., \$1,000 please enter as 1000 and 99% enter as 0.99 and so forth).

Time	10
Beta 0	0.05
Beta 1	0.10
Beta 2	0.10
Lambda 1	0.2
Lambda 2	0.2

STEP 3: Save the Models and Data:

You can save multiple analyses and notes in the profile for future retrieval.

Name: Example

Notes:

Save As

Edit

Save

Delete

Model
Economic Capital for Revolving Credit Exam...
Generalized Black Scholes Model Call Optio...
Generalized Black Scholes Model Put Option...
Binomial American Call Option Example
Example

STEP 4: Table and Chart Settings:

Rows: Select a VaR   From: To: Step:

Columns: Select a VaR   From: To: Step:

STEP 5: Run the Models:

Compute   Show: 4   decimals for   Result   0.0540

Figure 2.32: BIM Model

File Name: Yield Curve – Spline Interpolation and Extrapolation

Location: *Modeling Toolkit | Yield Curve | Spline Interpolation and Extrapolation*

Brief Description: This is the multidimensional cubic spline model for estimating and modeling the term structure of interest rates and yield curve approximation using a curve interpolation and extrapolation methods

Requirements: Modeling Toolkit, Risk Simulator

Modeling Toolkit Function Used: *MTCubicSpline*

The cubic spline polynomial interpolation and extrapolation model is used to "fill in the gaps" of missing spot yields and term structure of interest rates whereby the model can be used to both interpolate missing data points within a time series of interest rates (as well as other macroeconomic variables such as inflation rates and commodity prices or market returns) and also used to extrapolate outside of the given or known range, useful for forecasting purposes. In Figure 2.33, the actual U.S. Treasury risk-free rates are shown and entered into the model as known values. The timing of these spot yields is entered as Years (the known X value inputs), whereas the known risk-free rates are the known Y values. Using the *MTCubicSpline* function, we can now interpolate the in-between risk-free rates that are missing as well as the rates outside of the given input dates. For instance, the risk-free Treasury rates given include 1-month, 3-month, 6-month, 1-year, and so forth, until the 30-year rate. Using these data, we can interpolate the rates for, say, 5 months or 9 months, and so forth, as well as extrapolate beyond the 30-year rate.

Years	Spot Yields
0.0833	4.55%
0.2500	4.47%
0.5000	4.52%
1.0000	4.39%
2.0000	4.13%
3.0000	4.16%
5.0000	4.26%
7.0000	4.38%
10.0000	4.56%
20.0000	4.88%
30.0000	4.84%

These are the yields that are known and are used as inputs in the Cubic Spline Interpolation and Extrapolation model

Spline Interpolation and Extrapolation Results

Years	Yield	Notes
0.5	4.52%	Interpolate
1.0	4.39%	Interpolate
1.5	4.21%	Interpolate
2.0	4.13%	Interpolate
2.5	4.13%	Interpolate
3.0	4.16%	Interpolate
3.5	4.19%	Interpolate
4.0	4.22%	Interpolate
4.5	4.24%	Interpolate
5.0	4.26%	Interpolate
5.5	4.29%	Interpolate
6.0	4.32%	Interpolate
6.5	4.35%	Interpolate
7.0	4.38%	Interpolate
7.5	4.41%	Interpolate
8.0	4.44%	Interpolate
8.5	4.47%	Interpolate
9.0	4.50%	Interpolate
9.5	4.53%	Interpolate
10.0	4.56%	Interpolate
10.5	4.59%	Interpolate
11.0	4.61%	Interpolate
11.5	4.64%	Interpolate
12.0	4.66%	Interpolate
12.5	4.68%	Interpolate
13.0	4.70%	Interpolate
13.5	4.72%	Interpolate
14.0	4.74%	Interpolate

Daily Treasury Yield Curve Rates

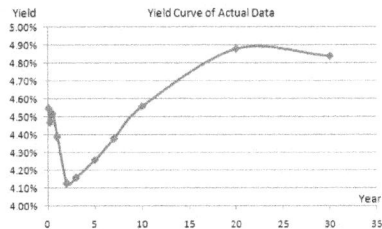

Figure 2.33: Cubic Spline Model

Illustrative Example: Yield Curve – Forward Rates from Spot Rates

File Name: Yield Curve – Forward Rates from Spot Rates

Location: *Modeling Toolkit | Yield Curve | Forward Rates from Spot Rates*

Brief Description: This is a bootstrap model used to determine the implied forward rate given two spot rates

Requirements: Modeling Toolkit, Risk Simulator

Modeling Toolkit Function Used: *MTForwardRate*

Given two spot rates (from Year 0 to some future time periods), you can determine the implied forward rate between these two time periods. For instance, if the spot rate from Year 0 to Year 1 is 8%, and the spot rate from Year 0 to Year 2 is 7% (both yields are known currently), the implied forward rate from Year 1 to Year 2 (that will occur based on current expectations) is 6%. This is simplified by using the *MTForwardRate* function in Modeling Toolkit (Figure 2.34).

FORWARD RATES
COMPUTING FORWARD RATES FROM SPOT RATES

Input Assumptions

Spot Rate 1	8.00%
Spot Rate 2	7.00%
Time of Spot Rate 1	1.00
Time of Spot Rate 2	2.00

Forward Rate   **6.00%**

Figure 2.34: Forward Rate Extrapolation

Illustrative Example: Yield Curve – Vasicek Model

File Name: Yield Curve – Vasicek Model

Location: *Modeling Toolkit | Yield Curve | Vasicek Model*

Brief Description: The Vasicek model is used to create the term structure of interest rates and to reconstruct the yield curve assuming the underlying interest rates are mean reverting and stochastic

Requirements: Modeling Toolkit, Risk Simulator

Modeling Toolkit Function Used: *MTVasicekBondYield*

This is the Vasicek model used to compute the term structure of interest rates and yield curve. The Vasicek model assumes a mean-reverting stochastic interest rate (Figure 2.35). The rate of reversion and long-run mean rates can be determined using Risk Simulator's statistical analysis tool. If the long-run rate is higher than the current short rate, the yield curve is upward sloping, and vice versa.

The yield curve is the time-series relationship between interest rates and the time to maturity of the debt. The more formal mathematical description of this relationship is called the term structure of interest rates. As discussed previously, the yield curve can take on various shapes. The normal yield curve means that yields rise as maturity lengthens and the yield curve is positively sloped, reflecting investor expectations for the economy to grow in the future (and, hence, an expectation that inflation rates will rise in the future). An inverted yield curve occurs when the opposite happens, where the long-term yields fall below short-term yields, and long-term investors will settle for lower yields now if they think the economy will slow or even decline in the future, indicative of a worsening economic situation in the future (and, hence, an expectation that inflation will remain low in the future). Another potential situation is a flat yield curve, signaling uncertainty in the economy. The yield curve can also be humped or show a smile or a frown. The yield curve over time can change in shape through a twist or bend, a parallel shift, or a movement on one end versus another.

As the yield curve is related to inflation rates as discussed above, and central banks in most countries have the ability to control monetary policy to target inflation rates, inflation rates are mean reverting in nature. This also implies that interest rates are mean reverting, as well as stochastically changing over time.

A Czech mathematician, Oldrich Vasicek, in a 1977 paper, proved that bond prices on a yield curve over time and various maturities are driven by the short end of the yield curve, or the short-term interest rates, using a risk-neutral martingale measure. In his work, the mean-reverting Ornstein–Uhlenbeck process was assumed; hence the resulting Vasicek model requires that a mean-reverting interest rate process be modeled (rate of mean reversion and long-run mean rates are both inputs in the Vasicek model).

VASICEK MODEL
YIELD CURVE CONSTRUCTION

Input Assumptions

Time to Maturity of the Bond or Debt (Years)	1.00
Riskfree Rate (Short Rate)	2.00%
Long-run Mean Rate	8.00%
Annualized Volatility of Interest Rate	2.00%
Market Price of Interest Rate Risk	0.00%
Rate of Mean Reversion	20.00%

Yield of Zero Coupon Bond 2.5562%

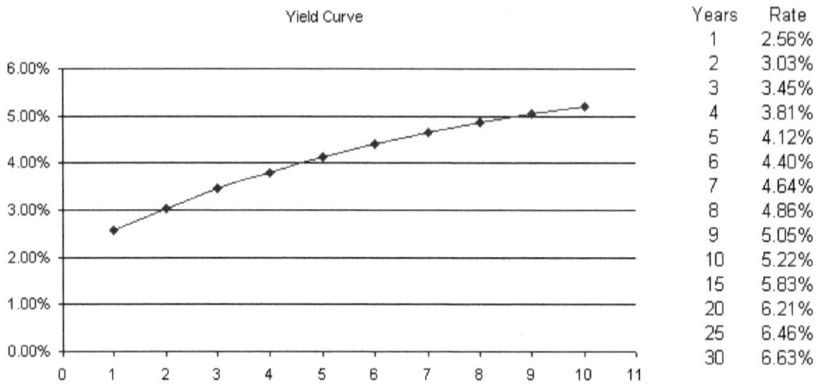

Years	Rate
1	2.56%
2	3.03%
3	3.45%
4	3.81%
5	4.12%
6	4.40%
7	4.64%
8	4.86%
9	5.05%
10	5.22%
15	5.83%
20	6.21%
25	6.46%
30	6.63%

Figure 2.35: Using the Vasicek Model to Generate a Yield Curve

Illustrative Example: Stochastic Forecasting of Interest Rates and Stock Prices

File Name: Forecasting – Stochastic Processes

Location: *Modeling Toolkit | Forecasting | Stochastic Processes*

Brief Description: This sample model illustrates how to simulate Stochastic Processes (Brownian Motion Random Walk, Mean-Reversion, Jump-Diffusion, and Mixed Models)

Requirements: Modeling Toolkit, Risk Simulator

A stochastic process is a sequence of events or paths generated by probabilistic laws. That is, random events can occur over time but are governed by specific statistical and probabilistic rules. The main stochastic processes include Random Walk or Brownian Motion, Mean-Reversion and Jump-Diffusion. These processes can be used to forecast a multitude of variables that seemingly follow random trends but yet are restricted by probabilistic laws. We can use Risk Simulator's *Stochastic Process* module to simulate and create such processes. These processes can be used to forecast a multitude of time-series data including stock prices, interest rates, inflation rates, oil prices, electricity prices, commodity prices, and so forth.

Stochastic Process Forecasting

To run this model, simply:

1. Select *Simulation | Forecasting | Stochastic Processes*.

2. Enter a set of relevant inputs or use the existing inputs as a test case (Figure 2.36).

3. Select the relevant process to simulate.

4. Click on *Update Chart* to view the updated computation of a single path or click *OK* to create the process.

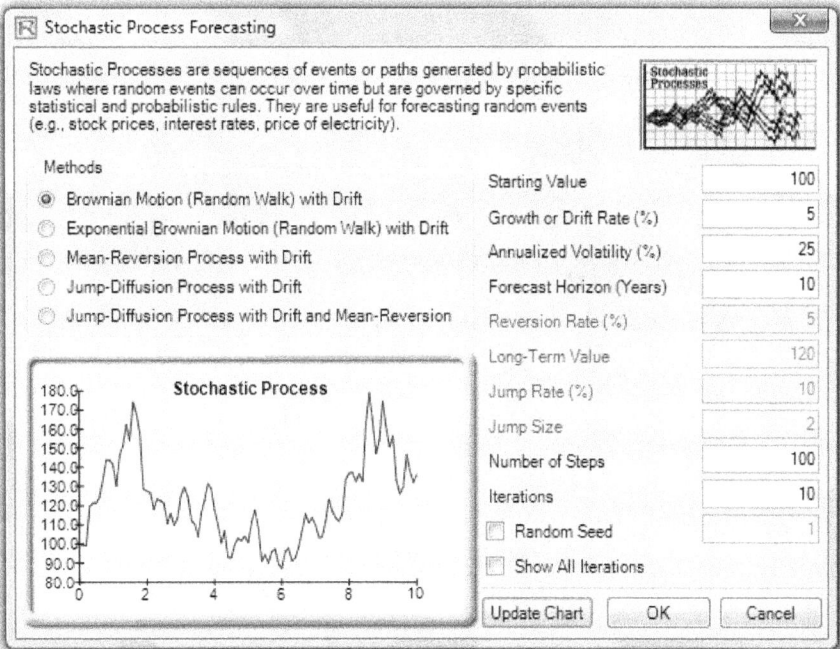

Figure 2.36: Running a Stochastic Process Forecast

PROBABILITY OF DEFAULT
AND VALUE AT RISK

Probability of Default – Bond Yields and Spreads (Market Comparable Approach)

File Name: Probability of Default – Yields and Spreads

Location: *Modeling Toolkit | Prob of Default | Bond Yields and Spreads (Market Comparable)*

Brief Description: Generates the probability of default on a bond or debt by looking at market traded instruments' yields (bond)

Requirements: Modeling Toolkit

Modeling Toolkit Functions Used: *MTProbabilityDefaultCumulativeBondYieldApproach, MTProbabilityDefaultHazardRate, MTProbabilityDefaultCumulativeSpreadApproach, MTProbabilityDefaultAdjustedBondYield, MTProbabilityDefaultCorrelation, MTProbabilityDefaultAverageDefaults, MTProbabilityDefaultPercentileDefaults*

This model looks at the computation of probability of default on a bond or debt by looking at market traded instruments. Probability of default measures the degree of likelihood that the borrower of a loan or debt (an obligor) will be unable to make the necessary scheduled repayments on the debt, thereby defaulting on it. If the obligor is unable to pay, the debt is in default, and the lenders have legal avenues to attempt a recovery of the debt or at least partial repayment of the entire debt. The higher the default probability a lender estimates a borrower to have, the higher the interest rate the lender will charge the borrower as compensation for bearing the higher default risk. Probability of default models are categorized as structural or empirical.

Structural models compute probability of default based on market data (e.g., bond yields and spreads, equity prices, market and book values of asset and liabilities, as well as the volatility of these variables). In contrast, empirical models or credit scoring models are used to quantitatively determine the probability that a loan or loan holder will default, where the loan holder is an individual, by looking at historical portfolios of loans held, where individual characteristics are assessed (e.g., age, educational level, debt to income ratio, etc.).

The bond yield comparable approach is clearly a structural model. In these models, given the annualized spot risk-free yields over time, the corresponding corporate bond yields (both are zero coupon bonds), and the expected recovery rate upon default, we can compute the implied cumulative default probability, the default probability in a particular year, and the hazard rates for each year (Figure 3.1).

In addition, the cumulative default probability between two years can also be computed using the same bond yield approach. Sometimes, only the risky bond or debt's spread (the premium charged above the risk-free rate) is known. Using this credit spread, the cumulative probability of default can also be determined. To obtain the probability of default in a given year, compute two cumulative default probabilities and get the difference.

This model also exemplifies the use of the Credit Risk Plus method employed by Credit Suisse Financial Products and is used to compute the average number of credit defaults per period given the total number of credit exposures in the portfolio, the cumulative probability of default on average, and the percentile Value at Risk for the portfolio. The Credit Risk Plus method can also be used to compute the percentile given some estimated average number of defaults per period.

The downside to this method is the need for bond yield data that are comparable to the debt or bond to be analyzed. In contrast, the subsequent chapters look at other structural and empirical models that do not require a bond market.

Probability of Default Analysis

Maturity	Risk-Free Zero Yield	Corporate Bond Zero Yield	Cumulative Default Probability	Default Probability Specific Year	Hazard Rate Specific Year
1	5.00%	5.25%	0.3121%	0.3121%	1.1675%
2	5.00%	5.50%	1.2438%	0.9317%	1.7093%
3	5.00%	5.70%	2.5976%	1.3539%	2.0181%
4	5.00%	5.85%	4.1786%	1.5809%	2.0952%
5	5.00%	5.95%	5.7987%	1.6201%	1.9410%
6	5.00%	6.00%	7.2794%	1.4807%	2.0952%
7	5.00%	6.05%	8.8580%	1.5785%	2.0027%
8	5.00%	6.08%	10.3466%	1.4886%	1.9564%
9	5.00%	6.10%	11.7822%	1.4356%	2.0181%
10	5.00%	6.12%	13.2445%	1.4623%	

Assumed Recovery Rate: 20.00%

Modeling Toolkit Function Used: MTProbabilityDefaultCumulativeBondYieldApproach

Computing the Cumulative Default Probability between two time periods:

From Year	5
To Year	10
Cumulative Default Probability	7.4458%

Computing the Cumulative Probability between two time periods using Bond Spreads:

First Credit Spread above Risk-Free	0.9500%
First Credit Spread's Maturity	5
Second Credit Spread above Risk-Free	1.1200%
Second Credit Spread's Maturity	10
First Credit Spread's Cumulative Default Probability	5.7987%
Second Credit Spread's Cumulative Default Probability	13.2445%
Cumulative Default Probability between First and Second Maturity	7.4458%

Modeling Toolkit Function Used: MTProbabilityDefaultCumulativeSpreadApproach

Figure 3.1: Bond Yield Approach to Probability of Default

Probability of Default – Empirical Model

File Name: Probability of Default – Empirical

Location: *Modeling Toolkit | Prob of Default | Empirical (Individuals)*

Brief Description: Computes the probability of default on loans of individuals given some historical data on existing loans (age, educational levels, years at employment, etc.) and applies a maximum likelihood estimation approach

Requirements: Modeling Toolkit, Risk Simulator

Probability of default measures the degree of likelihood that the borrower of a loan or debt (also called an obligor) will be unable to make the necessary scheduled repayments on the debt, thereby defaulting on it. Should the obligor be unable to pay, the debt is in default, and the lenders of the debt have legal avenues to attempt a recovery of the debt, or at least partial repayment of the entire debt. The higher the default probability a lender estimates a borrower to have, the higher the interest rate the lender will charge the borrower as compensation for bearing the higher default risk.

Probability of default models are categorized as structural or empirical. Structural models are presented over the next few sections, which look at a borrower's ability to pay based on market data such as equity prices, market and book values of asset and liabilities, as well as the volatility of these variables. Hence, they are used predominantly to estimate the probability of default of companies and countries. In contrast, empirical models or credit scoring models as presented here are used to quantitatively determine the probability that a loan or loan holder will default, where the loan holder is an individual, by looking at historical portfolios of loans held, where individual characteristics are assessed (e.g., age, educational level, debt to income ratio, and so forth). Other default models in the Modeling Toolkit handle corporations using market comparables and asset/liability valuations as seen in the next section.

The data here represent a sample of several hundred previous loans, credit, or debt issues. The data show whether each loan had defaulted or not, as well as the specifics of each loan applicant's age, education level (1–3 indicating high school, university, or graduate professional education), years with current employer, and so forth (Figure 3.2). The idea is to model these empirical data to see which

variables affect the default behavior of individuals, using Risk Simulator's *Maximum Likelihood* models. The resulting model will help the
bank or credit issuer compute the expected probability of default of
an individual credit holder having specific characteristics.

To run the analysis, select the data (include the headers) and
make sure that the data have the same length for all variables, without
any missing or invalid data. Then, click on *Risk Simulator | Forecasting
| Maximum Likelihood Models.* A sample set of results is provided in
the *MLE* worksheet in the model, complete with detailed instructions on how to compute the expected probability of default of an
individual.

Maximum Likelihood Estimates (MLE) on a binary multivariate
logistic analysis is used to model dependent variables to determine
the expected probability of success of belonging to a certain group.
For instance, given a set of independent variables (e.g., age, income,
education level of credit card or mortgage loan holders), we can
model the probability of default using MLE. A typical regression
model is invalid because the errors are heteroskedastic and non-
normal, and the resulting estimated probability estimates sometimes
will be above 1 or below 0. MLE analysis handles these problems
using an iterative optimization routine.

Use the MLE when the data are *ungrouped* (there is only one dependent variable, and its values are either 1 for success or 0 for
failure). If the data are *grouped* into unique categories (for instance,
the dependent variables are actually two variables, one for the *Total
Events* T and another *Successful Events* S), and if, based on historical
data for a given level of income, age, education level and so forth,
data on how many loans had been issued (T) and of those, how many
defaulted (S) are available, then use the *grouped* approach and apply
the *Weighted Least Squares* and *Unweighted Least Squares* method instead.

The coefficients provide the estimated MLE intercept and
slopes. For instance, the coefficients are estimates of the true population b values in the equation $Y = b_0 + b_1X_1 + b_2X_2 + ... + b_nX_n$.
The *standard error* measures how accurate the predicted coefficients
are, and the Z-statistics are the ratios of each predicted coefficient to
its standard error.

The Z-statistic is used in hypothesis testing, where we set the
null hypothesis (H_o) such that the real mean of the coefficient is
equal to zero, and the alternate hypothesis (H_a) such that the real

mean of the coefficient is not equal to zero. The Z-test is very important as it calculates if each of the coefficients is statistically significant in the presence of the other regressors. This means that the Z-test statistically verifies whether a regressor or independent variable should remain in the model or should be dropped. That is, the smaller the p-value, the more significant the coefficient. The usual significant levels for the p-value are 0.01, 0.05, and 0.10, corresponding to the 99%, 95%, and 90% confidence levels.

The coefficients estimated are actually the logarithmic odds ratios and cannot be interpreted directly as probabilities. A quick computation is first required. The approach is simple. To estimate the probability of success of belonging to a certain group (e.g., predicting if a debt holder will default given the amount of debt held), simply compute the estimated Y value using the MLE coefficients. For instance, if the model is, say, $Y = -2.1 + 0.005$ (Debt in thousands), then someone with a \$100,000 debt has an estimated Y of $-2.1 + 0.005(100) = -1.6$. Then, calculate the inverse antilog of the odds ratio by computing:

$$\frac{exp(\,estimated\ Y\,)}{1 + exp(\,estimated\ Y\,)} = \frac{exp(\,-1.6\,)}{1 + exp(\,-1.6\,)} = 0.1679$$

Such a person has a 16.79% chance of defaulting on the new debt. Using this probability of default, you can then use the *Credit Analysis – Credit Premium* model to determine the additional credit spread to charge this person given this default level and the customized cash flows anticipated from this debt holder.

PROBABILITY OF DEFAULT (EMPIRICAL USING MAXIMUM LIKELIHOOD)

Defaulted	Age	Education Level	Years with Current Employer	Years at Current Address	Household Income (Thousands $)	Debt to Income Ratio (%)	Credit Card Debt (Thousands $)	Other Debt (Thousands $)
1	41	3	17	12	176	9.3	11.36	5.01
0	27	1	10	6	31	17.3	1.36	4
0	40	1	15	14	55	5.5	0.86	2.17
0	41	1	15	14	120	2.9	2.66	0.82
1	24	2	2	0	28	17.3	1.79	3.06
0	41	2	5	5	25	10.2	0.39	2.16
0	39	1	20	9	67	30.6	3.83	16.67
0	43	1	12	11	38	3.6	0.13	1.24
1	24	1	3	4	19	24.4	1.36	3.28
0	36	1	0	13	25	19.7	2.78	2.15
0	27	1	0	1	16	1.7	0.18	0.09
0	25	1	4	0	23	5.2	0.25	0.94
0	52	1	24	14	64	10	3.93	2.47
0	37	1	6	9	29	16.3	1.72	3.01
0	48	1	22	15	100	9.1	3.7	5.4
1	36	2	9	6	49	8.6	0.82	3.4
1	36	2	13	6	41	16.4	2.92	3.81
0	43	1	23	19	72	7.6	1.18	4.29
0	39	1	6	9	61	5.7	0.56	2.91
0	41	3	0	21	26	1.7	0.1	0.34
0	39	1	22	3	52	3.2	1.15	0.51
0	47	1	17	21	43	5.6	0.59	1.82

Figure 3.2 Empirical Analysis of Probability of Default (continues)

Credit Risk (ERC)   Market Risk   Asset Liability Management   **Analytical Models**   Operational Risk   Key Risk Indicator (KRI)

Credit (Structural)   **Credit (Time Series)**   Credit (Portfolio)   Credit (Models)

STEP 1: Select the Analysis Category and the Model to run:

Analysis	Model
Probability of Default (PD)	**PD on Individuals and Retail**
Volatility	Limited Dependent Variables (Probit)
	Limited Dependent Variables (Tobit)

Probability of default measures the degree of likelihood that the borrower of a loan or debt (the obligor) will be unable to make the necessary scheduled repayments on the debt.

Maximum Likelihood Estimates (MLE) on a binary multivariate logistic analysis is used to model dependent variables to determine the expected probability of success of belonging to a certain group. For instance, given a set of independent variables (e.g., age, income, education level of credit card or mortgage loan holders), we can model the probability of default using MLE.

STEP 3: Save the Models and Data:

You can save multiple analyses and notes in the profile for future retrieval.

Name: Probability of Default Model on Retail Loans

Notes:

Save As	Model
	Sample Historical Volatility
Edit	Probability of Default Model on Retail Loans
	GARCH Volatility Model
Save	
Delete	

< >

STEP 2: Enter the required inputs:

Show **100** ▾ rows by **8** ▾ variables with **2** ▾ decimals for results

Computations   Charts

Enter numerical inputs only (e.g. $1,000 please enter as 1000 and 99% enter as 0.99 and so forth).

STEP 4: Run the Models:

Compute

	Y (DEP)	X (IND) 1	X (IND) 2	X (IND) 3	X (IND) 4	X (IND) 5	X (IND) 6	X (IN ^
1	1	41	3	17	12	176	9.3	11.
2	0	27	1	10	6	31	17.3	1.3
3	0	40	1	15	14	55	5.5	0.8
4	0	41	1	15	14	120	2.9	2.6
5	1	24	2	2	0	28	17.3	1.7
6	0	41	2	5	5	25	10.2	0.3
7	0	39	1	20	9	67	30.6	3.8
8	0	43	1	12	11	38	3.6	0.1
9	1	24	1	3	4	19	24.4	1.3
10	0	36	1	0	13	25	19.7	2.7
11	0	27	1	0	1	16	1.7	0.1 ∨

First run :				
Variable	Coefficients	Standard Error	Z-Statistic	p-Value
Intercept	0.555531	1.566307	0.354676	
0.722833				
Column1	-0.017680	0.048900	-0.361558	
0.717682				
Column2	-0.114134	0.374608	-0.304676	
0.760613				
Column3	-0.132858	0.080842	-1.643436	
0.100293				
Column4	-0.134936	0.070964	-1.901479	
0.057239				
Column5	-0.011330	0.030191	-0.375269	
0.707460				
Column6	0.017760	0.055762	0.318505	
0.750102				
Column7	0.629984	0.357091	1.764211	
0.077696				

Figure 3.2: Empirical Analysis of Probability of Default

File Name: Probability of Default – External Options Model

Location: *Modeling Toolkit | Prob of Default | External Options Model (Public Company)*

Brief Description: Computes the probability of default and distance to default of a publicly traded company by decomposing the firm's book value and market value of liability, assets, and volatility using a simultaneous equations options model with optimization

Requirements: Modeling Toolkit, Risk Simulator

Modeling Toolkit Functions Used: *MTMertonDefaultProbabilityII, MTMertonDefaultDistance, MTBlackScholesCall, MTProbabilityDefaultMertonImputedAssetValue, MTProbabilityDefaultMertonImputedAssetVolatility, MTProbabilityDefaultMertonRecoveryRate, MTProbabilityDefaultMertonMVDebt*

Probability of default models is a category of models that assesses the likelihood of default by an obligor. These models differ from regular credit scoring models in several ways. First of all, credit scoring models usually are applied to smaller credits (individuals or small businesses) whereas default models are applied more to larger credits (corporation or countries). Credit scoring models are largely statistical, regressing instances of default against various risk indicators, such as an obligor's income, home renter or owner status, years at a job, educational level, debt to income ratio, and so forth. An example of such a model is seen in the previous section, *Probability of Default – Empirical Model*, where the maximum likelihood approach is used on an advanced econometric regression model. Default models, in contrast, directly model the default process and typically are calibrated to market variables, such as the obligor's stock price, asset value, debt book value, or credit spread on its bonds. Default models find many applications within financial institutions. They are used to support credit analysis and to find the probability that a firm will default, to value counterparty credit risk limits, or to apply financial engineering techniques in developing credit derivatives or other credit instruments.

This model is used to solve the probability of default of a publicly traded company with equity and debt holdings and accounting for its volatilities in the market (Figure 3.3). It is currently used by

KMV and Moody's to perform credit risk analysis. This approach assumes that the book value of asset and asset volatility are unknown and solved in the model, and that the company is relatively stable and the growth rate of its assets are stable over time (e.g., not in start-up mode). The model uses several simultaneous equations in options valuation coupled with optimization to obtain the implied underlying asset's market value and volatility of the asset in order to compute the probability of default and distance to default for the firm.

It is assumed that at this point the reader is well versed in running simulations and optimizations in Risk Simulator. If not, it is suggested that the reader first spends some time on the *Simulation – Basic Simulation Model* as well as the *Continuous Portfolio Optimization* sections before proceeding with the procedures discussed next.

To run this model, enter in the required inputs such as the market value of equity (obtained from market data on the firm's capitalization, i.e., stock price times number of stocks outstanding), market value of equity (computed in the *Volatility* or *LPVA* worksheets in the model), book value of debt and liabilities (the firm's book value of all debt and liabilities), the risk-free rate (the prevailing country's risk-free interest rate for the same maturity), the anticipated growth rate of the company (the expected annualized cumulative growth rate of the firm's assets, estimated using historical data over a long period of time, making this approach more applicable to mature companies rather than start-ups), and the debt maturity (the debt maturity to be analyzed, or enter **1** for the annual default probability). The comparable option parameters are shown in cells G18 to G23. All these comparable inputs are computed except for Asset Value (the market value of asset) and the Volatility of Asset. You will need to input some rough estimates as a starting point so that the analysis can be run. The rule of thumb is to set the volatility of the asset in G22 to be one-fifth to half of the volatility of equity computed in G10, and the market value of asset (G19) to be approximately the sum of the market value of equity and book value of liabilities and debt (G9 and G11).

Then you need to run an optimization in Risk Simulator in order to obtain the desired outputs. To do this, set *Asset Value* and *Volatility of Asset* as the decision variables (make them continuous variables with a lower limit of 1% for volatility and $1 for asset, as both these inputs can take on only positive values). Set cell G29 as the objective to minimize as this is the absolute error value. Finally, the constraint is such that cell H33, the implied volatility in the default model, is set to exactly equal the numerical value of the equity volatility in cell G10. Run a static optimization using Risk Simulator.

If the model has a solution, the absolute error value in cell G29 will revert to zero (Figure 3.4). From here, the probability of default (measured in percent) and distance to default (measured in standard deviations) are computed in cells G39 and G41. Then the relevant credit spread required can be determined using the *Credit Analysis – Credit Premium* model or some other credit spread tables (such as using the *Internal Credit Risk Rating* model). The simpler alternative is to use Modeling Toolkit's prebuilt internally optimized functions (we embedded some artificial intelligence integrated with optimization of simultaneous stochastic equations to solve the problem) using

MTProbabilityDefaultMertonImputedAssetValue (cell I21) and

MTProbabilityDefaultMertonImputedAssetVolatility (cell I24)

for obtaining the probability of default (*MTProbabilityDefaultMertonII* in cell G39).

Real Options Valuation
www.realoptionsvaluation.com

DEFAULT PROBABILITY (EXTERNAL MARKET APPROACH)

This model is used to solve the probability of default of a publicly traded company with equity and debt holdings, and accounting for its volatilities in the market. This model is currently used by KMV and Moody's to perform credit risk analysis. This approach assumes that the book value of asset and asset volatility are unknown and solved.

STEP ONE:

Available market and corporate data stating that we have:

Market Value Equity	$3,000	(in millions)	*This value is obtained from market data on the firm's capitalization*
Market Equity Volatility	46.64%	(annualized)	*This value is computed in the Volatility or LPVA worksheets*
Book Value Liabilities and Debt	$10,000	(in millions)	*This is the firm's book value of debt and liabilities*
Risk-free Spot Rate	5.00%		*This is the prevailing risk-free interest rate for the same maturity*
Anticipated Growth Rate	7.00%		*This is the expected annualized cumulative growth rate of the firm's assets****
Maturity of Debt	1.00		*This is the debt maturity or enter 1 for the annual default probability*
			**** Usually this is set as the risk-free rate for a risk-neutral analysis*

Inputs in the real options model:

	Solved	Starting	Optimized	
Call Value	$2,491			*This is the value of the option and should be set to the equity value using optimization*
Asset Value*	$12,000	$12,000	$12,509	*This is the value to be solved* and is hence set as a decision variable in Risk Simulator*
Strike Value	$10,000		12509.10	*This is set as the book value of debt*
Maturity	1	*Using Modeling Toolkit Functions*		*For simplicity, we set this as 1 year, to obtain the 1-year default probability*
Volatility of Asset*	10.00%	10.00%	11.33%	*This is the value to be solved* and is hence set as a decision variable in Risk Simulator*
Risk-free Rate	5.0%	*Using Modeling Toolkit Functions*	11.33%	*This is the corresponding risk-free rate for the maturity of the option being analyzed*

Optimization parameters:

Call value:	$3,000	*This is the target result*
Computed value:	$2,491	*This is the computed result*
Minimize Absolute Difference	$509	*Objective to Minimize (we minimize this error function to solve the simultaneous equations)*

Optimization Constraints:

Set value   39.28%   to be exactly   46.64%   which is the equity volatility

Set Lower Bounds for Asset Value and Volatility of Asset at $1 and 1% (so they do not go negative)

STEP TWO:

Default Probability is computed using the Risk Simulator Distribution Analysis tool on:

Default Probability:	0.6695%	*This is the computed probability of default*
Distance to Default:	2.4732	*This is the computed distance to default in standard deviations*
Computed Expected Recovery Rate:	94.00%	
Computed Market Value of Debt:	9509.10	

Figure 3.3: Default Probability Model

DEFAULT PROBABILITY (EXTERNAL MARKET APPROACH)

This model is used to solve the probability of default of a publicly traded company with equity and debt holdings and accounting for its volatilities in the market. This model is currently used by KMV and Moody's to perform credit risk analysis. This approach assumes that the book value of asset and asset volatility are unknown and solved.

STEP ONE:

Available market and corporate data stating that we have:

Market Value Equity	$3,000	(in millions)
Market Equity Volatility	46.64%	(annualized)
Book Value Liabilities and Debt	$10,000	(in millions)
Risk-free Spot Rate	5.00%	
Anticipated Growth Rate	7.00%	
Maturity of Debt	1.00	

Inputs in the real options model:

	Solved	Starting	Optimized
Call Value	$3,000	$12,000	$12,509
Asset Value*	$12,509		
Strike Value	$10,000		12509.10
Maturity	1	Using Modeling Toolkit Functions	
Volatility of Asset*	11.33%	10.00%	11.33%
Risk-free Rate	5.0%	Using Modeling Toolkit Functions	

Optimization parameters:

Call value:	$3,000
Computed value:	$3,000
Minimize Absolute Difference:	$0

Optimization Constraints:
Set value: 46.64% to be exactly 46.64% which is the equity volatility
Set Lower Bounds for Asset Value and Volatility of Asset at $1 and 1% (so they do not go negative)

STEP TWO:

Default Probability is computed using the Risk Simulator Distribution Analysis tool on:

Default Probability:	0.5603%	This is the computed probability of default
Distance to Default:	2.5362	This is the computed distance to default in standard deviations
Computed Expected Recovery Rate:	94.00%	
Computed Market Value of Debt:	9509.10	

Figure 3.4: Default Probability Model Setup

Probability of Default – Merton Internal Options Model (Private Company)

File Name: Probability of Default – Merton Internal Model

Location: *Modeling Toolkit | Prob of Default | Merton Internal Model (Private Company)*

Brief Description: Computes the probability of default and distance to default of a privately held company by decomposing the firm's book value of liability, assets, and volatility

Requirements: Modeling Toolkit, Risk Simulator

Modeling Toolkit Functions Used: *MTMertonDefaultProbabilityII, MTMertonDefaultDistance*

This model is a structural model that employs the options approach to computing the *probability of default* and *distance to default* of a company assuming that the book values of asset and debt are known, as are the asset volatilities and anticipated annual growth rates. If the book value of assets or volatility of assets is not known and the company is publicly traded, use the *External Options* model in the previous section instead. This model assumes these inputs are known or the company is privately held and not traded. It essentially computes the probability of default or the point of default for the company when its liabilities exceed its assets, given the asset's growth rates and volatility over time (Figure 3.5). It is recommended that the reader review the previous section's model on an external publicly traded company before using this model. Methodological parallels exist between these two models, with this section building on the knowledge and expertise of the preceding one.

CREDIT RISK DEFAULT PROBABILITY (OPTIONS APPROACH)

VALUING DEFAULT PROBABILITY AND DISTANCE TO DEFAULT BASED ON OPTIONS MODELING OF INTERNAL DEBT

Input Assumptions

Asset Book Value	$12.0000
Debt Book Value	$10.0000
Maturity	1.0000
Risk-free Rate	5.00%
Volatility of Asset	10.00%

Probability of Default   1.1507%
Distance to Default   2.2732

Function: MTProbabilityDefaultMertonII
Function: MTProbabilityDefaultMertonDefaultDistance

Figure 3.5: Credit Default Risk Model with Options Modeling

Probability of Default – Merton Market Options Model (Industry Comparable)

File Name: Probability of Default – Merton Market Options Model

Location: *Modeling Toolkit | Prob of Default | Merton Market Options Model (Industry Comparable)*

Brief Description: Computes the probability of default and distance to default of a publicly or privately held company by decomposing the firm's book value of liability, assets, and volatility while benchmarking the company's returns to some external benchmark or index

Requirements: Modeling Toolkit, Risk Simulator

Modeling Toolkit Function Used: *MTMertonDefaultProbabilityI*

This models the probability of default for both public and private companies using an index or set of comparables (the market), assuming that the company's asset and debt book values are known, as well as the asset's annualized volatility. Based on this volatility and the correlation of the company's assets to the market, we can determine the probability of default. This model is similar to the models in the preceding two sections, which should be reviewed before attempting to run the model illustrated here, as the theoretical constructs of this model are derived from those two structural models.

MERTON MODEL OF DEBT DEFAULT PROBABILITY

VALUING THE PROBABILITY OF DEFAULT BASED ON MARKET RELATIONSHIPS

Input Assumptions	
Asset Value	$100.0000
Debt Value	$50.0000
Time to Maturity	1.00
Risk-free Rate	5.00%
Volatility of Asset	20.00%
Market Volatility	10.00%
Market Return	8.00%
Correlation	0.00
Probability of Default	**0.0150%**

Function: MTProbabilityDefaultMertonI

Figure 3.6 Merton Market Options Model (continues)

Credit (Structural) Credit (Time Series) Credit (Portfolio) Credit (Models)

STEP 1: Select the Analysis Category and the Model to run:

Analysis	Model
Exposure at Default (EAD)	**PD using Market Comparables**
Loss Given Default (LGD)	PD using Bond Yields and Spreads
Probability of Default (PD)	
Volatility	

Probability of default measures the degree of likelihood that the borrower of a loan or debt (the obligor) will be unable to make the necessary scheduled repayments on the debt.

Given the annualized spot risk-free yields over time, the corresponding corporate bond yields (both are zero coupon bonds), and the expected recovery rate upon default, we can compute the cumulative default probability, the default probability in a particular year, and the hazard rates for each year.

STEP 2: Enter the required inputs:

Show 3 ▲▼ rows and 6 ▲▼ decimals for results.

Computations Charts   Enter numerical inputs only (e.g. $1,000 please enter as 1000 and 99% enter as 0.99 and so forth).

STEP 3: Save the Models and Data:

You can save multiple analyses and notes in the profile for future retrieval.

Name: Probability of Default (Market Comps) Example

Notes:

	Model
Save As	EAD using Credit Conversion Factor CCF
	Credit Risk Plus Average Defaults Example
Edit	EAD using LEQ, CCF, EADF
	Loss Given Default (LGD) Example
Save	Probability of Default (Market Comps) Exa...
	Probability of Default (Bond Spreads) Exa...
Delete	Implied Volatility from a Call Option

STEP 4: Run the Models: Compute

N	Probability Of Default	Name	Asset Value	Book Value of Li...	Risk-Free Rate	Maturity	Asset Volatility	Market Equity V...	Market Return	Correlation
1	0.000150	Company 1	100,000	50,000	0.05	1	0.20	0.10	0.06	0
2	0.147610	Company 2	15,000	13,000	0.05	3	0.15	0.25	0.12	0.1
3	0.009802	Company 3	20,000	10,000	0.02	1	0.30	0.45	0.14	0.4

Figure 3.6: Merton Market Options Model

Value at Risk – Optimized and Simulated Portfolio VaR

File Name: Value at Risk – Optimized and Simulated Portfolio VaR

Location: *Modeling Toolkit | Value at Risk | Optimized and Simulated Portfolio VaR*

Brief Description: Computes the Value at Risk (VaR) of a portfolio of assets and uses Monte Carlo simulation to perform historical simulation to determine the tail-end confidence interval for determining VaR

Requirements: Modeling Toolkit, Risk Simulator

This model uses Monte Carlo simulation and optimization routines in Risk Simulator to minimize the Value at Risk (VaR) of a portfolio of assets (Figure 3.7).

VALUE AT RISK WITH ASSET ALLOCATION OPTIMIZATION MODEL

Asset Class Description	Annualized Returns	Volatility Risk	Allocation Weights	Required Minimum Allocation	Required Maximum Allocation
S&P 500	7.10%	9.80%	10.00%	10.00%	40.00%
Small Cap	9.51%	14.35%	27.30%	10.00%	40.00%
High Yield	15.90%	22.50%	22.70%	10.00%	40.00%
Govt Bonds	4.50%	7.25%	40.00%	10.00%	40.00%
		Total Weight:	100.00%		

Correlation Matrix	S&P 500	Small Cap	High Yield	Govt Bonds
S&P 500	1.0000	0.7400	0.6500	0.5500
Small Cap	0.7400	1.0000	0.4200	0.3100
High Yield	0.6500	0.4200	1.0000	0.2300
Govt Bonds	0.5500	0.3100	0.2300	1.0000

Covariance Matrix	S&P 500	Small Cap	High Yield	Govt Bonds
S&P 500	0.0096	0.0104	0.0143	0.0039
Small Cap	0.0104	0.0206	0.0136	0.0032
High Yield	0.0143	0.0136	0.0506	0.0038
Govt Bonds	0.0039	0.0032	0.0038	0.0053

Starting Value	$1,000,000.00
Term (Years)	5.00

Annualized Return	8.72%	Profit/Loss	$87,151.94
Portfolio Risk	9.84%	Return to Risk Ratio	88.59%
Ending Value	$1,087,151.94		

Specifications of the optimization model:

Objective:	*Maximize Return to Risk Ratio (E28)*
Decision Variables:	*Allocation Weights (E6:E9)*
Restrictions on Decision Variables:	*Minimum and Maximum Required (F6:G9)*
Constraints:	*Portfolio Total Allocation Weights 100% (E10 is set to 100%)*

Figure 3.7: Computing Value at Risk (VaR) with Simulation

First, simulation is used to determine the 90% left-tail VaR. This means that there is a 10% chance that losses will exceed this VaR for a specified holding period. With an equal allocation of 25% across the four-asset classes, the VaR is determined using simulation (Figure 3.8). The annualized returns are uncertain and hence simulated. The VaR is then read off the forecast chart. Then optimization is run to find the best portfolio subject to the 100% total allocation across the four projects that will maximize the portfolio's bang for the buck (returns to risk ratio). The resulting optimized portfolio is then simulated once again, and the new VaR is obtained (Figure 3.9). The VaR of this optimized portfolio is a lot less than the non-optimized portfolio.

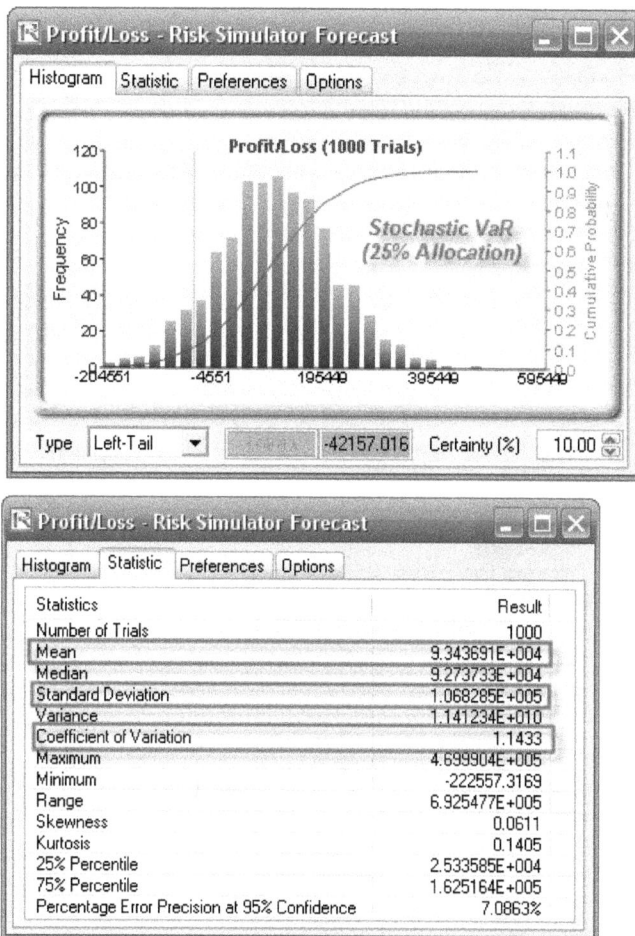

Figure 3.8: Non-optimized Value at Risk

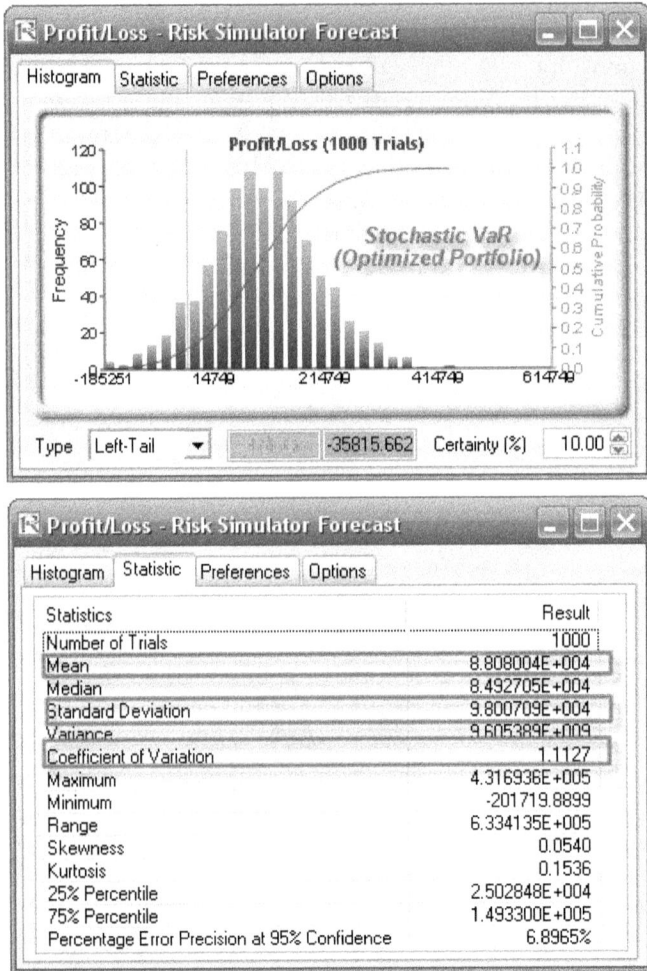

Figure 3.9: Optimal Portfolio's Value at Risk Through Optimization and Simulation

File Name: Value at Risk – Options Delta Portfolio VaR

Location: *Modeling Toolkit | Value at Risk | Options Delta Portfolio VaR*

Brief Description: Computes the Value at Risk (VaR) of a portfolio of options and uses closed-form structural models to determine the VaR, after accounting for the cross-correlations among the various options

Requirements: Modeling Toolkit, Risk Simulator

Modeling Toolkit Functions Used: *MTVaROptions, MTCallDelta*

There are two examples in this *Value at Risk* (VaR) model. The first example illustrates how to compute the portfolio Value at Risk of a group of options, given the options' deltas (Figure 3.10). The option delta is the instantaneous sensitivity of the option's value to the stock price for more details on computing an option's delta sensitivity measure). Given the underlying stock price of the option, the quantity of options held in the portfolio, each option's delta levels, and the daily volatility, we can compute the portfolio's VaR measure. In addition, given a specific holding period (typically between 1 and 10 days) or risk horizon days and the percentile required (typically between 90% and 99.95%), we can compute the portfolio's VaR for that holding period and percentile. If the option's delta is not available, use the *MTCallDelta* function instead, or see the *Given Option Inputs* worksheet.

The second example (Figure 3.11) illustrates how to compute the portfolio VaR of a group of options, given the option inputs (stock price, strike price, risk-free rate, maturity, annualized volatilities, and dividend rate). The option delta is then computed using the *MTCallDelta* function. The delta measure is the instantaneous sensitivity of the option's value to the stock price. Given the underlying stock price of the option, the quantity of options held in the portfolio, each option's delta levels, and the daily volatility, we can compute the portfolio's VaR measure. In addition, given a specific holding period (typically between 1 and 10 days) or risk horizon days and the percentile required (typically between 90% and 99.95%), we can compute the portfolio's VaR for that holding period and percentile. Finally, the daily volatility is computed by dividing the annualized volatility by the square root of trading days per year.

VALUE AT RISK (DELTA OPTIONS PORTFOLIO)

Asset Allocation	Stock Price	Quantity Held	Delta	Daily Volatility
Asset A	$120.00	10000	0.1000	2.00%
Asset B	$30.00	200000	0.1000	1.00%
Asset C	$75.00	5000	0.2000	3.00%
Asset D	$48.00	10000	0.2500	4.00%
Asset E	$98.00	12500	0.2900	5.00%

Correlation Matrix	Asset A	Asset B	Asset C	Asset D	Asset E
Asset A	1.0000	0.1000	0.1000	0.1000	0.1000
Asset B	0.1000	1.0000	0.1000	0.1000	0.1000
Asset C	0.1000	0.1000	1.0000	0.1000	0.1000
Asset D	0.1000	0.1000	0.1000	1.0000	0.1000
Asset E	0.1000	0.1000	0.1000	0.1000	1.0000

Horizon Days for VaR	5
VaR Percentile	95.00%

Portfolio Value at Risk	$78,638.72

Figure 3.10: Delta Options VaR with Known Options Delta Values

VALUE AT RISK (DELTA OPTIONS PORTFOLIO)

Asset Allocation

	Stock Price	Strike Price	Maturity in Years	Annualized Risk-Free Rate	Annualized Volatility	Annualized Dividend Rate	Quantity	Delta	Daily Volatility
Asset A	$120.00	$100.00	1.00	5.00%	31.62%	0.00%	1250	0.8140	2.00%
Asset B	$30.00	$30.00	1.00	5.00%	15.81%	0.00%	30000	0.6537	1.00%
Asset C	$50.00	$50.00	2.00	5.00%	25.00%	0.00%	5000	0.6771	1.58%
Asset D	$75.00	$70.00	3.00	5.00%	23.60%	0.10%	7500	0.7659	1.49%
Asset E	$36.00	$31.00	5.00	5.00%	18.90%	0.20%	10000	0.8627	1.20%

Correlation Matrix

	Asset A	Asset B	Asset C	Asset D	Asset E
Asset A	1.0000	0.1000	0.1000	0.1000	0.1000
Asset B	0.1000	1.0000	0.1000	0.1000	0.1000
Asset C	0.1000	0.1000	1.0000	0.1000	0.1000
Asset D	0.1000	0.1000	0.1000	1.0000	0.1000
Asset E	0.1000	0.1000	0.1000	0.1000	1.0000

Horizon Days for VaR	5
VaR Percentile	95.00%
Trading Days Per Year	250

Portfolio Value at Risk $43,093.78

Figure 3.11: Delta Options VaR with Options Input Parameters

Value at Risk – Portfolio Operational and Credit Risk VaR Capital Adequacy

File Name: Value at Risk – Portfolio Operational and Capital Adequacy

Location: *Modeling Toolkit | Value at Risk | Portfolio Operational and Capital Adequacy*

Brief Description: Illustrates how to use Risk Simulator for distributional fitting, to find the best-fitting distributions for credit risk and operational risk parameters, and how to run Monte Carlo simulation on these credit and operational risk variables to determine the total capital required under a 99.50% Value at Risk

Requirements: Modeling Toolkit, Risk Simulator

This model shows how operational risk and credit risk parameters are fitted to statistical distributions and their resulting distributions are modeled in a portfolio of liabilities to determine the Value at Risk (VaR) 99.50th percentile certainty for the capital requirement under Basel III/IV/IV requirements. It is assumed that the historical data of the operational risk impacts (*Historical Data* worksheet) are obtained through econometric modeling of the *Key Risk Indicators*.

The *Distributional Fitting Report* worksheet is a result of running a distributional fitting routine in Risk Simulator to obtain the appropriate distribution for the operational risk parameter. Using the resulting distributional parameter, we model each liability's capital requirements within an entire portfolio. Correlations can also be inputted if required, between pairs of liabilities or business units. The resulting Monte Carlo simulation results show the VaR capital requirements. Note that an appropriate empirically based historical VaR cannot be obtained if distributional fitting and risk-based simulations were not first run. Only by running simulations will the VaR be obtained.

Procedure

To perform distributional fitting, follow the steps below:

1. In the *Historical Data* worksheet (Figure 3.12), select the data area (cells C5:L104) and click on *Risk Simulator | Analytical Tools | Distributional Fitting (Single Variable)*.

2. Browse through the fitted distributions and select the best-fitting distribution (in this case, the exponential distribution in Figure 3.13) and click OK.

Basel II – Credit Risk and Capital Requirement (Portfolio-Based)

This model applies the Basel II requirements on capital adequacy and modeling the operational risk of probability of default on 100 loans as well as the loss given default. These values are fitted based on the bank's historical loss data (Historical Data and Distributional Fitting Report sheets) using Risk Simulator. Then, the relevant historical simulation assumptions are set in this model (Credit Risk sheet) and a Monte Carlo risk-based simulation was run in Risk Simulator to determine the expected capital required and 99.50% Value at Risk (VaR). A simulation has to be run in order to determine the VaR.

Market Factor	2.000

	Rating level	P (Default) - Long term
	1	0.5%
Weighting:	2	1.0%
Macro	50%	3	1.5%
Micro	50%	4	2.0%
	5	2.5%
Correlation	100%	6	3.0%
	7	5.0%

	Static	Stochastic with Risk-Simulation
Expected Value of Total Capital	$11,734.54	$11,112.81
VaR 99.50% of Total Capital	$30,888.34	$25,959.60

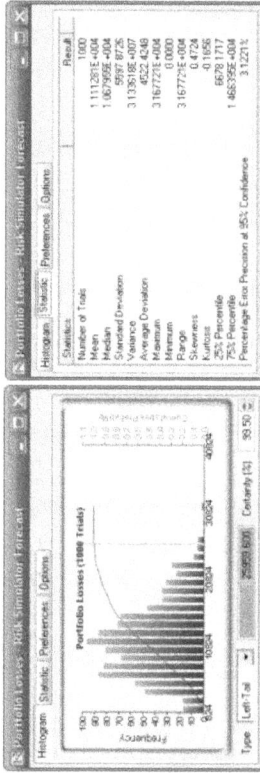

Without running historical simulations, the 99.50% VaR cannot be obtained directly. The only recourse is to apply a theoretical distributional analysis using the fitted distributions' empirical parameters and estimating the theoretical cumulative density function value at 99.50%, and computing the relevant theoretical confidence level. This approach is at best an overestimation of the required capital (thereby requiring too much capital) and at worst, wrong.

Bank loan	Size of loan	Rating grade	P (Default) - Long term	Operational Risk Factor	P (Default) - Now	Default?	Loss Given Default (LGD%)		Losses	
							Static	Stochastic	Static	Stochastic
1	$ 13,274.73	5	2.5%	2.000	5.00%	0	30.0%	30.0%	$ 199.12	$ -
2	$ 14,215.77	6	3.0%	2.000	6.00%	0	30.0%	30.0%	$ 255.88	$ -
3	$ 9,003.59	1	0.5%	2.000	1.00%	0	30.0%	30.0%	$ 27.01	$ -
4	$ 1,324.27	3	1.5%	2.000	3.00%	0	30.0%	30.0%	$ 11.92	$ -
5	$ 11,203.14	1	0.5%	2.000	1.00%	0	30.0%	30.0%	$ 33.61	$ -
6	$ 5,480.61	4	2.0%	2.000	4.00%	0	30.0%	30.0%	$ 65.77	$ -
7	$ 9,853.12	5	2.5%	2.000	5.00%	0	30.0%	30.0%	$ 147.80	$ -
8	$ 12,356.22	3	1.5%	2.000	3.00%	0	30.0%	30.0%	$ 111.21	$ -
9	$ 8,255.80	4	2.0%	2.000	4.00%	0	30.0%	30.0%	$ 99.07	$ -
10	$ 1,662.99	2	1.0%	2.000	2.00%	0	30.0%	30.0%	$ 9.98	$ -
11	$ 7,175.82	3	1.5%	2.000	3.00%	0	30.0%	30.0%	$ 64.58	$ -
							Sum		$11,734.54	$ -
								Static 99.50%	$ 30,888.34	

Figure 3.12: Sample Historical Bank Loans

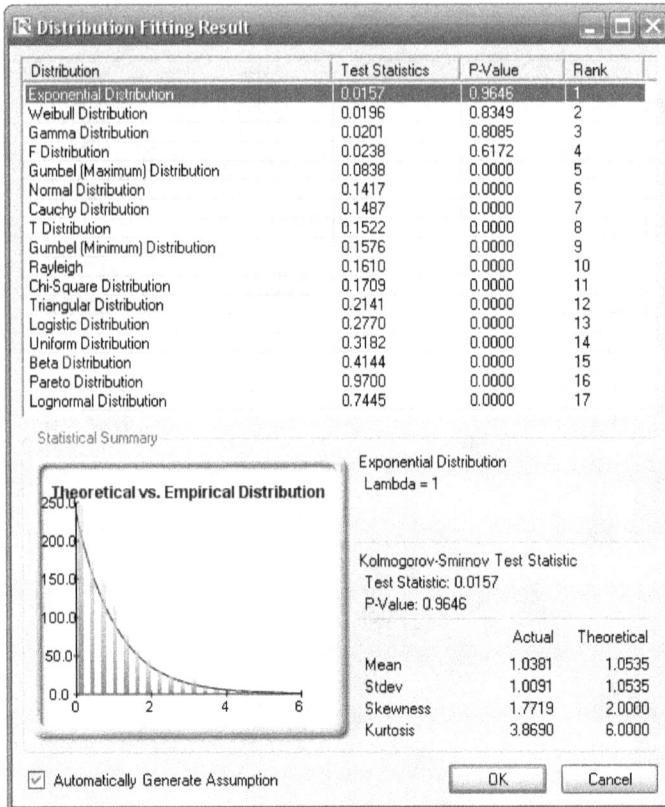

Figure 3.13: Data Fitting Results

To run a simulation in the portfolio model:

1. You may now set the assumptions on the *Operational Risk Factors* with the exponential distribution (fitted results show *Lambda* = 1) in the *Credit Risk* worksheet. Note that the assumptions have been set for you in advance. You may set them by going to cell F27 and clicking on *Risk Simulator | Set Input Assumption*, selecting Exponential distribution and entering 1 for the *Lambda* value, and clicking OK. Continue this process for the remaining cells in column F or simply perform a Risk Simulator Copy and Risk Simulator Paste on the remaining cells:

   a. Note that since the cells in column F have assumptions set, you will first have to clear them if you wish to reset and copy/paste parameters. You can do so by first selecting cells F28:F126 and clicking on the Remove Parameter icon or selecting *Risk Simulator | Remove Parameter*.

b. Then select cell F27, click on the Risk Simulator Copy icon or select *Risk Simulator | Copy Parameter*, and then select cells F28:F126 and click on the Risk Simulator Paste icon or select *Risk Simulator | Paste Parameter*.

2. Next, additional assumptions can be set such as the probability of default using the Bernoulli distribution (column H) and *Loss Given Default* (column J). Repeat the procedure in Step 3 if you wish to reset the assumptions.

3. Run the simulation by clicking on the RUN icon or clicking on *Risk Simulator | Run Simulation*.

4. Obtain the Value at Risk by going to the forecast chart once the simulation is done running and selecting Left-Tail and typing in 99.50. Hit TAB on the keyboard to enter the confidence value and obtain the VaR of $25,959 (Figure 3.14).

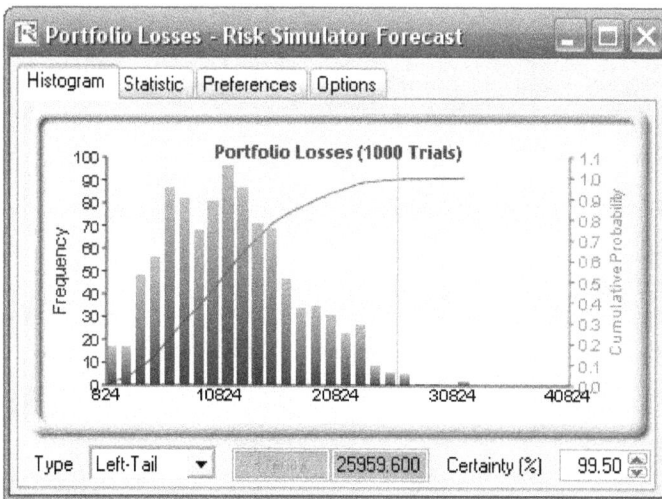

Figure 3.14: Simulated Forecast Results (continues)

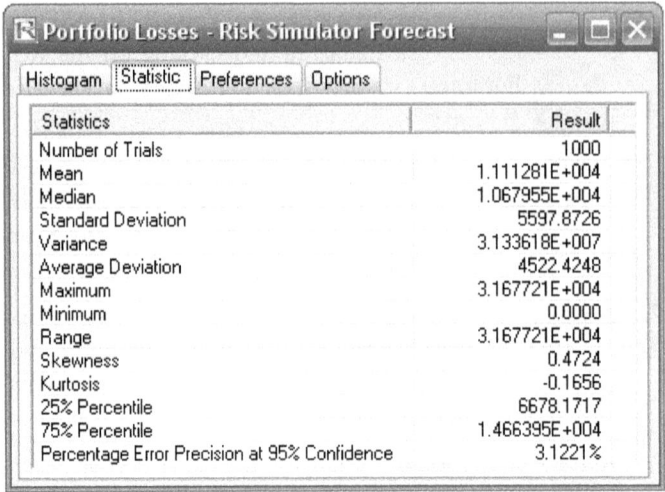

Statistics	Result
Number of Trials	1000
Mean	1.111281E+004
Median	1.067955E+004
Standard Deviation	5597.8726
Variance	3.133618E+007
Average Deviation	4522.4248
Maximum	3.167721E+004
Minimum	0.0000
Range	3.167721E+004
Skewness	0.4724
Kurtosis	-0.1656
25% Percentile	6678.1717
75% Percentile	1.466395E+004
Percentage Error Precision at 95% Confidence	3.1221%

Figure 3.14: Simulated Forecast Results

Value at Risk – Right-Tail Capital Requirements

File Name: Value at Risk – Right Tail Capital Requirements

Location: *Modeling Toolkit | Value at Risk | Right Tail Capital Requirements*

Brief Description: Illustrates how to use Risk Simulator for running a risk-based correlated Monte Carlo simulation to obtain the right-tailed Value at Risk for Basel III/IV/IV requirements

Requirements: Modeling Toolkit, Risk Simulator

This model shows the capital requirements per Basel III/IV/IV requirements (99.95th percentile capital adequacy based on a specific holding period's Value at Risk). Without running risk-based historical and Monte Carlo simulation using Risk Simulator, the required capital is $37.01M (Figure 3.15) as compared to only $14.00M required using a correlated simulation (Figure 3.16). This is due to the cross-correlations between assets and business lines and can only be modeled using Risk Simulator. This lower VaR is preferred as banks can now be required to hold less required capital and can reinvest the remaining capital in various profitable ventures, thereby generating higher profits.

TAIL VALUE AT RISK MODEL (BASEL II REQUIREMENT)

Line of Business	Mean Required Capital	99.95th Percentile	Capital Required	Allocation Weights	Minimum Allowed	Maximum Allowed	
Business 1	$10.50	$36.52	$26.01	10.00%	5.00%	15.00%	3.48
Business 2	$11.12	$47.52	$36.39	10.00%	5.00%	15.00%	4.27
Business 3	$11.77	$48.99	$37.22	10.00%	5.00%	15.00%	4.16
Business 4	$10.77	$37.34	$26.56	10.00%	5.00%	15.00%	3.47
Business 5	$13.49	$49.52	$36.03	10.00%	5.00%	15.00%	3.67
Business 6	$14.24	$55.59	$41.35	10.00%	5.00%	15.00%	3.91
Business 7	$15.60	$60.24	$44.64	10.00%	5.00%	15.00%	3.86
Business 8	$14.95	$64.69	$49.74	10.00%	5.00%	15.00%	4.33
Business 9	$14.15	$61.02	$46.87	10.00%	5.00%	15.00%	4.31
Business 10	$10.08	$35.37	$25.29	10.00%	5.00%	15.00%	3.51
Portfolio Total	$12.67	$49.68	$37.01	100.00%			
Total Capital Required			$14.00				

Correlation Matrix

	1	2	3	4	5	6	7	8	9	10
1										
2	-0.20									
3	-0.13	0.35								
4	-0.05	0.01	0.00							
5	0.23	0.50	0.15	0.00						
6	0.00	0.00	-0.15	0.00	0.03					
7	0.25	0.00	-0.26	0.01	0.10	-0.10				
8	0.36	-0.25	-0.60	-0.30	0.00	0.00	-0.15			
9	-0.01	-0.20	0.16	0.04	-0.01	0.01	0.00	0.00		

Figure 3.15: Right-Tail VaR Model

Procedure

1. To run the model, click on *Risk Simulator | Run Simulation* (if you had other models open, make sure you first click on *Risk Simulator | Change Profile*, and select the *Tail VaR* profile before starting).

2. When simulation is complete, select Left-Tail in the forecast chart and enter in 99.95 in the *Certainty* box and hit TAB on the keyboard to obtain the value of $14.00M Value at Risk for this correlated simulation.

3. Note that the assumptions have been set for you in advance in the model in cells C6:C15. However, you may set them again by going to cell C6 and clicking on *Risk Simulator | Set Input Assumption*, selecting your distribution of choice or using the default *Normal Distribution* (as a quick example) or perform a distributional fitting on historical data and click OK. Continue this process for the remaining cells in column C. You may also decide to first *Remove Parameters* of these cells in column C and set your own distributions. Further, correlations can be set manually when assumptions are set (Figure 3.17) or by going to *Risk Simulator | Edit Correlations* (Figure 3.18) after all the assumptions are set.

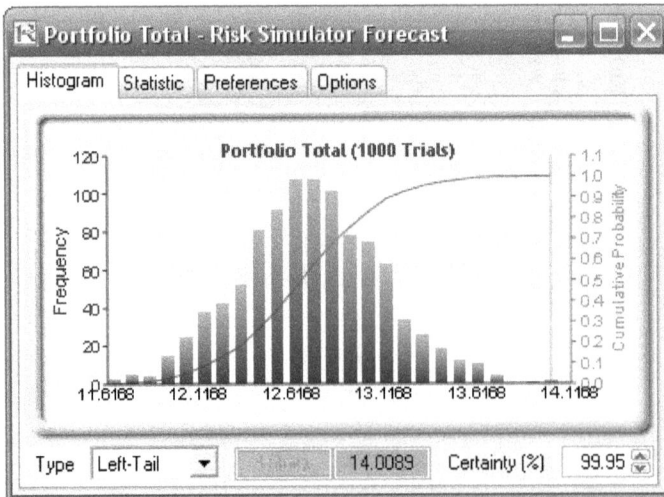

Figure 3.16: Simulated Results of the Portfolio VaR

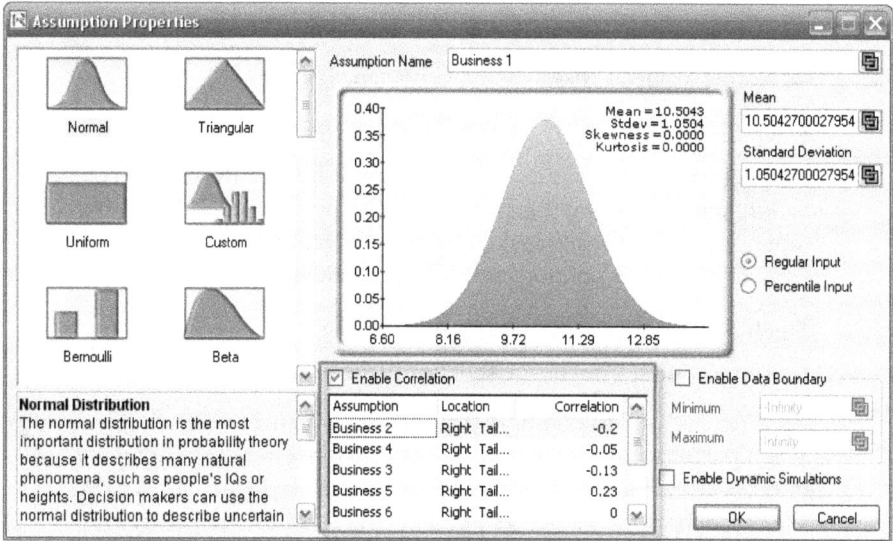

Figure 3.17: Setting Correlations One at a Time

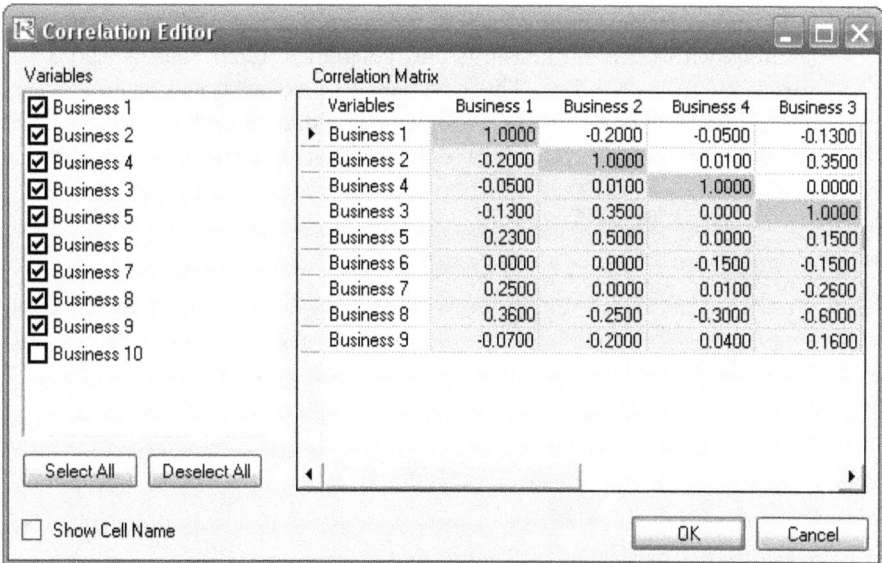

Figure 3.18: Setting Correlations Using the Correlation Matrix Routine

Value at Risk – Static Covariance Method

File Name: Value at Risk – Static Covariance Method

Location: *Modeling Toolkit | Value at Risk | Static Covariance Method*

Brief Description: Computes a static Value at Risk (VaR) using a correlation and covariance method, to obtain the portfolio's VaR after accounting for the individual component's returns, volatility, cross-correlations, holding period, and VaR percentile

Requirements: Modeling Toolkit, Risk Simulator

Modeling Toolkit Function Used: *MTVaRCorrelationMethod*

This model is used to compute the portfolio's Value at Risk (VaR) at a given percentile for a specific holding period, after accounting for the cross-correlation effects between the assets (Figure 3.19). The daily volatility is the annualized volatility divided by the square root of trading days per year. Typically, positive correlations tend to carry a higher VaR compared to zero correlation asset mixes, whereas negative correlations reduce the total risk of the portfolio through the diversification effect (Figure 3.20). The approach used is a portfolio VaR with correlated inputs, where the portfolio has multiple asset holdings with different amounts and volatilities. Each asset is also correlated to each other. The covariance or correlation structural model is used to compute the VaR given a holding period or horizon and percentile value (typically 10 days at 99% confidence).

VALUE AT RISK (VARIANCE-COVARIANCE METHOD)

Asset Allocation	Amount	Daily Volatility
Asset A	$1,000,000.00	1.20%
Asset B	$2,000,000.00	2.00%
Asset C	$3,000,000.00	1.89%
Asset D	$4,000,000.00	3.25%
Asset E	$5,000,000.00	4.20%

Correlation Matrix	Asset A	Asset B	Asset C	Asset D	Asset E
Asset A	1.0000	0.1000	0.1000	0.1000	0.1000
Asset B	0.1000	1.0000	0.1000	0.1000	0.1000
Asset C	0.1000	0.1000	1.0000	0.1000	0.1000
Asset D	0.1000	0.1000	0.1000	1.0000	0.1000
Asset E	0.1000	0.1000	0.1000	0.1000	1.0000

Horizon (Days)	10
Percentile	99.00%

Value at Risk (Daily)	$655,915.30
Value at Risk (Horizon)	$2,074,186.30

Daily Value at Risk (Positive Correlations)	$2,074,186.30
Daily Value at Risk (Zero Correlations)	$1,889,345.26
Daily Value at Risk (Negative Correlations)	$1,684,340.28

Figure 3.19: Computing Value at Risk Using the Covariance Method

Correlation Matrix	Asset A	Asset B	Asset C	Asset D	Asset E
Asset A	1.0000	0.1000	0.1000	0.1000	0.1000
Asset B	0.1000	1.0000	0.1000	0.1000	0.1000
Asset C	0.1000	0.1000	1.0000	0.1000	0.1000
Asset D	0.1000	0.1000	0.1000	1.0000	0.1000
Asset E	0.1000	0.1000	0.1000	0.1000	1.0000

Correlation Matrix	Asset A	Asset B	Asset C	Asset D	Asset E
Asset A	1.0000	0.0000	0.0000	0.0000	0.0000
Asset B	0.0000	1.0000	0.0000	0.0000	0.0000
Asset C	0.0000	0.0000	1.0000	0.0000	0.0000
Asset D	0.0000	0.0000	0.0000	1.0000	0.0000
Asset E	0.0000	0.0000	0.0000	0.0000	1.0000

Correlation Matrix	Asset A	Asset B	Asset C	Asset D	Asset E
Asset A	1.0000	-0.1000	-0.1000	-0.1000	-0.1000
Asset B	-0.1000	1.0000	-0.1000	-0.1000	-0.1000
Asset C	-0.1000	-0.1000	1.0000	-0.1000	-0.1000
Asset D	-0.1000	-0.1000	-0.1000	1.0000	-0.1000
Asset E	-0.1000	-0.1000	-0.1000	-0.1000	1.0000

Figure 3.20: Value at Risk Results with Different Correlation Levels

Volatility – Implied Volatility

File Name: Volatility – Implied Volatility

Location: *Modeling Toolkit | Volatility | Implied Volatility*

Brief Description: Computes the implied volatilities using an internal optimization routine, given the fair market values of a call or put option as well as all their required inputs

Requirements: Modeling Toolkit, Risk Simulator

Modeling Toolkit Functions Used: *MTImpliedVolatilityCall, MTImpliedVolatilityPut*

This implied volatility computation is based on an internal iterative optimization, which means it will work under typical conditions (without extreme volatility values, i.e., too small or too large). It is always good modeling technique to recheck the imputed volatility using an options model to make sure the answer coincides before adding more sophistication to the model. That is, given all the inputs in an option analysis as well as the option value, the volatility can be imputed. See Figure 3.21.

IMPLIED VOLATILITY FUNCTION

Asset	$100.00
Strike	$95.00
Maturity	0.50
Riskfree	8.00%
Volatility	25.00%
DividendRate	3.00%
Call Option	$10.9126
Put Option	$3.6764
Implied Volatility Calculation	
Call Option	25.00%
Put Option	25.00%

Figure 3.21: Getting the Implied Volatility from Options

File Name: Volatility – Volatility Computations

Location: *Modeling Toolkit | Volatility, and Applying Log Cash Flow Returns, Log Asset Returns, Probability to Volatility, EWMA, and GARCH Models*

Brief Description: Uses Risk Simulator to apply Monte Carlo simulation to compute a project's volatility measure

Requirements: Modeling Toolkit, Risk Simulator

There are several ways to estimate the volatility used in the option models. The most common and valid approaches are:

Logarithmic Cash Flow Returns Approach or Logarithmic Stock Price Returns Approach: This method is used mainly for computing the volatility of liquid and tradable assets, such as stocks in financial options. However, sometimes it is used for other traded assets, such as the price of oil or electricity. The drawback is that discounted cash flow models with only a few cash flows generally will overstate the volatility, and this method cannot be used when negative cash flows occur. Thus, this volatility approach is applicable only for financial instruments and not for real options analysis. The benefits include its computational ease, transparency, and modeling flexibility. In addition, no simulation is required to obtain a volatility estimate. The approach is simply to take the annualized standard deviation of the logarithmic relative returns of the time-series data as the proxy for volatility. The Modeling Toolkit function **MTVolatility** is used to compute this volatility, where the time series of stock prices can be arranged in either chronological or reverse chronological order when using the function. See the *Log Cash Flow Returns* example model in the Volatility section of Modeling Toolkit for details.

Exponentially Weighted Moving Average (EWMA) Models: This approach is similar to the logarithmic cash flow returns approach. It uses the **MTVolatility** function to compute the annualized standard deviation of the natural logarithms of relative stock returns. The difference here is that the most recent value will have a higher weight than values farther in the past. A lambda, or weight variable, is required (typically, industry standards set this at 0.94). The most recent volatility is weighted at this lambda value, and the period before that is (1 – lambda), and so forth. See the *EWMA* example model in the Volatility section of Modeling Toolkit for details.

Logarithmic Present Value Returns Approach: This approach is used mainly when computing the volatility on assets with cash flows. A typical application is in real options. The drawbacks of this method are that simulation is required to obtain a single volatility, and it is not applicable for highly traded liquid assets, such as stock prices. The benefits include the ability to accommodate certain negative cash flows. Also, this approach applies more rigorous analysis than the logarithmic cash flow returns approach, providing a more accurate and conservative estimate of volatility when assets are analyzed. In addition, within, say, a cash flow model, you can set up multiple simulation assumptions (insert any types of risks and uncertainties, such as related assumptions, correlated distributions and nonrelated inputs, multiple stochastic processes, etc.) and allow the model to distill all the interacting risks and uncertainties in these simulations. You then obtain the single-value volatility, which represents the integrated risk of the project. See the *Log Asset Returns* example model in the Volatility section of Modeling Toolkit for details.

Management Assumptions and Guesses: This approach is used for both financial options and real options. The drawback is that the volatility estimates are very unreliable and are only subjective best guesses. The benefit of this approach is its simplicity—using this method, you can easily explain to management the concept of volatility, both in execution and interpretation. Most people understand what probability is but have a hard time understanding what volatility is. Using this approach, you can impute one from the other. See the *Probability to Volatility* example model in the Volatility section of Modeling Toolkit for details.

Generalized Autoregressive Conditional Heteroskedasticity (GARCH) Models: These methods are used mainly for computing the volatility of liquid and tradable assets, such as stocks in financial options. However, sometimes they are used for other traded assets, such as the price of oil or electricity. The drawbacks are that these models require a lot of data and advanced econometric modeling expertise is required. In addition, these models are highly susceptible to user manipulation. The benefit is that rigorous statistical analysis is performed to find the best-fitting volatility curve, providing different volatility estimates over time. The *EWMA* model is a simple weighting model; the *GARCH* model is a more advanced analytical and econometric model that requires advanced algorithms, such as generalized method of moments, to obtain volatility forecasts.

This section only provides a high-level review of all these methods as they pertain to hands-on applications. For detailed technical details on volatility estimates, including the theory and step-by-step interpretation of the method, refer to Chapter 7 of Dr. Johnathan Mun's *Real Options Analysis,* Third Edition (Thomson–Shore, 2016).

Procedure

1. For the Log Cash Flow or Log Returns Approach, make sure that your data are all positive (this approach cannot apply negative values). The Log Cash Flow Approach worksheet illustrates an example computation of downloaded Microsoft stock prices (Figure 3.22). You can perform *Edit | Copy* and *Edit | Paste Special | Values Only* using your own stock closing prices to compute the volatility. The *MTVolatility* function is used to compute volatility. Enter in the positive integer for periodicity as appropriate (e.g., to annualize the volatility using monthly stock prices, enter in 12, or 52 for weekly stock prices, etc.), as seen in the example model.

Downloaded Weekly Historical Stock Prices of Microsoft

Volatility Computations

Date	Open	High	Low	Close	Volume	Adj. Close*	LN Relative Returns	Moving Average Volatilities			
27-Dec-04	27.01	27.10	26.68	26.72	52388840	26.64	-0.0108	17.87%			
20-Dec-04	27.01	27.17	26.78	27.01	77413174	26.93	0.0019	17.84%			
13-Dec-04	27.10	27.40	26.80	26.96	108628300	26.88	-0.0045	17.85%			
6-Dec-04	27.10	27.44	26.91	27.08	83312720	27.00	-0.0055	18.00%	*One-Year Annualized Volatility Analysis*		
29-Nov-04	26.64	27.44	26.61	27.23	83103200	27.15	0.0235	18.13%			
22-Nov-04	26.75	26.82	26.10	26.60	61834599	26.52	-0.0098	18.03%	Average	21.89%
15-Nov-04	27.34	27.50	26.84	26.86	75375960	26.78	-0.0011	18.10%	Median	22.30%
8-Nov-04	29.18	30.20	29.13	29.97	109385736	26.81	0.0223	18.20%			
1-Nov-04	28.16	29.36	27.96	29.31	85044019	26.22	0.0468	18.28%			
25-Oct-04	27.67	28.54	27.55	27.97	70791679	25.02	0.0084	17.71%			
18-Oct-04	28.07	28.89	27.58	27.74	74671318	24.81	-0.0092	17.80%			
11-Oct-04	28.20	28.27	27.80	27.99	48396360	25.04	0.0000	19.68%			
4-Oct-04	28.44	28.59	27.97	27.99	52998320	25.04	-0.0091	19.69%			
27-Sep-04	27.17	28.32	27.04	28.25	61783760	25.27	0.0346	19.68%			
20-Sep-04	27.44	27.74	27.07	27.29	59162520	24.41	-0.0082	19.62%			
13-Sep-04	27.53	27.57	26.74	27.51	51599880	24.61	0.0008	20.52%			
7-Sep-04	27.29	27.51	27.14	27.49	51935175	24.59	0.0139	21.30%			
30-Aug-04	27.30	27.68	26.85	27.11	45125980	24.25	-0.0127	21.25%			
23-Aug-04	27.27	27.67	27.09	27.46	40526880	24.56	0.0123	22.29%			
16-Aug-04	27.03	27.50	26.89	27.20	52571740	24.26	0.0066	22.29%			
9-Aug-04	27.26	27.75	26.86	27.02	51244080	24.10	-0.0041	22.42%			
2-Aug-04	28.27	28.55	27.06	27.14	56739100	24.20	-0.0488	22.42%			
26-Jul-04	28.36	28.81	28.13	28.49	65555220	25.41	0.0163	21.97%			
19-Jul-04	27.62	29.89	27.60	28.03	114579322	25.00	0.0198	22.11%			
12-Jul-04	27.67	28.36	27.25	27.48	57970740	24.51	-0.0138	22.02%			
6-Jul-04	28.32	28.33	27.55	27.86	61197249	24.85	-0.0250	22.04%			
28-Jun-04	28.60	28.84	28.17	28.57	66214339	25.48	0.0000	22.07%			
21-Jun-04	28.22	28.66	27.81	28.57	82202478	25.48	0.0079	22.30%			
14-Jun-04	26.55	28.50	26.53	28.35	97727643	25.28	0.0574	22.48%			
7-Jun-04	26.02	26.79	25.97	26.77	55540250	23.87	0.0311	22.71%			
1-Jun-04	26.13	26.28	25.86	25.95	49284475	23.14	-0.0107	22.86%			
24-May-04	26.05	26.35	25.60	26.23	51927460	23.39	0.0129	23.19%			
17-May-04	25.47	26.27	25.42	25.89	56652040	23.09	0.0013	23.21%			
10-May-04	25.63	26.19	25.43	25.86	58864200	23.06	0.0030	23.87%			
3-May-04	26.19	26.60	25.75	25.78	60847680	22.99	-0.0134	24.07%			
26-Apr-04	27.45	27.55	25.96	26.13	77381899	23.30	-0.0527	24.05%			
19-Apr-04	25.08	27.72	25.06	27.54	102244677	24.56	0.0903	23.67%			
12-Apr-04	25.48	25.77	25.10	25.16	56472679	22.44	-0.0124	21.92%			
5-Apr-04	25.81	25.98	25.35	25.48	52838950	22.72	-0.0144	22.50%			
29-Mar-04	25.25	25.90	24.85	25.85	69704180	23.05	0.0322	22.76%			
22-Mar-04	24.48	25.51	24.01	25.03	92829802	22.32	0.0158	22.59%			

Figure 3.22 Historical Stock Prices and Volatility Estimates

2. For the Log Present Value Approach, we allow negative cash flows. In fact, this approach is preferred to the Log Cash Flow approach when modeling volatilities in a real options world. First, set some assumptions in the model or use the preset assumptions as is. The Intermediate X Variable is used to compute the project's volatility (Figure 3.23). Run the simulation and view the Intermediate Variable X's forecast chart. Go to the Statistics tab and obtain the Standard Deviation (Figure 3.24). Annualize it by multiplying the value with the square root of the number of periods per year (in this case, the annualized volatility is 11.64% as the periodicity is annual, otherwise multiply the standard deviation by the square root of 4 if quarterly data is used, the square root of 12 if monthly data is used, etc.).

Log Present Value Approach

Input Parameters		Results	
Discount Rate (Cash Flow)	15.00%	Present Value (Cash Flow)	$286.66
Discount Rate (Impl. Cost)	5.00%	Present Value (Impl. Cost)	$189.58
Tax Rate	10.00%	Net Present Value	$97.09

	2002	2003	2004	2005	2006
Revenue	$100.00	$200.00	$300.00	$400.00	$500.00
Cost of Revenue	$40.00	$80.00	$120.00	$160.00	$200.00
Gross Profit	$60.00	$120.00	$180.00	$240.00	$300.00
Operating Expenses	$22.00	$44.00	$66.00	$88.00	$110.00
Depreciation Expense	$5.00	$10.00	$15.00	$20.00	$25.00
Interest Expense	$3.00	$6.00	$9.00	$12.00	$15.00
Income Before Taxes	$30.00	$60.00	$90.00	$120.00	$150.00
Taxes	$3.00	$6.00	$9.00	$12.00	$15.00
Income After Taxes	$27.00	$54.00	$81.00	$108.00	$135.00
Non-Cash Expenses	$12.00	$12.00	$12.00	$12.00	$12.00
Cash Flow	$39.00	$66.00	$93.00	$120.00	$147.00
Implementation Cost	$25.00	$25.00	$50.00	$50.00	$75.00

Volatility Estimates (Logarithmic PV Approach)

PV (0)	$39.00	$57.39	$70.32	$78.90	$84.05
PV (1)	N/A	$66.00	$80.87	$90.74	$96.65
Static PV (0)	$39.00	$63.65	$81.21	$93.10	$100.51
Variable X	-0.1216				
Volatility	Simulate to obtain volatility				

Figure 3.23: Using the PV Asset Approach to Model Volatility

Variable X - Risk Simulator Forecast	
Histogram Statistic Preferences Options	

Statistics	Result
Number of Trials	1000
Mean	-0.1334
Median	-0.1301
Standard Deviation	0.1164
Variance	0.0136
Average Deviation	0.0925
Maximum	0.1818
Minimum	-0.5553
Range	0.7372
Skewness	-0.2310
Kurtosis	0.0957
25% Percentile	-0.2101
75% Percentile	-0.0554
Percentage Error Precision at 95% Confidence	5.4083%

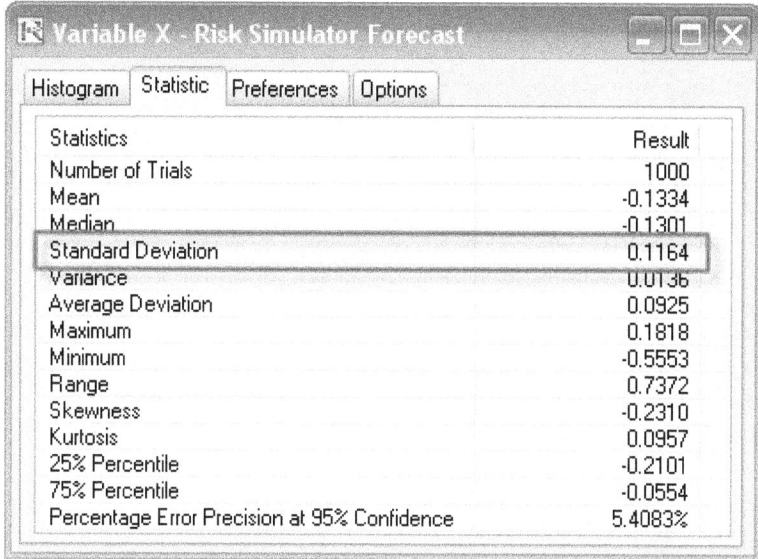

Figure 3.24: Volatility Estimates Using the PV Asset Approach and Simulation

3. The Volatility to Probability approach can provide rough estimates of volatility, or you can use it to explain to senior management the concept of volatility. To illustrate, say your model has an expected value of $100M, and the best-case scenario as modeled or expected or anticipated by subject matter experts or senior management is $150M with a 10% chance of exceeding this value. We compute the implied volatility as 39.02% (Figure 3.25).

Probability to Volatility (Best-Case Scenario)

Expected NPV of the Asset:	$100.00
Alternate Best-Case Scenario NPV:	$150.00
Percentile of Best-Case Scenario:	90.00%
Implied Volatility Estimate:	39.02%

Figure 3.25: Probability to Volatility Approximation Approach

Clearly this is a rough estimate, but it is a good start if you do not wish to perform elaborate modeling and simulation to obtain a volatility measure. Further, this approach can be reversed. That is, instead of getting volatility from probability, you can get probability from volatility. This reversed method is very powerful in explaining to senior management the concept of volatility. To illustrate, we use the *Worst-Case Scenario* model next.

Suppose you run a simulation model and obtain an annualized volatility of 35% and need to explain what this means to management. Well, 35% volatility does not mean that there is a 35% chance of something happening, nor does it mean that the expected value can go up 35%, and so forth. Management has a hard time understanding volatility, whereas probability is a simpler concept. For instance, if you say that there is a 10% chance of something happening (such as a product being successful in the market), management understands this to mean that 1 out of 10 products will be a superstar. You can take advantage of this fact and impute the probability from the analytically computed volatility to explain the concept in a simplified manner. Using the *Probability to Volatility Worst-Case Scenario* model, assume that the worst case is defined as the 10% left tail (you can change this if you wish), and that your analytical model provides a 35% volatility. Simply click on Tools | Goal Seek and set the cell F24 (the volatility cell) to change to the value 35% (your computed volatility) by *changing the alternate worst-case scenario* cell (F21). Clicking OK returns the value $55.15 in cell F21. This means that a 35% volatility can be described as a project with an expected NPV of $100M. It is risky enough that the worst-case scenario can occur less than 10% of the time, and if it does, it will reduce the project's NPV to $55.15M. In other words, there is a 1 in 10 chance the project will be below $55.15M or 9 out of 10 times it will make at least $55.15M (Figure 3.26).

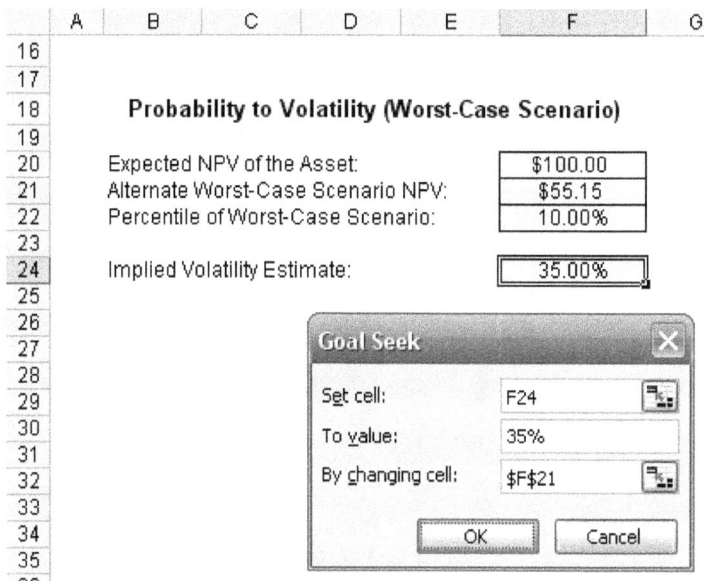

Figure 3.26: Sample Computation Using the Volatility to Probability Approach

1. For the EWMA and GARCH approaches, time-specific multiple volatility forecasts are obtained. That is, a term structure of volatility can be determined using these approaches. GARCH models are used mainly in analyzing financial time-series data, in order to ascertain their conditional variances and volatilities. These volatilities are then used to value the options as usual, but the amount of historical data necessary for a good volatility estimate remains significant. Usually, several dozen—and even up to hundreds—of data points are required to obtain good GARCH estimates. GARCH is a term that incorporates a family of models that can take on a variety of forms, known as GARCH(p,q), where p and q are positive integers that define the resulting GARCH model and its forecasts. In most cases for financial instruments, a GARCH(1,1) is sufficient and is most generally used.

For instance, a GARCH (1,1) model takes the form of

$$y_t = x_t\gamma + \varepsilon_t$$
$$\sigma_t^2 = \omega + \alpha\varepsilon_{t-1}^2 + \beta\sigma_{t-1}^2$$

where the first equation's dependent variable (y_t) is a function of exogenous variables (x_t) with an error term (ε_t). The second equation estimates the variance (squared volatility σ_t^2) at time t, which depends on a historical mean (ω), news about volatility from the previous period, measured as a lag of the squared residual from the mean equation (ε_{t-1}^2), and volatility from the previous period (σ_{t-1}^2). The exact modeling specification of a GARCH model is beyond the scope of this book. Suffice it to say that detailed knowledge of econometric modeling (model specification tests, structural breaks, and error estimation) is required to run a GARCH model, making it less accessible to the general analyst. The other problem with GARCH models is that the model usually does not provide a good statistical fit. That is, it is impossible to predict the stock market and, of course, equally if not harder to predict a stock's volatility over time. Figure 3.27 shows a GARCH (1,1) on a sample set of historical stock prices using the *MTGARCH* model.

	A	B	I	J
1			Computed Alpha	0.082019894
2	User Data		Couted Beta	0.914890346
3	Period	Inputs	Computed Omega	0.000000968
4	1	459.11		0.00%
5	2	460.71	Periods/Year	0.00%
6	3	460.34	252	17.80%
7	4	460.68		17.10%
8	5	460.83		16.44%
9	6	461.68		15.80%
10	7	461.66		15.22%
11	8	461.64		14.64%
12	9	465.97		14.09%
13	10	469.38		14.21%
14	11	470.05		14.08%
15	12	469.72		13.57%
16	13	466.95		13.08%
17	14	464.78		12.89%
18	15	465.81		12.61%
19	16	465.86		12.20%
20	17	467.44		11.78%

Figure 3.27: Sample GARCH (1,1) Model

In order to create GARCH forecasts, start the Modeling Toolkit and open the *Volatility | GARCH* model. You will see a model that resembles Figure 3.28. Follow the next procedures to create the volatility estimates:

1. Enter the Stock Prices in chronological order (e.g., cells I6:I17).

2. Use the MTGARCH function call in Modeling Toolkit. For instance, cell K3 has the following function call: "MTGARCH($I$6:$I$17,$I$19,1,3)" where the stock price inputs are in cells I6:I17, the periodicity is 12 (i.e., there are 12 months in a year, to obtain the annualized volatility forecasts), and the predictive base is 1, and we forecast for a sample of 3 periods into the future. Because we will copy and paste the function down the column, make sure that absolute addressing is used, i.e., $I$6 and not relative addressing, I6.

3. Copy cell K3 and paste the function on cells K3:K20 (select cell K3 and drag the fill handle to copy the function down the column). You do this because the first three values are the GARCH estimated parameters of Alpha, Beta, and Gamma, and at the bottom (e.g., cells K18:K20) are the forecast values.

4. With the entire column selected (cells K3:K20 selected), hit F2 on the keyboard, and then hold down Shift+Ctrl and hit Enter. This will update the entire matrix with GARCH forecasts.

Alternatively, and probably a simpler method, is to use Risk Simulator's *Forecast GARCH* module as seen in Figure 3.29, select the data location of raw stock prices, and enter in the required parameters (see below for a description of these parameters). The result is a GARCH volatility report seen in Figure 3.30.

Note that the GARCH function has several inputs as follow:

Stock Prices: This is the time series of stock prices in chronological order. Typically, dozens of data points are required for a decent volatility forecast.

Periodicity: This is a positive integer indicating the number of periods per year (e.g., 12 for monthly data, 252 for daily trading data, etc.), assuming you wish to annualize the volatility. To obtain periodic volatility, enter 1.

Predictive Base: This is the number of periods (the time-series data) back to use as a base to forecast volatility. The higher this number, the longer the historical base is used to forecast future volatility.

Forecast Period: This is a positive integer indicating how many future periods beyond the historical stock prices you wish to forecast.

Variance Targeting: This variable is set as False by default (even if you do not enter anything here) but can be set as True. False means the omega variable is automatically optimized and computed. The suggestion is to leave this variable empty. If you wish to create mean-reverting volatility with variance targeting, set this variable as True.

P: This is the number of previous lags on the mean equation.

Q: This is the number of previous lags on the variance equation.

			GARCH (1,1)
	Alpha		0.1939450
	Beta		0.0000000
Periods (Months)	Stock Price	Omega	0.0013381
Jan	10.25		0.00%
Feb	13.25		0.00%
Mar	15.36		41.16%
Apr	15.95		25.86%
May	16.15		13.92%
Jun	15.45		12.81%
Jul	14.55		14.36%
Aug	15.50		15.63%
Sep	16.00		15.93%
Oct	16.20		13.57%
Nov	16.90		12.81%
Dec	17.50		14.22%
			13.74%
Periodicity	12		13.74%
			13.74%

Figure 3.28: Setting Up a GARCH Model

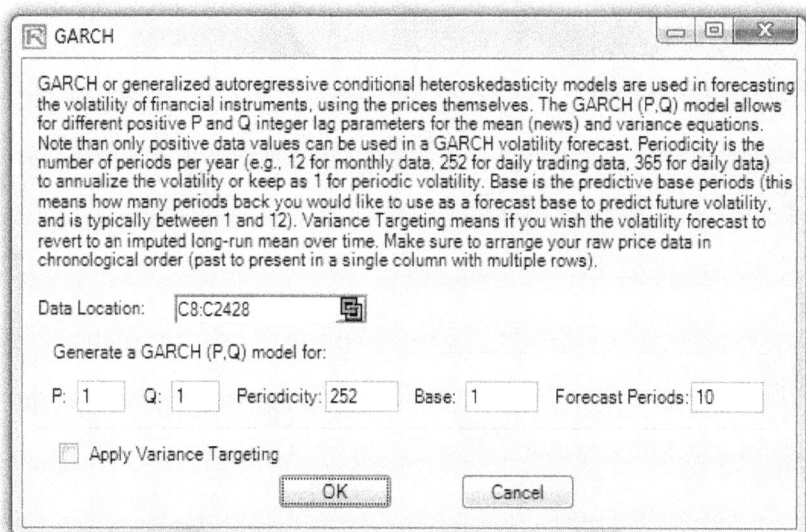

Figure 3.29: Running a GARCH Model in Risk Simulator

GARCH: Generalized Autoregressive Conditional Heteroskedasticity (Volatility Forecast)

GARCH models are used mainly for computing the volatility on liquid and tradable assets such as stocks in financial options; this model is sometimes used for other traded assets such as price of oil and price of electricity. The drawback is that a lot of data is required: advanced econometric modeling expertise is required, and this approach is highly susceptible to user manipulation. The benefit is that rigorous statistical analysis is performed to find the best-fitting volatility curve, providing different volatility estimates over time. GARCH is a term that incorporates a family of models that can take on a variety of forms, known as GARCH (P,Q), where P and Q are positive integers that define the resulting GARCH model and its forecasts. In most cases for financial instruments, a GARCH (1,1) is sufficient and is most generally used.

GARCH Model (P, Q)	1,1		Periodicity (Periods/Year)	252
Optimized Alpha	0.0820		Predictive Base	1
Optimized Beta	0.9149		Forecast Periods	10
Optimized Omega	0.0000		Variance Targeting	FALSE

Period	Data	Volatility
0	459.11	
1	460.71	
2	460.34	17.80%
3	460.68	17.10%
4	460.83	16.44%
5	461.68	15.80%
6	461.66	15.22%
7	461.64	14.64%
8	465.97	14.09%
9	469.38	14.21%
10	470.05	14.08%
11	469.72	13.57%
12	466.95	13.08%
13	464.78	12.89%
14	465.81	12.61%
15	465.86	12.20%
16	467.44	11.78%
17	468.32	11.48%
18	470.39	11.12%
19	468.51	10.94%
20	470.42	10.73%
21	470.40	10.55%
22	472.78	10.21%
23	478.64	10.15%
24	481.14	11.32%
25	480.81	11.19%
26	481.19	10.82%
27	480.19	10.47%
28	481.46	10.18%

GARCH or generalized autoregressive conditional heteroskedasticity models are used in forecasting the volatility of financial instruments, using the prices themselves. The GARCH (P,Q) model allows for different positive P and Q integer lag parameters for the mean (news) and variance equations. Note than only positive data values can be used in a GARCH volatility forecast. Periodicity is the number of periods per year (e.g., 12 for monthly data, 252 for daily trading data, 365 for daily data) to annualize the volatility or keep as 1 for periodic volatility. Base is the predictive base periods (this means how many periods back you would like to use as a forecast base to predict future volatility, and is typically between 1 and 12). Variance Targeting means if you wish the volatility forecast to revert to an imputed long-run mean over time. Make sure to arrange

Real Options Valuation
www.realoptionsvaluation.com

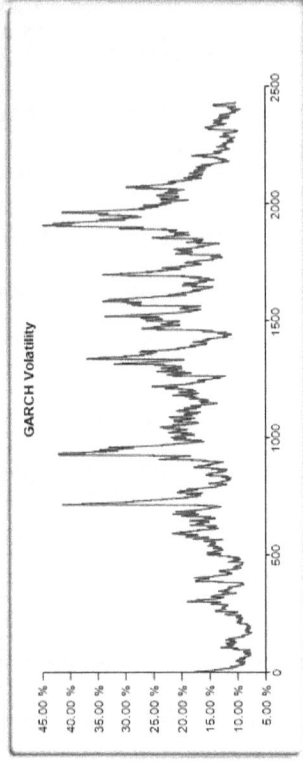

Figure 3.30: GARCH Forecast Results

COMPLIANCE WITH GLOBAL STANDARDS: BASEL, COSO, ISO, NIST, AND SARBOX

ERM methods deployed by any organization should at least consider compliance with global standards if not exactly mirroring COSO (Committee of Sponsoring Organizations of the Treadway Commission, with respect to their organizing committees at AAA, AICPA, FEI, IMA, and IIA), International Standards ISO 31000:2009, the U.S. Sarbanes–Oxley Act, the Basel III/IVI/IV requirements for Operational Risk (from the Basel Committee through the Bank of International Settlements), and NIST 800-37. The parallels and applications of ROV methodologies closely mirror, and at times exceed, these regulatory and international standards.

Figures 4.1–4.10 illustrate some examples of compliance with ISO 31000:2009, Figures 4.11–4.20 show compliance with Basel III/IV/IV and Basel IV requirements, and Figures 4.21–4.29 show compliance with COSO requirements. These figures and the summary lists that follow assume that the reader is already familiar with the integrated risk management or IRM methodology employed throughout this book.

- The IRM methodology we employ is in line with ISO 31000:2009 Clauses 2.3 and 2.8 requiring a risk management process (Figure 4.1), as well as Clause 5 (5.4.2 requiring risk identification where we use tornado analysis and scenario analysis; 5.4.3. requiring quantitative risk analysis where we apply Monte Carlo risk simulations; 5.4.4 where existing Excel-based evaluation models are used and overlaid with IRM methodologies such as simulations; etc.).

- ISO 31000:2009 Clause 5.4.4 looks at the risk tolerance levels and comparing various risk levels in a portfolio optimization and efficient frontier analysis employed in our IRM methodology (Figure 4.2).

- Figure 4.3 shows quantified consequences and the likelihoods (probabilities and confidence levels) of potential events that can occur using simulations, as required in ISO 31000:2009 Clauses 2.1 and 5.4.3.

- ISO 31000:2009 Clause 5.4.3 requires viewing the analysis from the perspectives of various stakeholders, multiple consequences, and multiple objectives to develop a combined level of risk. These perspectives are achieved through a multicriteria optimization and efficient frontier analysis (Figure 4.4) in the IRM process.

- ISO 31000:2009 Clause 3F requires that historical data and experience as well as stakeholder feedback and observation coupled with expert judgment be used to forecast future risk events. The IRM process employs a family of 16 forecasting methods (Figure 4.5 shows an example of the ARIMA model) coupled with risk simulations with high fidelity to determine the best goodness-of-fit when historical data exist, or using subject matter expert estimates and stakeholder assumptions, we can apply the Delphi method and custom distribution to run risk simulations on the forecasts.

- ISO 31000:2009 Clauses 3C, 5.4.3, 5.5, and 5.5.2 require risk evaluations on risk treatments, options to execute when different types of risks are involved, and selecting and implementing various risk treatment strategic options that are not solely reliant on economics. The IRM's strategic real options methodology allows users to model multiple path-independent and path-dependent implementation strategies or alternate courses of action that are generated to mitigate downside risks and take advantage of upside potentials (Figure 4.6).

- Figure 4.7 illustrates how ISO 31000:2009 Clauses 3D, 3E, and 5.4.3 are satisfied using the IRM process of probability distribution fitting of uncertain variables and how their interdependencies (correlations) are executed.

- Risk controls are required in ISO 31000:2009 Clauses 2.26, 4.43, and 5.4.3 (Figure 4.8). The control charts and Risk Effectiveness calculations in PEAT ERM help decision makers identify if a particular risk mitigation strategy and response that was enacted had sufficiently and statistically significantly affected the outcomes of future risk states.

- Scenarios, cascading, and cumulative effects (consequences) are also the focus of ISO 31000:2009 Clause 5.4.2. The IRM method uses tornado analysis, scenario analysis, dynamic sensitivity analysis, and risk simulations (Figure 4.9) to identify which inputs have the highest impact on the organization's risks and model their impacts on the total risks of the organization.

- ISO 31000:2009 Clause 5.2 requires proper communication of risk exposures and consequences, and an understanding of the basis and reasons of each risk. The PEAT ERM Risk Dashboards provide details and insights for a better understanding of the issues governing each of the risk issues in an organization (Figure 4.10).

Integrated Risk Management Process

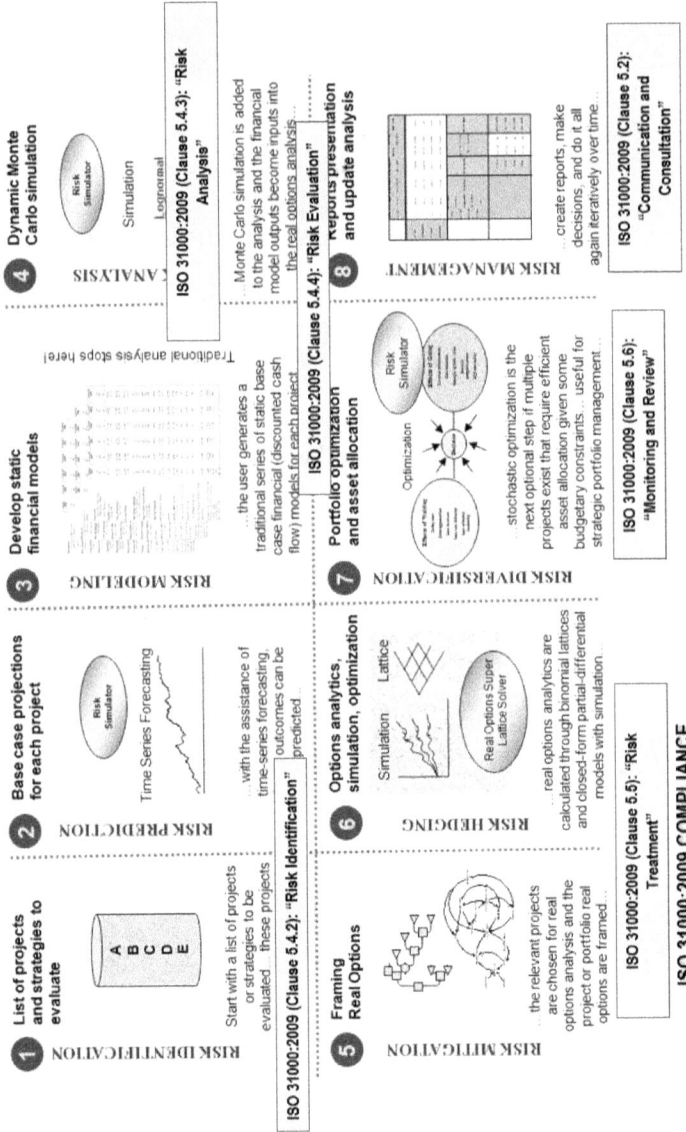

ISO 31000:2009 (Clause 2.3): "Risk Management Framework"

1 List of projects and strategies to evaluate

RISK IDENTIFICATION

Start with a list of projects or strategies to be evaluated ... these projects

ISO 31000:2009 (Clause 5.4.2): "Risk Identification"

2 Base case projections for each project

RISK PREDICTION

Time Series Forecasting

Risk Simulator

... with the assistance of time-series forecasting, outcomes can be predicted ...

3 Develop static financial models

RISK MODELING

Traditional analysis stops here!

... the user generates a traditional series of static base case financial (discounted cash flow) models for each project ...

4 Dynamic Monte Carlo simulation

ANALYSIS

Risk Simulator

Simulation

Lognormal

ISO 31000:2009 (Clause 5.4.3): "Risk Analysis"

Monte Carlo simulation is added to the analysis and the financial model outputs become inputs into the real options analysis ...

5 Framing Real Options

RISK MITIGATION

... the relevant projects are chosen for real options analysis and the project or portfolio real options are framed ...

ISO 31000:2009 (Clause 5.5): "Risk Treatment"

ISO 31000:2009 COMPLIANCE

6 Options analytics, simulation, optimization

RISK HEDGING

Simulation   Lattice

Real Options Super Lattice Solver

... real options analytics are calculated through binomial lattices and closed-form partial-differential models with simulation ...

7 Portfolio optimization and asset allocation

RISK DIVERSIFICATION

Optimization

Risk Simulator

... stochastic optimization is the next optional step if multiple projects exist that require efficient asset allocation given some budgetary constraints ... useful for strategic portfolio management ...

ISO 31000:2009 (Clause 5.6): "Monitoring and Review"

8 Reports presentation and update analysis

RISK MANAGEMENT

ISO 31000:2009 (Clause 5.4.4): "Risk Evaluation"

... create reports, make decisions, and do it all again iteratively over time ...

ISO 31000:2009 (Clause 5.2): "Communication and Consultation"

Figure 4.1: ISO 31000:2009—IRM

Investment Efficient Frontiers analysis provides for a variety of budget scenarios when considering portfolios of options

ISO 31000:2009 (Clause 5.4.4): "Risk evaluation involves **comparing the level of risk found** during the analysis process with **risk criteria established** when the context was considered. Based on this comparison, the need for treatment can be considered. Decisions should take account of the wider context of the risk and include consideration of the **tolerance of the risk borne** by parties other then the org that benefits from the risk."

Budget	Comprehensive Score	Tactical Score	Military Score	Allowed Projects	ROI-RANK Objective
$3,800.00	33.15	62.64	56.58	10	$470,235.60
$4,800.00	36.33	68.85	66.86	11	$521,645.92
$5,800.00	38.40	70.46	75.69	12	$623,557.79
$6,800.00	39.94	72.14	82.31	13	$659,947.99
$7,800.00	39.76	70.05	86.54	14	$676,279.81

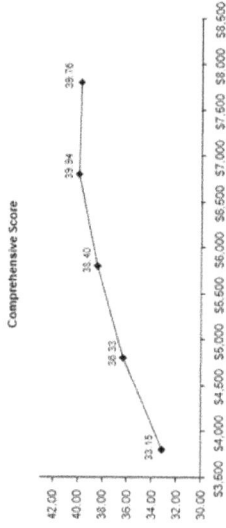

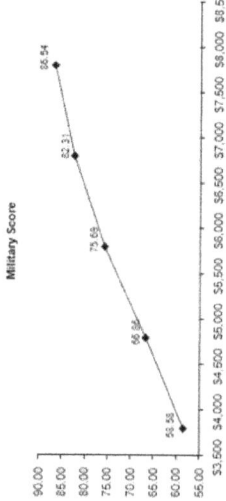

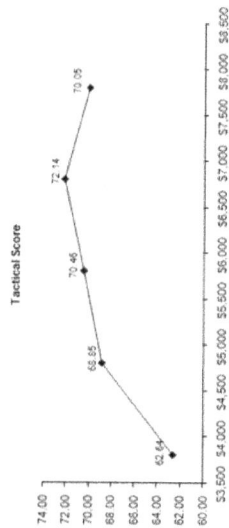

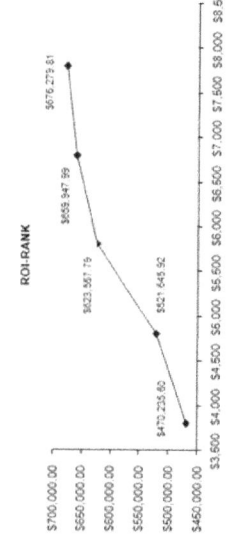

Figure 4.2: ISO 31000:2009—Risk Tolerance

Risk Simulation provides the decision maker with additional data

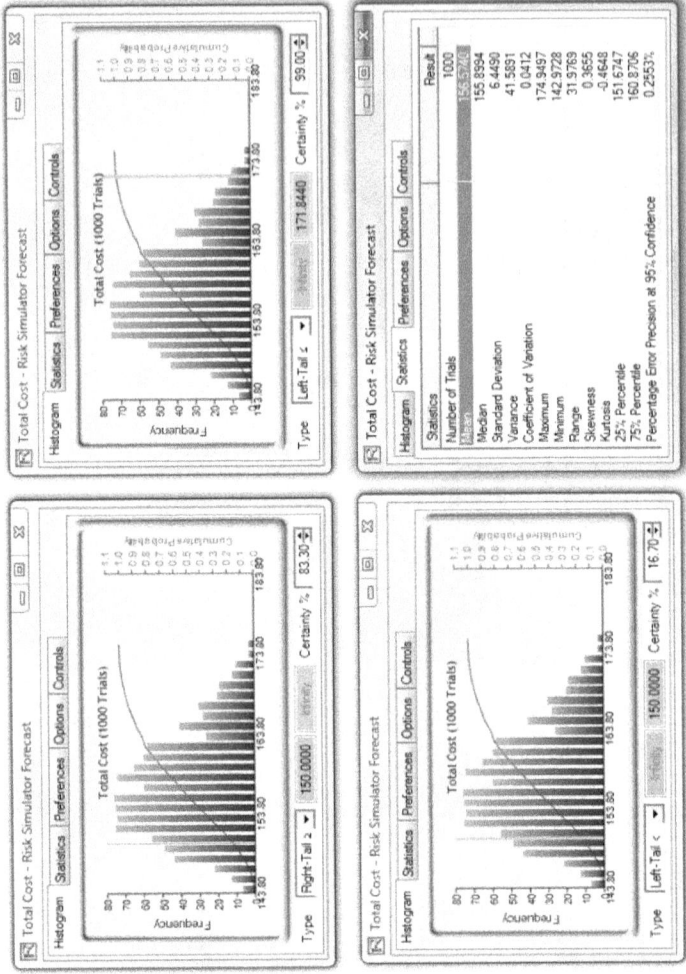

ISO 31000:2009 (Clause 5.4.3): "Factors that affect **consequences and likelihood** should be identified. Risk is analyzed by determining consequences and their likelihood, and other attributes of the risk."

ISO 31000:2009 (Clause 2.1): "Risk is often characterized by reference to **potential events** (2.17) **and consequences** (2.18), or a combination of these."

Figure 4.3: ISO 31000:2009—Consequences and Likelihood

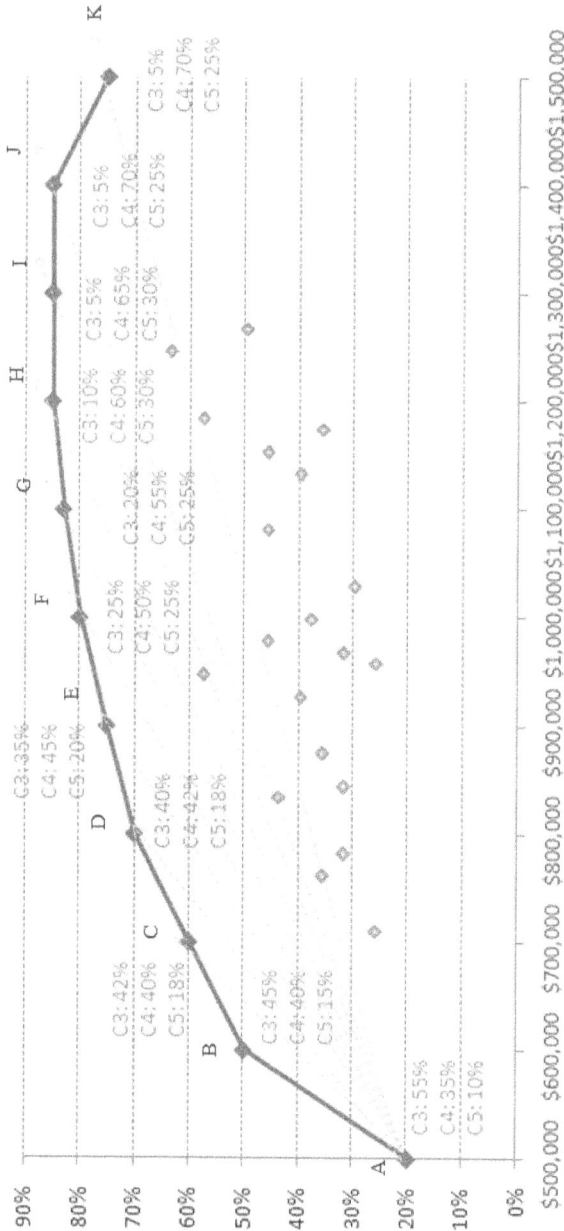

Optimal Portfolio Efficient Frontier

ISO 31000:2009 (Clause 5.4.3): "An event can have **multiple consequences** and can affect **multiple objectives**. The way in which consequences and likelihood are expressed and the way in which they are **combined determine a level of risk...**"

Figure 4.4: ISO 31000:2009—Multiple Stakeholder Objectives and Consequences

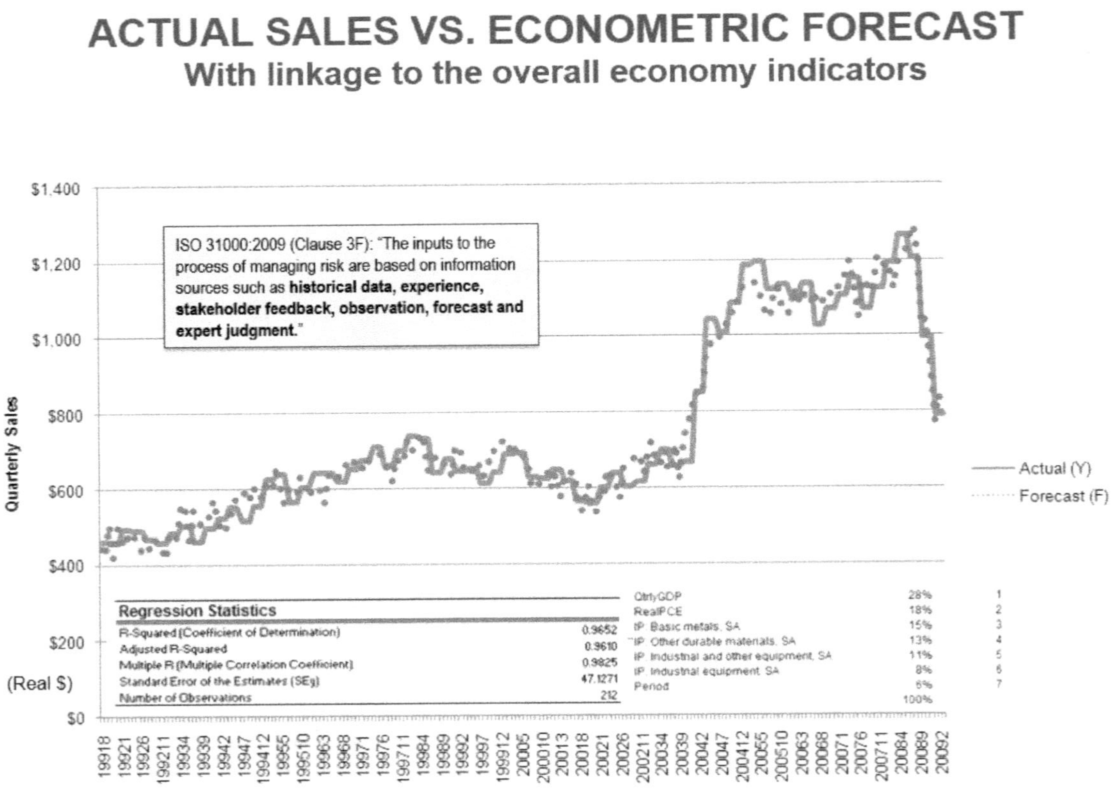

ACTUAL SALES VS. ECONOMETRIC FORECAST
With linkage to the overall economy indicators

ISO 31000:2009 (Clause 3F): "The inputs to the process of managing risk are based on information sources such as **historical data, experience, stakeholder feedback, observation, forecast and expert judgment.**"

Figure 4.5: ISO 31000:2009—Historical Data and Future Forward Forecast

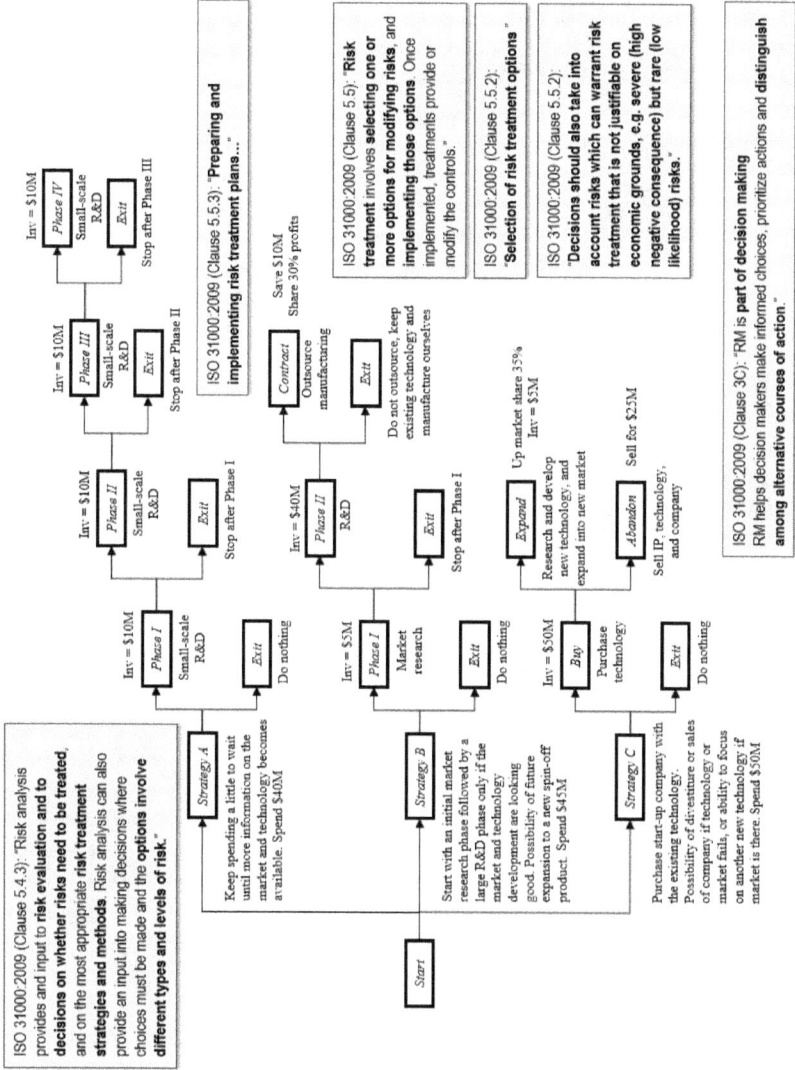

Figure 4.6: ISO 31000:2009—Multiple Options, Strategies, and Alternatives

Monte Carlo Simulation and Model Fitting

Correlated historical and Monte Carlo simulation

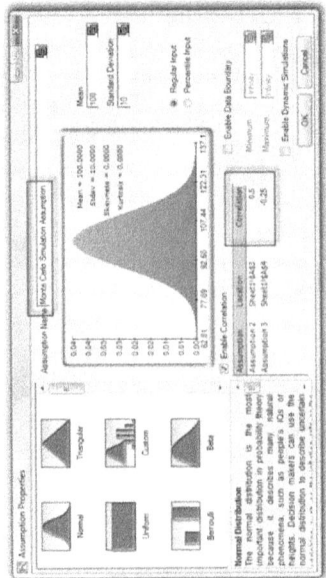

Finding the right distribution of your historical data

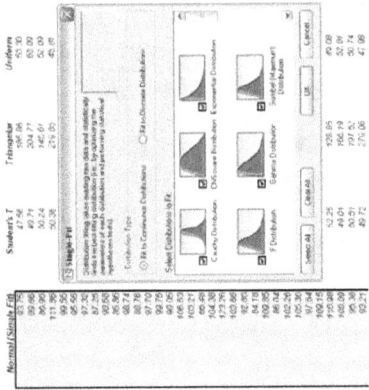

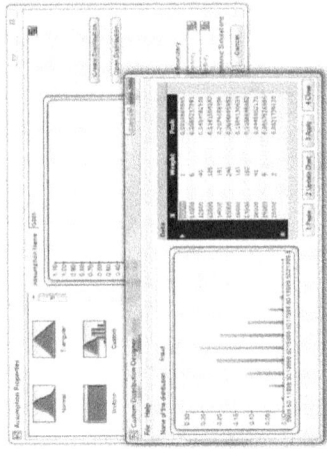

ISO 31000:2009 (Clause 3E): "A systematic, timely and structured approach to RM contributes to efficiency and to consistent, comparable and reliable results."

ISO 31000:2009 (Clause 3D): "RM explicitly takes account of uncertainty, the nature of that uncertainty, and how it can be addressed."

ISO 31000:2009 (Clause 5.4.3): "It is also important to consider the interdependence of different risks and their sources."

Figure 4.7: ISO 31000:2009 Structured Approach, Probability Fitting, and Correlations

Operational Risk Controls

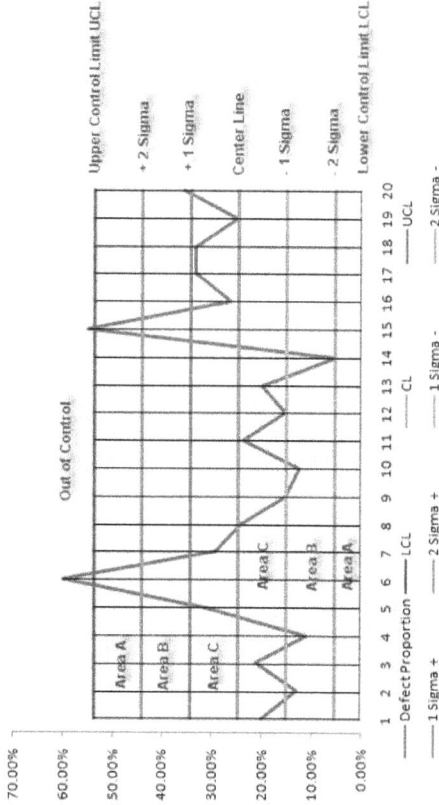

Figure 4.8: ISO 31000:2009—Risk Control Efficiency and Effectiveness

ISO 31000:2009 (Clause 2.26): **"Controls...measures that modify risk..."**

ISO 31000:2009 (Clause 4.4.3): "Implementing and maintaining the RM process and ensuring the **adequacy, effectiveness and efficiency of any controls.**"

ISO 31000:2009 (Clause 5.4.3): "**Existing controls and their effectiveness and efficiency** should also be taken into account. The way in which consequences and likelihood are expressed and the way in which they are combined determine a **level of risk** should reflect the type of risk, the information available and the purpose for which the risk assessment output is to be used. These should all be consistent with the risk criteria.

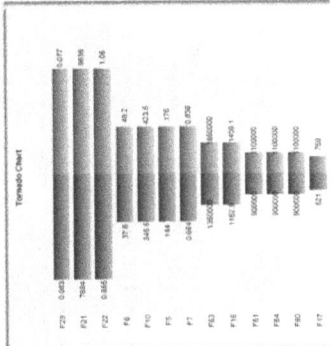

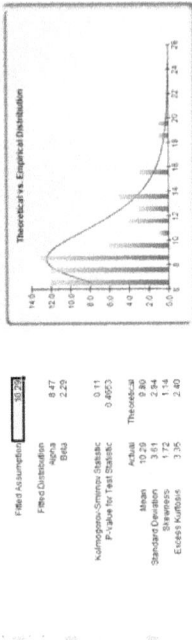

ISO 31000:2009 (Clause 5.4.2): "Risk Identification:
Risk identification should include examination of the
**knock-on effect of particular consequences,
including cascade and cumulative effects.** It is
necessary to consider possible **causes and scenario**
that show what consequence can occur."

Figure 4.9: ISO 31000:2009—Consequences, Cascades, and Scenarios

Management Dashboards

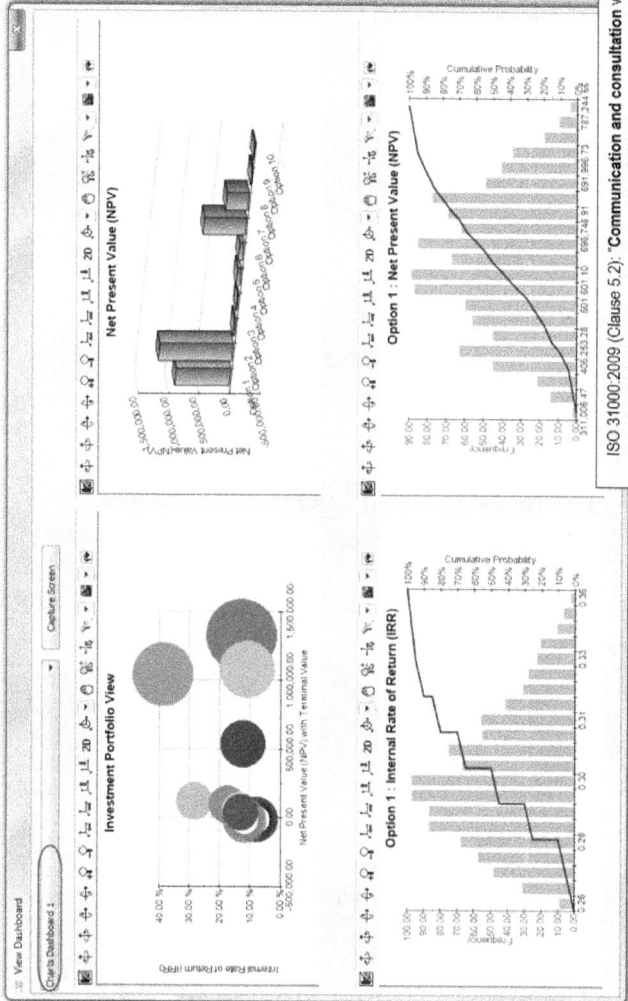

You can retrieve any of the saved dashboards and these dashboards will be populated only if the appropriate models have been run....

ISO 31000:2009 (Clause 5.2): "Communication and consultation with external and internal stakeholders should take place during all stages of the RM process. These should address issues relating to the risk itself, its causes, its consequences (if known), and the measures being taken to treat it. Stakeholders need to understand the basis on which decisions are made, and the reasons why particular actions are required."

Figure 4.10: ISO 31000:2009—Communication and Consultation

COMPLIANCE WITH BASEL III/IV/IV AND BASEL IV FRAMEWORK

The following provides a quick summary of Basel III/IV/IV and Basel IV compliance when using the IRM methodology:

- Figure 4.11 shows Monte Carlo risk simulations applied to determine confidence levels, percentiles, and probabilities of occurrence using historically fitted data or forecast expectations. These methods are in line with Basel III/IV/IV and Basel IV requirements Sections 16 and 161 concerning the use of historical simulations, Monte Carlo simulations, and 99th percentile confidence intervals.

- Figure 4.12 shows a correlated simulation of a portfolio of assets and liabilities, where asset returns are correlated against one another in a portfolio and optimization routines were run on the simulated results. These processes provide compliance with Basel III/IV/IV and Basel IV requirements Sections 178, 232, and 527(f) involving correlations, Value at Risk (VaR) models, portfolios of segments, and pooled exposures (assets and liabilities).

- Figure 4.13 shows Value at Risk percentile and confidence calculations using structural models and simulation results that are in line with Basel III/IV/IV and Basel IV requirements Sections 179, 527(c), and 527(f).

- Figure 4.14 shows the computations of probability of default (PD) as required in the Basel Accords, specifically Basel III/IV/IV and Basel IV Section 733 and Annex 2's Section 16. PD can be computed using structural models or based on historical data through running basic ratios to more advanced binary logistic models.

- Figure 4.15 shows the simulation and generation of interest rate yield curves using Risk Simulator and Modeling Toolkit models. These methods are in line with Basel III/IV/IV and Basel IV requirements Section 763 requiring the analysis of interest rate fluctuations and interest rate shocks.

- Figure 4.16 shows additional models for volatile interest rates, financial markets, and other liquid instruments' instantaneous shocks using Risk Simulator's stochastic process models. These analyses conform to Basel III/IV/IV and Basel IV requirements Sections 155, 527(a), and 527(b).

- Figure 4.17 shows several forecast models with high predictive and analytical power, which is a part of the Risk Simulator family of forecast methods. Such modeling provides compliance with Basel III/IV/IV and Basel IV requirements Section 417 requiring models of good predictive power.

- Figure 4.18 shows the list of financial and credit models available in the ROV Modeling Toolkit and ROV Real Options SLS software applications. These models conform to Basel III/IV/IV and Basel IV requirements Sections 112, 203, and 527(e) requiring the ability to value and model over-the-counter (OTC) derivatives, nonlinear equity derivatives and convertibles, hedges, and embedded options.

- Figure 4.19 shows the modeling of foreign exchange instruments and hedges to determine the effectiveness of foreign exchange hedging vehicles and their impact on valuation, portfolio profitability, and Value at Risk, in line with Basel III/IV/IV and Basel IV Sections 131 and 155 requiring the analysis of different currencies, correlations, volatility, and hedges.

- Figure 4.20 shows the option-adjusted spread (OAS), credit default swaps (CDS), and credit spread options (CSO) models in ROV Modeling Toolkit. These models provide compliance with Basel III/IV/IV and Basel IV requirements Sections 140 and 713 pertaining to modeling and valuing credit derivatives and credit hedges.

Basel III Compliance

Monte Carlo Simulation and Model Fitting

Finding the right distribution of your historical data

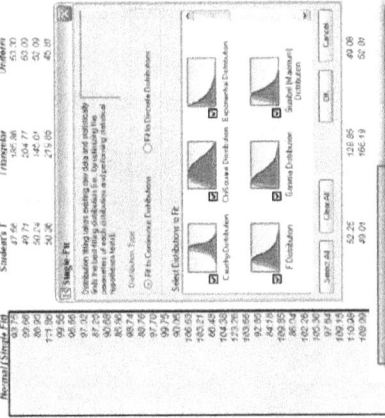

Correlated historical and Monte Carlo simulation

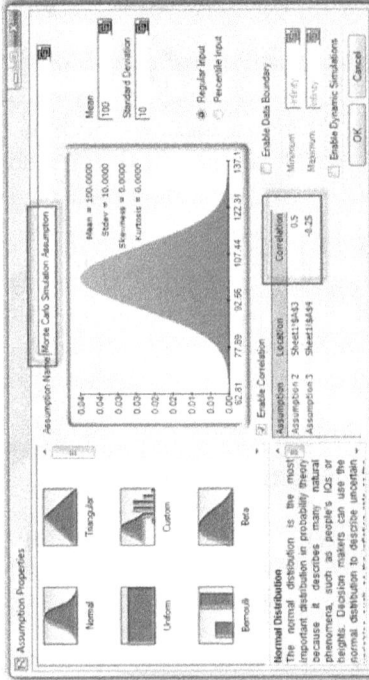

Normal Distribution

The normal distribution is the most important distribution in probability theory because it describes many natural phenomena, such as people's IQs or heights. Decision makers can use the normal distribution to describe uncertain...

Basel III & III Section 161:

No particular type of model is prescribed. So long as each model used captures all the material risks run by the bank, banks will be free to use models based on, for example, **historical simulations and Monte Carlo simulations**.

Basel II & III Section 16:

After reviewing a variety of methodologies, the Committee decided to use **Monte Carlo simulations** to calibrate both the monitoring and trigger levels for each **credit risk assessment category**. In particular, the proposed monitoring levels were derived from the **99th percentile confidence interval** and the trigger level benchmark from the 99.9th percentile confidence interval.

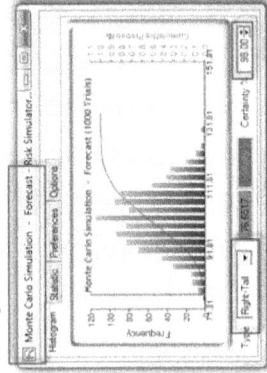

Figure 4.11: Basel III/IV/IV and Basel IV Confidence Levels, Monte Carlo Simulations, and Credit Risk

Basel III Compliance

Correlated Portfolio Optimization

TAIL VALUE AT RISK MODEL (BASEL II REQUIREMENT)

Line of Business	Mean Required Capital	99.95th Percentile	Capital Required	Allocation Weights	Minimum Allowed	Maximum Allowed	
Business 1	$10.50	$36.52	$26.01	10.00%	5.00%	15.00%	3.48
Business 2	$11.12	$47.52	$36.39	10.00%	5.00%	15.00%	4.27
Business 3	$11.77	$48.99	$37.22	10.00%	5.00%	15.00%	4.16
Business 4	$10.77	$37.34	$26.56	10.00%	5.00%	15.00%	3.47
Business 5	$13.49	$49.52	$36.03	10.00%	5.00%	15.00%	3.67
Business 6	$14.24	$55.59	$41.35	10.00%	5.00%	15.00%	3.91
Business 7	$15.60	$60.24	$44.64	10.00%	5.00%	15.00%	3.86
Business 8	$14.95	$54.69	$49.74	10.00%	5.00%	15.00%	4.33
Business 9	$14.15	$60.02	$46.67	10.00%	5.00%	15.00%	4.31
Business 10	$10.08	$35.37	$25.29	10.00%	5.00%	15.00%	3.51

Portfolio Total $12.67 $49.68 $37.01 100.00%

Total Capital Required $14.00

Correlation Matrix

This model shows the capital requirements per Basel II (99.95 percentile capital adequacy) based on a specific holding period). Without running risk-based historical and Monte Carlo simulation using Risk Simulator, the required capital is $37.01M as compared to only $14.00M is required. This is due to the cross-correlations between assets and business lines, and can only be modeled using Risk Simulator. To run the model click on Simulation and select Run Simulation. If you had other models open, make sure you first click on Simulation, Change Simulation Profile, and select the Tail VaR profile before starting). This model will not run unless Risk Simulator is installed.

Basel II & III Section 178:

As an alternative to the use of standard or own-estimate haircuts, banks may be permitted to use a **VaR models** approach to reflect the price volatility of the exposure and collateral for repo-style transactions, taking into account **correlation** effects between security positions. This approach would apply to repo-style transactions covered by bilateral netting agreements on a counterparty-by-counterparty basis.

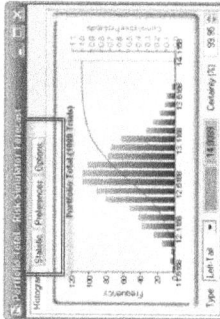

Basel II & III Section 232

The exposure must be one of a large pool of exposures, which are managed by the bank on a pooled basis ... Furthermore, it must not be managed individually in a way comparable to corporate exposures, but rather as part of a **portfolio** segment or pool of exposures with similar risk characteristics for purposes of risk assessment and quantification.

Basel II & III Section 527 (f):

Subject to supervisory review, equity portfolio correlations can be integrated into a bank's internal risk measures. The use of explicit correlations (e.g., utilization of a **variance/covariance VaR model**) must be fully documented and supported using empirical analysis. The appropriateness of implicit **correlation** assumptions will be evaluated by supervisors in their review of model documentation and estimation techniques.

Figure 4.12: Basel III/IV/IV and Basel IV Correlated Portfolios and Correlated Simulations

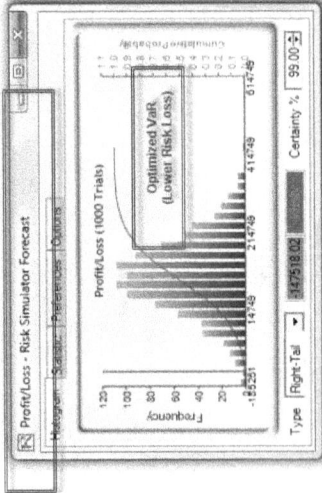

Figure 4.13: Basel III/IV/IIV and Basel IV Value at Risk and Percentiles

Financial Engineering: Credit Risk

Probability of Default

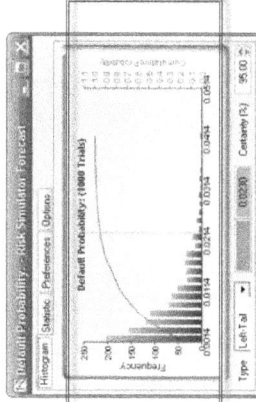

STEP ONE:

Default Probability and Credit Risk Model for Basel II

Available market and corporate data stating that we have:

Market Capitalization	$3,000	(in millions)	This value is obtained from market data on the firm's capitalization.
Equity Volatility (computed)	45.64%	(annualized)	This value is computed on the Volatility or LPVA worksheets.
Total Liabilities	$10,000	(in millions)	This is the firm's book value of debt.

Inputs in the real options model:

	Solved	Starting	Optimized	
Call Value	$2,491			This is the value of the option and should be set to the equity value using optimization.
Asset Value*	$12,500	$12,400	$12,509	This is the value to be solved* and is hence set as a decision variable in Risk Simulator.
Strike Value	$10,000			This is set as the book value of debt.
Maturity	1			For simplicity, we set this as 1 year, to obtain the 1-year default probability.
Volatility of Asset*	10.00%	5.0%	11.53%	This is the value to be solved* and is hence set as a decision variable in Risk Simulator.
Risk-free Rate	5.0%			This is the corresponding risk-free rate for the maturity of the option being analyzed.
Dividend Rate	0%			For simplicity, we assume a zero dividend rate.

Optimization parameters:

Call value	$3,000	This is the target result.
Computed value	$2,491	This is the computed result.
Minimize Absolute Difference	$509	Objective to Minimize this error function (we minimize this error function to solve the simultaneous equations)

Decision Variable Constraints:	Min	Max	
Asset Value	$10,000	$15,000	These are decision variable constraints, set at appropriate levels based on the input parameters
Volatility	5%	35%	These are decision variable constraints, set at appropriate levels based on the input parameters

Optimization Constraints		
Set value	39.29% to be exactly	46.64% which is the equity volatility

STEP TWO:

Default Probability is computed using the Risk Simulator Distribution Analysis tool on:

Anticipated Growth	7%	Enter in the expected annualized cumulative growth rate of the firm's assets
Standardized Value	-2.4732	This an intermediate computed value
Default Probability	0.6695%	This is the computed probability of default

| **Distance to Default:** | **2.47** | This is the computed distance to default in standard deviations |

Basel II & III Annex 2 - Section 16:

After reviewing a variety of methodologies, the Committee decided to use **Monte Carlo simulations** to calibrate both the monitoring and trigger levels for each **credit risk assessment** category. In particular, the proposed monitoring levels were derived from the **99th percentile confidence interval** and the trigger level benchmark from the 99.9th percentile confidence interval

Basel II & III Section 733:

Credit risk. Banks should have methodologies that enable them to assess the **credit risk** involved in exposures to **individual borrowers or counterparties** as well as at the **portfolio** level. For more sophisticated banks, the credit review assessment of capital adequacy, at a minimum, should cover four areas: risk rating systems, portfolio analysis/aggregation, securitization/complex credit derivatives, and large exposures and risk concentrations.

Figure 4.14: Basel III/IV/IV and Basel IV Credit Risk Analysis

Financial Engineering: Market Risk

Interest Rate and Yield Curve Analytics

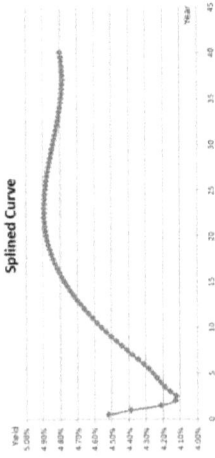

YIELD CURVE - INTERPOLATION MODEL

This is the Glass Interpolation model for generating the term structure of interest rates and yield curve estimation. This model requires several input parameters whereby their estimations require some econometric modeling techniques to calculate their values.

Function Used: B2YieldCurveBM (Beta 0, Beta 1, Beta 2, Lambda 1, Lambda 2)

Yield Curve

VASICEK MODEL
YIELD CURVE CONSTRUCTION

This is the Vasicek model used to compute the term structure of interest rates and yield curve. The Vasicek model assumes a mean-reverting stochastic interest rate. The rate of reversion and long-run mean rates can be determined using Risk Simulator's statistical analysis tool. If the long-run rate is higher than the current short rate, the yield curve is upward sloping, and vice versa.

Input Assumptions

Time to Maturity of the Bond or Debt (Years)	1.00
Riskfree Rate (Short Rate)	2.00%
Long-run Mean Rate	8.00%
Annualized Volatility of Interest Rate	2.00%
Market Price of Interest Rate Risk	0.00%
Rate of Mean Reversion	20.00%

Yield of Zero Coupon Bond 2.5562% Function call: B2BondVasicekBondYield (Maturity Riskfree Longterm Rate, Volatility, Market Price of Risk, Rate of Mean Reversion)

Years	Rate
1	2.56%
2	3.03%
3	3.45%
4	3.81%
5	4.12%
6	4.40%
7	4.64%
8	4.86%
9	5.05%
10	5.22%
15	5.83%
20	6.21%
25	6.46%
30	6.63%

Yield Curve

Daily Treasury Yield Curve Rates

Splined Curve

Basel II & III Section 763:
The revised guidance on interest rate risk recognizes banks' internal systems as the principal tool for the measurement of **interest rate risk** in the banking book and the supervisory response. To facilitate supervisors' monitoring of **interest rate risk exposures** across institutions, banks would have to provide the results of their internal measurement systems, expressed in terms of economic value relative to capital, using a standardized **interest rate shock**.

Figure 4.15: Basel III/IV/IV Interest Rate Risk and Market Shocks

Financial Engineering: Market Risk

Stochastic Forecasting

- ARIMA
- GARCH Volatility
- Brownian Motion Random Walk
- Cubic Spline Yield Curves
- Implied Yield Curves from Debt
- Mean-Reverting Interest Rates
- Jump-Diffusion Prices
- Mixed Stochastic Processes
- Time-Series Decomposition

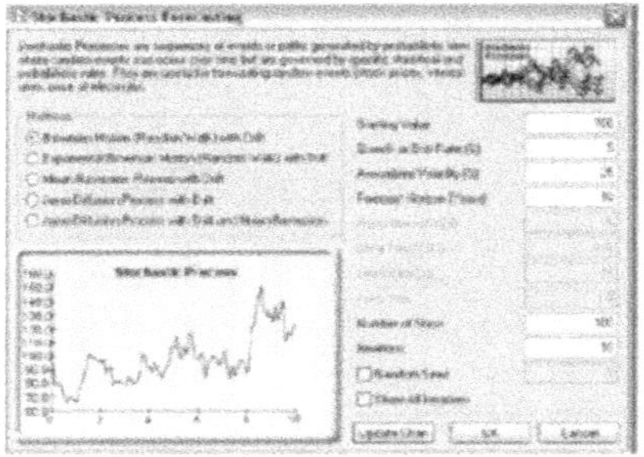

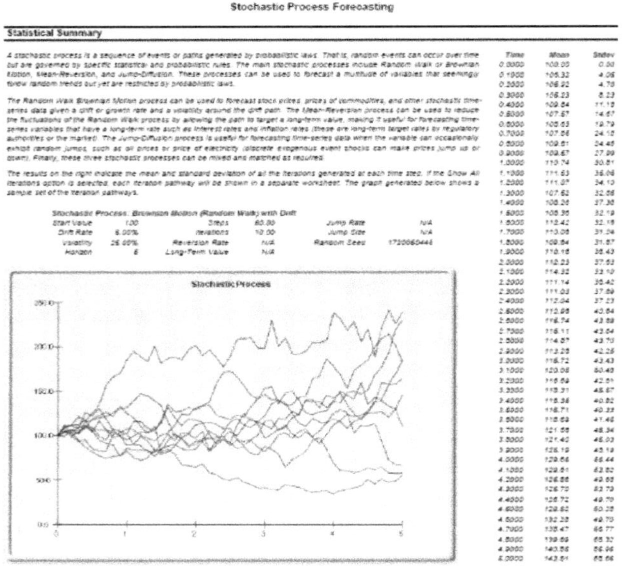

Basel II & III Section 527 (a) and (b):
The capital charge is equivalent to the **potential loss** on the institution's equity portfolio arising from an assumed **instantaneous shock** equivalent to the 99th percentile, one-tailed confidence interval of the difference between quarterly returns and an appropriate risk-free rate computed over a long-term sample period. The **estimated losses** should be robust to **adverse market movements** relevant to the long-term risk profile of the institution's specific holdings.

Basel II & III Section 155:
Banks must **estimate the volatility** of the collateral instrument or foreign exchange mismatch individually, estimated volatilities for each transaction must not take into account the **correlations** between unsecured exposure, collateral and **exchange rates.**

Figure 4.16: Basel III/IV/IV and Basel IV Volatility and Adverse Instantaneous Shocks

Data and Relationship Modeling

Econometric Analysis –
ARIMA, Regressions, GARCH

Modeling and forecasting cross-sectional, time-series, and
...ed panel data, and applications of volatility forecasts

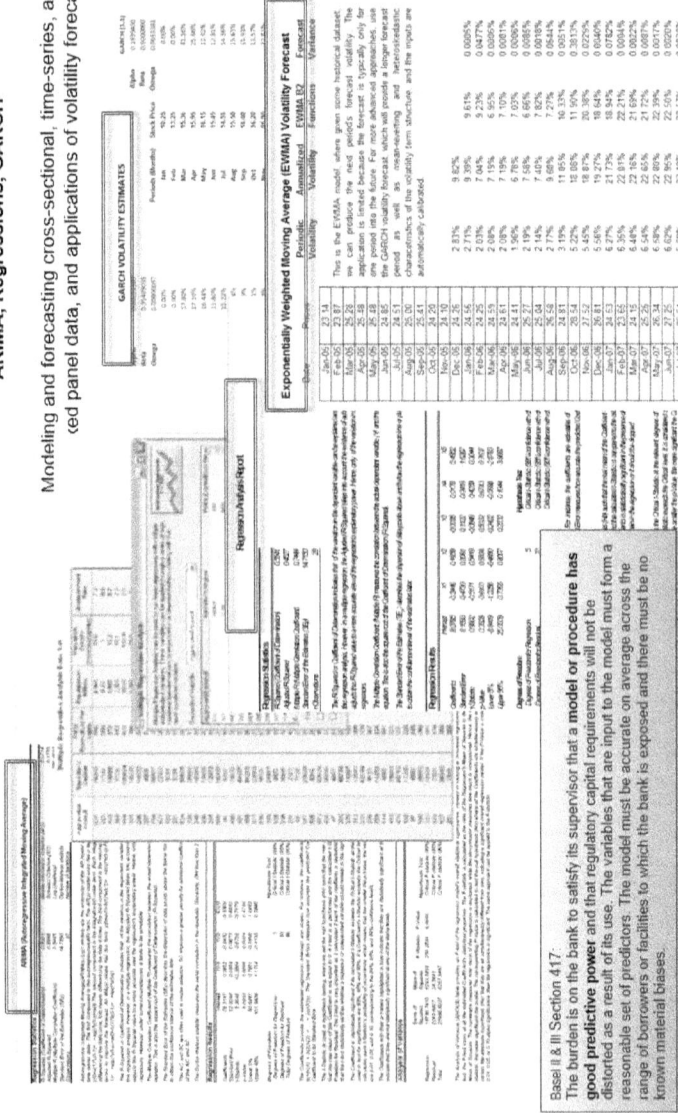

GARCH VOLATILITY ESTIMATES

Exponentially Weighted Moving Average (EWMA) Volatility Forecast

This is the EWMA model where some historical dataset
we can predict the next period's forecast volatility. The
application is limited because the forecast is typically only for
one period into the future. For more advanced approaches, use
the GARCH volatility forecast which will provide a longer forecast
period as well as mean-reverting and heteroskedastic
characteristics of the volatility, term structure and the inputs are
automatically calibrated.

Regression Analysis Report

Figure 4.17: Basel III/IV/IV and Basel IV Forecast Models with Strong Predictive Power

Financial Engineering

Exotic and Specialized Options

All these models are in the Basel III Modeling Toolkit

American and European Options
Asian Arithmetic
Asian Geometric
Asset or Nothing
Barrier Options
Binary Digital Options
Cash or Nothing
Credit Spread Options
Commodity Options
Complex Chooser
Currency Options
Double Barriers
Exchange Assets
Extreme Spread
Foreign Equity Linked Forex
Foreign Equity Domestic Currency
Foreign Equity Fixed Forex
Foreign Takeover Options
Forward Start
Futures and Forward Options
Gap Options
Graduated Barriers
Implied Trinomial Lattices

Index Options
Inverse Gamma Out-of-the-money Options
Jump Diffusion
Leptokurtic and Skewed Options
Lookback Fixed Strike Partial Time
Lookback Fixed Strike
Lookback Floating Strike Partial Time
Lookback Floating Strike
Min and Max of Two Assets
Option Collar
Options on Options
Perpetual Options
Simple Chooser
Spread on Futures
Supershares
Time Switch
Trading Day Corrections
Two Asset 3D Options
Two Assets Barrier
Two Assets Cash
Two Assets Correlated
Uneven Dividends
Writer Extendible

Real Options - Dual-Asset Rainbow Option Pentanomial Lattice
Real Options - Exotic Complex Floating American Chooser
Real Options - Exotic Complex Floating European Chooser
Real Options - Expand Contact Abandon American and European Out
Real Options - Expand Contract Abandon Bermudan Option
Real Options - Expand Contract Abandon Customized Option 1
Real Options - Expand Contract Abandon Customized Option B
Real Options - Expansion American and European Option
Real Options - Expansion Bermudan Option
Real Options - Expansion Customized Option
Real Options - Jump Diffusion Calls and Puts using Quadranomial Latt
Real Options - Mean Reverting Calls and Puts using Trinomial Lattices
Real Options - Multiple Asset Competing Options (3D Binomial)
Real Options - Multiple Phased Complex Sequential Compound Option
Real Options - Multiple Phased Sequential Compound Option
Real Options - Multiple Phased Simultaneous Compound Option
9 Puts using Trinomial Lattices
ed Sequential Compound Option
ised Simultaneous Compound Option
- High-Tech Manufacturing Strategy A
- High-Tech Manufacturing Strategy B
- High-Tech Manufacturing Strategy C
- Oil and Gas - Strategy A
- Oil and Gas - Strategy B
- Oil and Gas - Strategy A
- PG Stage-Gate Process A
- PG Stage-Gate Process B
- Switching Options 1 Strategy A
- Switching Options 1 Strategy B

Employee Stock Options - Simple American Call
Employee Stock Options - Simple Bermudan Call with Vesting
Employee Stock Options - Simple European Call
Employee Stock Options - Suboptimal Exercise
Employee Stock Options - Vesting, Blackout, Suboptimal, Forfeiture
Exotic Options - American Call Option with Dividends
Exotic Options - Accruals on Basket of Assets
Exotic Options - American Call Option on Foreign Exchange
Exotic Options - American Call Option on Index Futures
Exotic Options - Barrier Option - Down and In Lower Barrier
Exotic Options - Barrier Option - Down and Out Lower Barrier
Exotic Options - Barrier Option - Up and In Upper Barrier Call
Exotic Options - Barrier Option - Up and In, Down and In Double Barrier Call
Exotic Options - Barrier Option - Up and In, Up and Out Barrier Call
Exotic Options - Barrier Option - Up and Out, Grown and Out Double Barrier Call
Exotic Options - Basic American, European, wrived Bermudan Call Option
Exotic Options - Choozer Option
Exotic Options - Equity Linked Notes
Exotic Options - European Call Option with Dividends
Exotic Options - Range Accruals
Options Analysis - Plain Vanilla Call Option I
Options Analysis - Plain Vanilla Call Option B
Options Analysis - Plain Vanilla Call Option III
Options Analysis - Plain Vanilla Call Option IV
Options Analysis - Plain Vanilla Put Option
Real Options - Abandonment American Option
Real Options - Abandonment Bermudan Option
Real Options - Abandonment Customized Option
Real Options - Abandonment European Option

Quadranomial - Jump Diffusion American Call Option
Quadranomial - Jump Diffusion American Put Option
Quadranomial - Jump Diffusion European Call Option
Quadranomial - Jump Diffusion European Put Option
Trinomial - American Call Option
Trinomial - American Put Option
Trinomial - European Call Option
Trinomial - European Put Option
Trinomial - Mean Reverting American Call Option
Trinomial - Mean Reverting American Put Option
Trinomial - Mean Reverting European Call Option
Trinomial - Mean Reverting European Put Option
Trinomial - American Rainbow Call Option
Pentanomial - American Rainbow Put Option
Pentanomial - Dual Reverse Strike American Call (2D Binomial)
Pentanomial - Dual Reverse Strike American Put (3D Binomial)
Pentanomial - Dual Strike American Call (3D Binomial)
Pentanomial - Dual Strike American Put (3D Binomial)
Pentanomial - Rainbow Call Option
Pentanomial - Rainbow Put Option
Pentanomial - Exchange of Two Assets American Put (3D Binomial)
Pentanomial - Maximum of Two Assets American Call (3D Binomial)
Pentanomial - Maximum of Two Assets American Put (3D Binomial)
Pentanomial - Maximum of Two Assets American Call (3D Binomial)
Pentanomial - Portfolio American Call (3D Binomial)
Pentanomial - Portfolio American Put (3D Binomial)
Pentanomial - Spread of Two Assets American Call (3D Binomial)
Pentanomial - Spread of Two Assets American Put (3D Binomial)

Binary Digital Instruments
Inverse Floater Bond Lattice
Options Trading Strategies
Options Adjusted Spreads on Debt
Options on Debt
C128 and Points
Convertible Bonds
Valuation of a Warrant - Combined Value
Valuation of a Warrant - Put Only
Valuation of a Warrant - Warrant Only

Basel II & III Section 112
The comprehensive approach for the treatment of collateral will also be applied to calculate the counterparty risk charges for OTC **derivatives** and repo-style transactions booked in the trading book

Basel II & III Section 527 (e)
Institutions must use an internal model that is appropriate for the risk profile and complexity of their equity portfolio. Institutions with material holdings with values that are highly **non-linear** in nature (e.g. **equity derivatives, convertibles**) must employ an internal model designed to capture appropriately the risks associated with such instruments.

Basel II & III Section 203
For the **hedge**, **embedded options** which may reduce the term of the hedge should be taken into account so that the shortest possible effective maturity is used. Where a **call** is at the discretion of the **protection seller**, the maturity will always be at the first call date. If the **call** is at the discretion of the protection buying bank but the terms of the arrangement at origination of the **hedge**.

Figure 4.18: Basel III/V/IV and Basel IV Modeling OTC Derivatives and Exotic Convertibles

Foreign Exchange Risk

Hedging Foreign Exchange Exposure with Currency Options

Months	Jan	Feb	Mar	April	May	Jun
FX Spot Rate (HKD/USD)	7.80	7.40	7.80	7.80	7.30	7.30
FX Strike Rate (HKD/USD)	7.80	7.80	7.80	7.80	7.80	7.80
Maturity (Years)	0.5833	0.5000	0.4167	0.3333	0.2500	
Risk Free Rate US	6.08%	6.08%	6.08%	6.08%	6.08%	
Risk Free Rate HK	5.08%	5.08%	5.08%	5.08%	5.08%	
Volatility	15.00%	15.00%	15.00%	15.00%	15.00%	15.00%
Quantity of Options Hedge Position	10,000,000	10,000,000	10,000,000	10,000,000	10,000,000	10
Currency Put Option Value (HKD/USD)	0.3229	0.5191	0.3795	0.5533	0.7912	
Market Value of Hedge	3,229,135	5,191,009	3,794,813	5,532,845	7,012,279	
Intrinsic Value	0	4,000,000	2,000,000	5,000,000	7,000,000	
Time Value	3,229,135	1,191,009	1,794,813	532,845	12,229	

FINANCIAL STATEMENTS IMPACTS - MARK TO MARKET

Balance Sheet (in 000's)	Jan	Feb	Mar	April	May	Jun
Derivative Contract	3,229,135	5,191,009	3,794,813	5,532,845	7,012,279	7,000,000
Other Comp Income (SE)		4,000,000	2,000,000	5,000,000	7,000,000	7,000,000
Income Statement (in 000's)						
Hedge Effectiveness gain or loss per period	(2,038,128)					
Hedge Effectiveness sum of all periods		(2,538,128)	603,805	(1,281,969)	(528,615)	
Market Cost of Hedge (Current Period)						
Income from Option Exercise						
Net Valuation of Hedging						
Income from Hedging						
Income from No Hedge						
Loss Distribution from Hedging						
Loss Distribution from No Hedge						

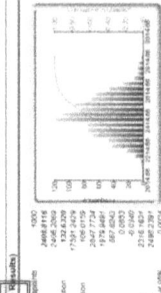

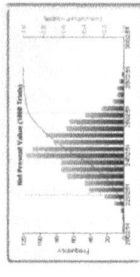

EQUITY LINKED FOREIGN EXCHANGE OPTIONS IN DOMESTIC CURRENCY

Input Assumptions

Fixed Exchange Rate	1.50
Asset Price	$70.00
Strike Price	1.25
Maturity	0.50
Domestic Risk Free Rate	5.00%
Foreign Risk Free	6.00%
Dividend Rate	1.00%
Volatility of Asset	25.00%
Volatility of Currency	15.00%
Correlation	0.25

Foreign Equity Linked Call Option	$11.5633
Foreign Equity Linked Put Option	$0.1777

Equity Linked Foreign Exchange Options are options whose underlying asset is in a foreign equity market, and the option holder can hedge the fluctuations of the foreign exchange rate. The resulting valuation is in the domestic currency.

Foreign Exchange Rate Hedged at 0.85 (Simulation Results)

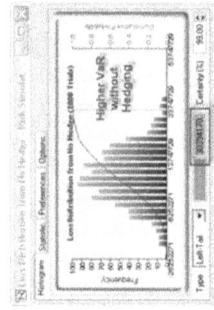

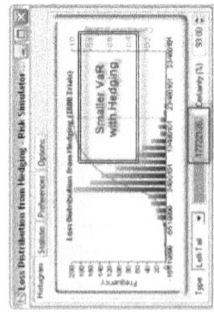

Basel II & III Section 131: Additionally where the exposure and collateral are held in **different currencies** an additional downwards adjustment must be made to the volatility adjusted collateral amount to take account of **possible future fluctuations in exchange rates.**

Basel II & III Section 155: Banks must estimate the **volatility** of the collateral instrument or **foreign exchange mismatch** individually. estimated **volatilities** for each transaction must not take into account the **correlations** between unsecured exposure, collateral and **exchange rates.**

Figure 4.19: Basel III/IV/IV and Basel IV Modeling Foreign Exchange Fluctuations

Credit Derivatives

OPTIONS ADJUSTED SPREAD WITH YIELD CURVE AND VOLATILITY TERM STRUCTURE

Face Value	$100.00	Coupon Per Period	$2.50	Delta T	0.5000
Maturity	4	Market Price of Debt	$100.00	Straight Spread	0.0000%	Modeling Toolkit Functions:
Total Steps	8	Callable Price	$101.00	Callable Spread	0.0000%	2.3387%
		Callable Step	6			2.3895%

Compute Spreads

Certain types of debt come with an option-embedded provision, for instance a bond might be callable if the market price exceeds a certain value, but the issuer can only recall the debt at par value. In addition, if it more profitable for the issuing company to call the debt and reissue new debt at the lower rates or prevailing allowable and legally required spreads, the firm will most probably do so. Clearly the certain embedded provisions make the price of the bond to increase or decrease. You can enter in the required price and compute the option adjusted spread i.e. the additional premium that should be charged on the option provision.

Short Rate Lattice

Interest Rates (Yields)	2.60%	2.60%	2.60%	2.60%	2.60%	2.60%	2.60%	2.60%
Interest Volatilities	N/A	20.00%	20.00%	20.00%	20.00%	20.00%	20.00%	20.00%

Steps	0	1	2	3	4	5	6	7
	2.60%	2.95%	3.14%	3.40%	3.60%	4.19%	4.61%	5.07%
		2.34%	2.57%	2.83%	3.11%	3.43%	3.77%	4.15%
			2.11%	2.32%	2.55%	2.81%	3.09%	3.40%
				1.90%	2.09%	2.30%	2.53%	2.79%
					1.71%	1.88%	2.07%	2.28%
						1.54%	1.68%	1.87%
							1.39%	1.53%
								1.25%

Straight

Price Lattice	Using Function:	110.06						
	110.06	107.95	106.01	104.26	102.72	101.45	100.48	99.87
		110.04	108.60	106.13	104.43	102.95	101.72	100.78
			108.55	107.68	105.85	104.19	102.74	101.53
				108.97	107.62	105.22	103.59	102.15
					107.99	106.57	104.29	102.56
						106.77	104.95	103.09
							105.34	103.43
								103.71

Callable Debt

Price Lattice	Using Function:	110.03						
	110.03	108.25	106.63	105.15	103.77	102.32	100.48	99.87
		110.68	107.99	106.48	105.21	104.20	103.50	100.78

Real Options Valuation

Modeling Toolkit Functions:
2.3387%
2.3895%

CREDIT DEFAULT SWAP (CDS) SPREADS

Input Assumptions

Bond Yield	7.00%
Annual Coupon Rate	10.00%
Coupon Payments Per Year	2
Risk-free Yield	5.00%
Recovery Rate at Default	80.00%

Credit Default Swap Spread	1.7699%

A credit default swap or CDS which allows the holder of the instrument to sell a bond or debt at par value when a credit event or default occurs. This model computes the valuation of the CDS spread. A CDS does not protect against movements of the credit spread (only a credit spread option can do that), but

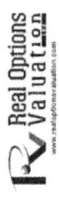

CREDIT SPREAD OPTIONS (CSO)

Input Assumptions

Credit Spread	3.00%
Strike Spread	2.90%
Duration (Spread to Currency Conversion Rate)	1000.00
Probability of Default	2.50%
Maturity	1.00
Risk-free Rate	5.00%
Volatility	25.00%

Credit Spread Call Option	$3.2102
Credit Spread Put Option	$2.2828

B2CreditSpreadCallOption
B2CreditSpreadPutOption

Credit spread options or CSO are exotic options where the payoff depends on a credit spread or the price of the underlying asset that is sensitive to interest rate movements such as floating or inverse floating rate notes and debt. A CSO call provides a return to the holder if the prevailing reference credit spread exceeds the predetermined strike rate, and the duration input variable is used to translate the percentage spread into a notional currency amount. The CSO expires when there is a credit default event

Input Assumptions

Forward Asset Price at Maturity	$1,000.00
Strike Price	$900.00
Probability of Default	2.50%
Maturity	1.00
Risk-free Rate	5.00%
Volatility	25.00%

Credit Asset Spread Call Option	$141.6406
Credit Asset Spread Put Option	$48.8957

CSO can only protect against any movements in the reference spread and not a default event. Only a credit default swap (CDS) can do that. Typically, to hedge against defaults and spread movements, both CDS and CDO are used. In some cases when the CSO covers a reference entity's underlying asset value and not the spread itself, the credit asset spread options are used instead.

Real Options Valuation
www.realoptionsvaluation.com

Basel II & III Section 140: Where guarantees or credit derivatives are direct, explicit, irrevocable and unconditional, and supervisors are satisfied that banks fulfill certain minimum operational conditions relating to risk management processes they may allow banks to take account of such **credit protection in calculating capital requirements.**

Basel II & III Section 713: Specific risk capital charges for positions **hedged by credit derivatives.** Full allowance will be recognized when the values of two legs (i.e. long and short) always move in the opposite direction and broadly to the same extent.

Figure 4.20: Basel III/IV/IV Credit Derivatives and Hedging

COMPLIANCE WITH COSO
INTEGRATED RISK FRAMEWORK

The following provides a quick summary of COSO Integrated ERM Framework compliance when using the IRM methodology:

- Figure 4.21 shows the PEAT ERM module's Risk Register tab where mitigation costs and benefits (gross risks reduced to residual risk levels), likelihood and impact measures, and spreads with varying precision levels ready for Monte Carlo risk simulation are situated, in compliance with COSO ERM Framework Sections 5 and 6.

- Figure 4.22 shows the PEAT ERM module where the likelihood and impact within a risk map is generated, in compliance with COSO AT/Exhibit 5.13.

- Figure 4.23 shows compliance with COSO AT/Exhibit 6.5 and COSO ERM Integrated Framework Section 6, where entity-wide portfolio and business unit, department, and functional areas' gross and residual risks are computed.

- Figure 4.24, a sample of the Risk Dashboard reports, also shows compliance with COSO AT/Exhibit 6.5 and COSO ERM Integrated Framework Section 6, where entity-wide portfolio and business unit, department, and functional areas' gross and residual risks are computed and compared against each other.

- Figure 4.25 shows the PEAT DCF module's efficient frontier model, consistent with COSO AT/Exhibit 3.7 requiring an analysis of the capital investment in relation to the returns within a diversified (optimized) portfolio.

- Figure 4.26 shows the PEAT ERM and DCF module's simulated results, where Value at Risk, percentiles, and statistical probabilities can be obtained, in compliance with COSO AT/Exhibit 5.5 requiring a range of outcomes based on distributional assumptions, and COSO ERM Integrated Framework Exhibit 5.2 requiring historical or simulated outcomes of future behaviors under probabilistic models.

- Figure 4.27 shows compliance with COSO AT/Exhibit 3.1 requiring the use of scenario modeling and stress testing.

- Figure 4.28 shows the CMOL module in PEAT where scenario analysis, stress testing, and gap analysis are performed, in compliance with COSO AT/Exhibit 5.10, to complement probabilistic models.

- Figure 4.29 shows compliance with COSO AT/Exhibits 5.8 and 5.9 requiring the modeling of operational and credit loss distributions with back-testing or historical simulation, sensitivity analysis, and Value at Risk calculations.

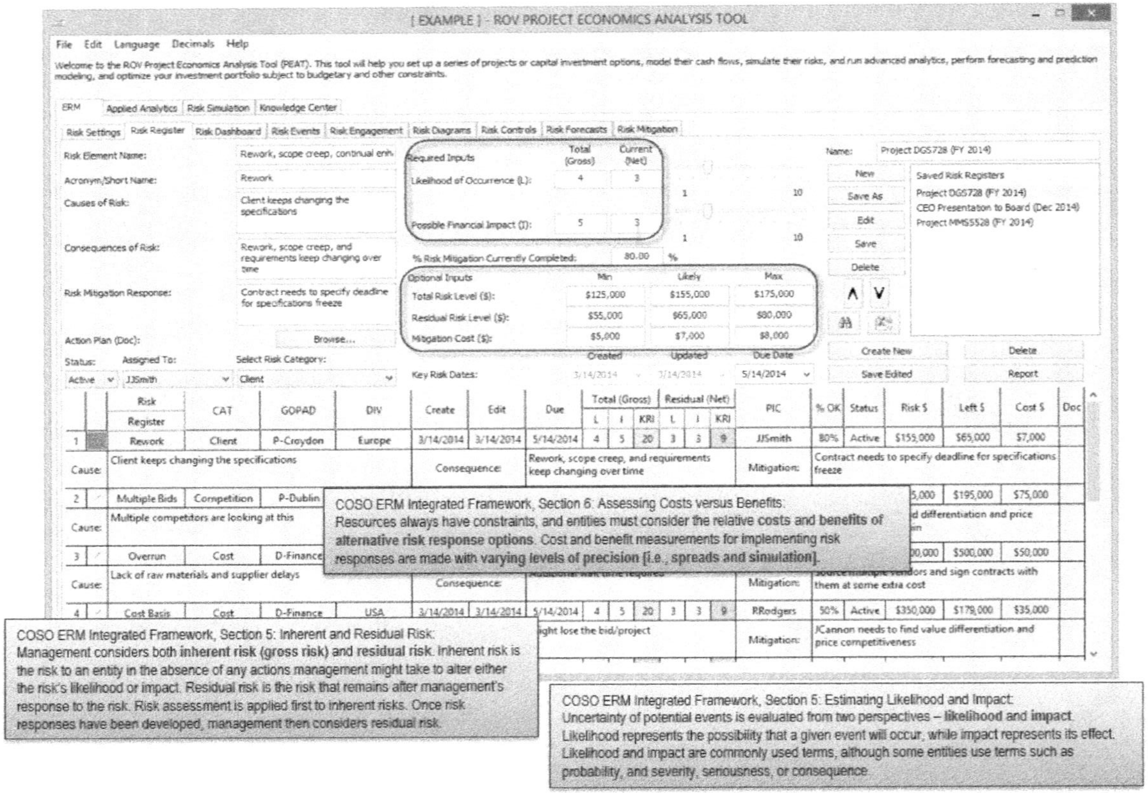

Figure 4.21: PEAT ERM and COSO Integrated Framework

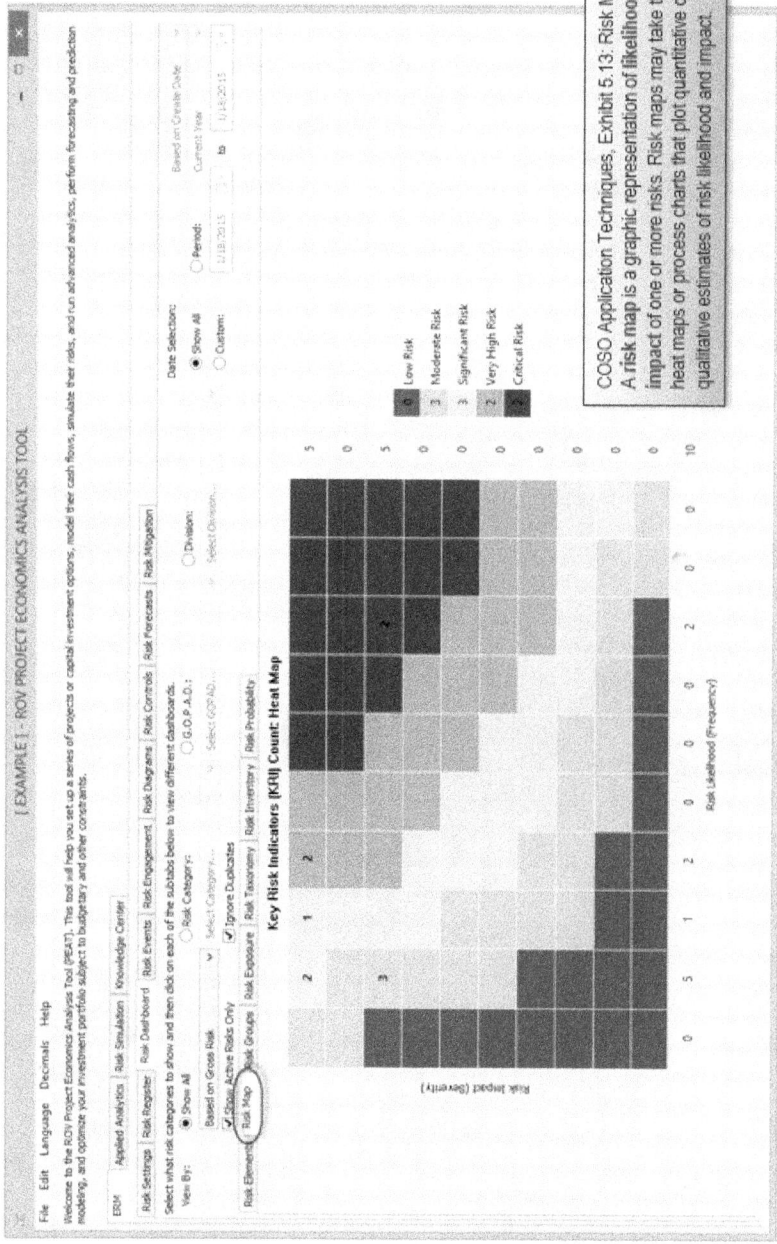

Figure 4.22: PEAT ERM Heat Map and Risk Matrix

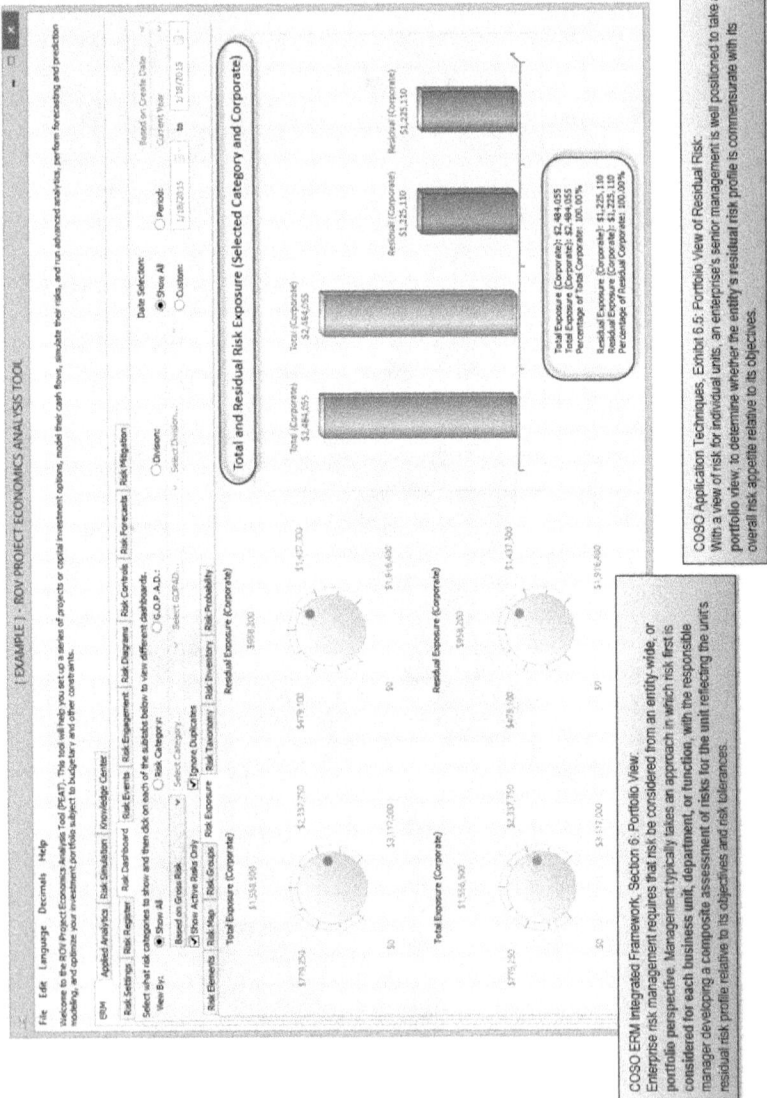

Figure 4.23: PEAT ERM Corporate Portfolio View of Gross and Residual Risk

[EXAMPLE] - ROV PROJECT ECONOMICS ANALYSIS TOOL

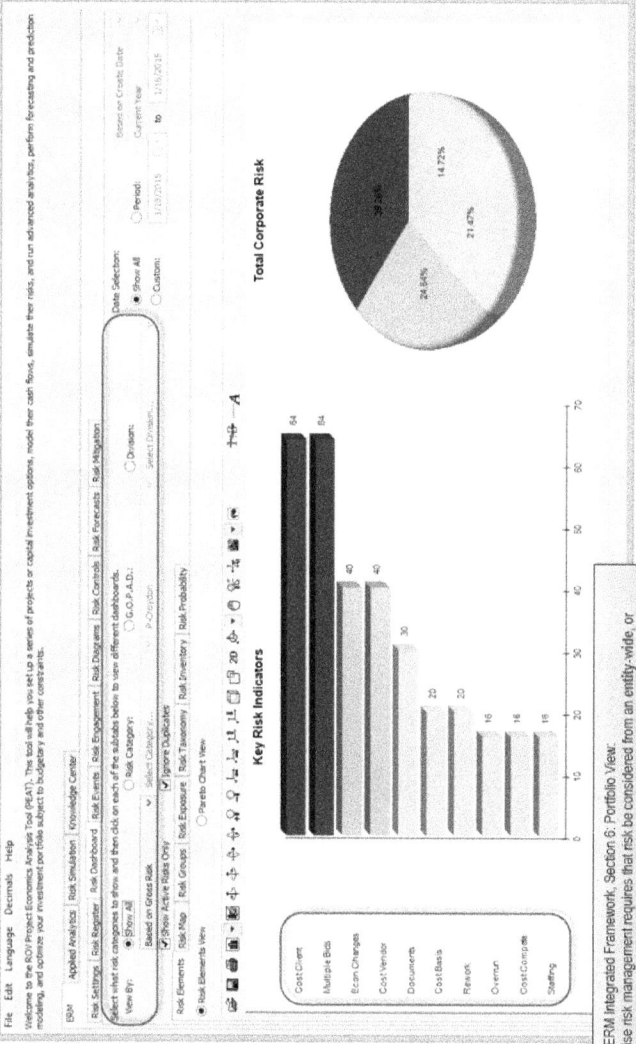

File Edit Language Decimals Help

Welcome to the ROV Project Economics Analysis Tool (PEAT). This tool will help you set up a series of projects or capital investment options, model their cash flows, simulate their risks, and run advanced analytics, perform forecasting and prediction modeling, and optimize your investment portfolio subject to budgetary and other constraints.

ERM

Risk Settings | Applied Analytics | Risk Simulation | Risk Dashboard | Knowledge Center

Risk Register | Risk Events | Risk Engagement | Risk Diagrams | Risk Controls | Risk Forecasts | Risk Mitigation

Select what risk categories to show and then click on each of the subtabs below to view different dashboards.

View By:
- Show All
- Based on Gross Risk

Risk Category:
Select Category...

- G.O.P.A.D.I.
- P.O.nyDion

Division:
Select Division...

Date Selection:
- Show All
- Custom

Period: 1/22/2015 to 1/16/2015

Based on Credits Date
Current Year

Show Active Risks Only
Ignore Duplicates

Risk Elements: Risk Map | Risk Groups | Risk Exposure | Risk Taxonomy | Risk Inventory | Risk Probability

- Risk Elements View
- Pareto Chart View

Key Risk Indicators

Cost Client — 64
Multiple Bids — 64
Ecsm Changes — 40
Cost Vendor — 40
Documents — 30
Cost Basis — 20
Rework — 20
Overrun — 16
Cost Compete — 16
Staffing — 18

(axis: 0, 10, 20, 30, 40, 50, 60, 70)

Total Corporate Risk

39.3%
24.94%
21.42%
14.72%

COSO ERM Integrated Framework, Section 6: Portfolio View.
Enterprise risk management requires that risk be considered from an entity-wide, or portfolio perspective. Management typically takes an approach in which risk first is considered for each business unit, department, or function, with the responsible manager developing a composite assessment of risks for the unit reflecting the unit's residual risk profile relative to its objectives and risk tolerances.

COSO Application Techniques, Exhibit 6.5: Portfolio View of Residual Risk:
With a view of risk for individual units, an enterprise's senior management is well positioned to take a portfolio view, to determine whether the entity's residual risk profile is commensurate with its overall risk appetite relative to its objectives.

Figure 4.24: PEAT ERM View by Department, Business Unit, Function, and Portfolio

COSO Application Techniques, Exhibit 3.7: Efficient Frontier.
The analysis illustrates how a company views capital at risk versus return in relation to risk appetite. The company strives to diversify its portfolio to earn a return that lines up along the target profile

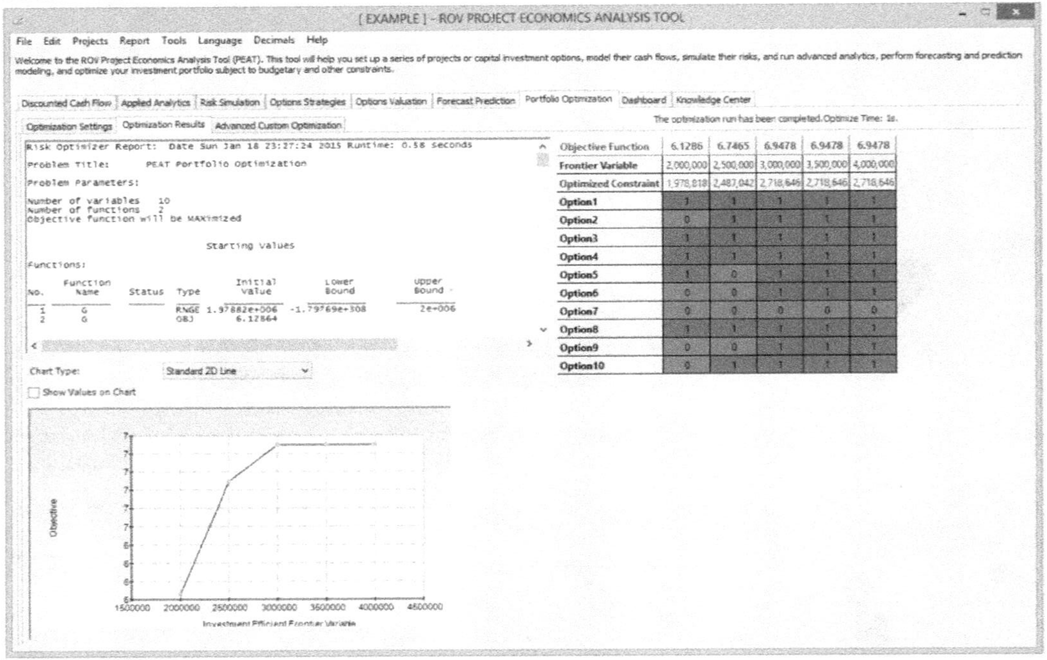

Figure 4.25: PEAT DCF Module's Portfolio Optimization and Efficient Frontier

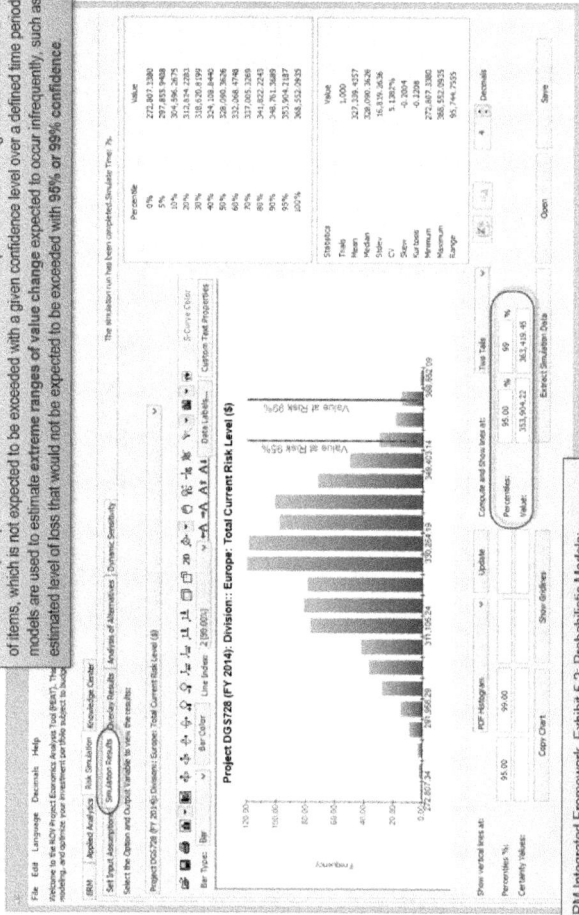

COSO Application Techniques, Exhibit 5.5: Value at Risk:
Value-at-risk (VaR) models are based on distributional assumptions about change in the value of an item or group of items, which is not expected to be exceeded with a given confidence level over a defined time period. These models are used to estimate extreme ranges of value change expected to occur infrequently, such as the estimated level of loss that would not be expected to be exceeded with **95% or 99% confidence.**

COSO ERM Integrated Framework, Exhibit 5.2: Probabilistic Models:
Probabilistic models associate a range of events and the resulting impact with the likelihood of those events based on **certain assumptions.** Likelihood and impact are assessed based on **historical data or simulated outcomes** reflecting **assumptions of future behavior.** Examples of probabilistic models include value at risk, cash flow at risk, earnings at risk, and development of credit and operational loss distributions.

COSO Application Techniques, Exhibit 5.5: Quantitative Probability Models:
Probability-based techniques measure the likelihood and impact of **a range of outcomes** based on distributional assumptions of the behavior of events.

Figure 4.26: PEAT ERM and DCF Module's Risk Simulation and Value at Risk

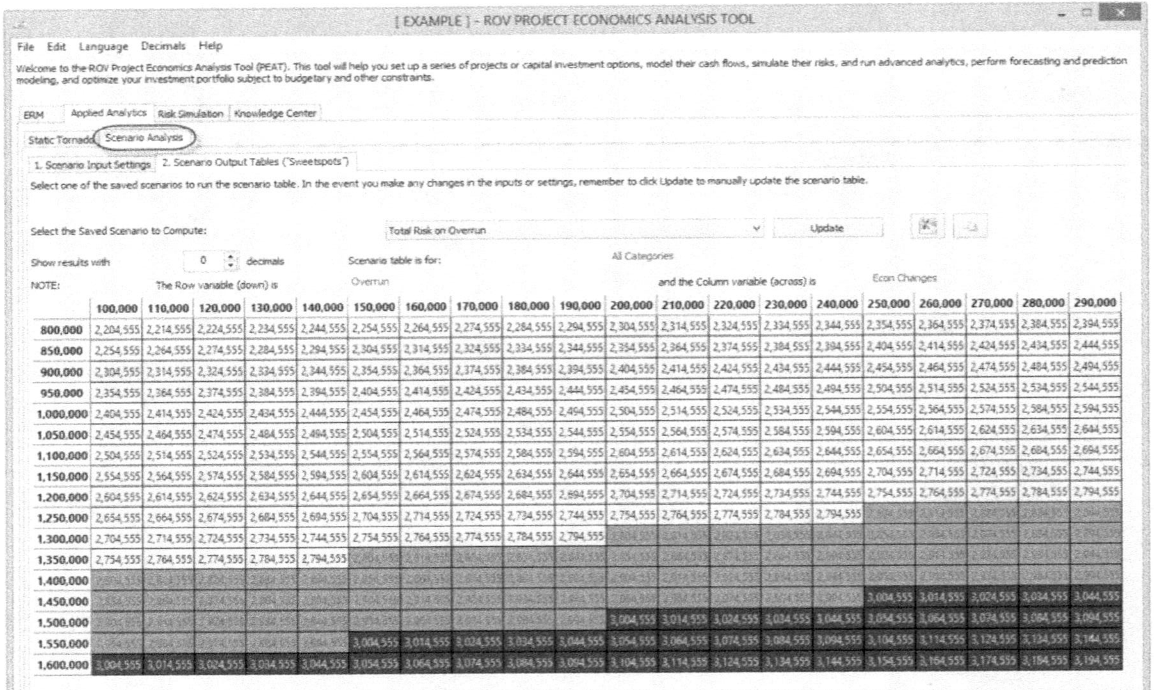

Figure 4.27: PEAT ERM and DCF Module's Scenario Analysis and Heat Map Regions

COSO Application Techniques, Exhibit 3.1: Scenarios, Stress Testing, Modeling

Using scenario analysis, modeling, and stress testing, management compared the results of each option in relation to the impact on return on capital employed. Management identified the distribution of potential return outcomes.

Credit Risk (ERC)   Market Risk   Asset Liability Management   Analytical Models   Operational Risk   KRI Dashboard

Interest Rate Risk   Liquidity Risk

Input Assumptions   Scenario Analysis   Stress Testing   Gap Analysis   Charts

ASSETS	Month 1	Month 2	Month 3	Month 4	Month 5	Month 6	Month 7	Month 8	Month 9	Month 10	Month 11	Month 12
Month												
LOANS												
Available	21.95%	2.13%	13.32%	23.54%	-2.51%	-22.69%	13.12%	-10.69%	0.72%	2.00%	6.20%	6.96%
Individual Firm Notes	-8.26%	-2.88%	-0.95%	0.38%	4.32%	2.87%	1.44%	1.99%	-0.95%	4.75%	-1.76%	-1.72%
Discounted Notes	-8.26%	-2.88%	-0.95%	0.38%	4.32%	2.87%	1.44%	1.99%	-0.95%	4.75%	-1.76%	-1.72%
Mortgages	0.39%	0.47%	0.05%	-0.23%	-0.22%	-0.41%	-0.52%	-0.82%	-1.01%	-0.97%	-0.80%	-0.83%
Pledges	-0.05%	2.52%	-1.79%	-1.82%	-3.76%	-3.17%	-4.79%	-3.62%	-3.47%	-3.51%	-4.03%	-3.43%
Cards	7.92%	0.27%	7.46%	-4.09%	10.82%	3.96%	9.76%	-2.48%	-0.16%	1.20%	17.39%	0.69%
Personal	4.19%	2.91%	-1.19%	-0.56%	-0.45%	-1.09%	-1.26%	-0.89%	-0.31%	1.54%	2.26%	1.15%

LIABILITIES	Month 1	Month 2	Month 3	Month 4	Month 5	Month 6	Month 7	Month 8	Month 9	Month 10	Month 11	Month 12
Month												
REGULAR DEPOSITS												
Public Sector	41.75%	-19.84%	-1.39%	10.22%	-7.67%	8.14%	-12.88%	7.85%	-2.84%	-10.50%	0.49%	15.82%
Private Sector	17.24%	-8.16%	-0.32%	3.79%	-4.86%	3.87%	-1.05%	3.97%	-2.46%	-6.84%	1.63%	7.83%
TIME DEPOSITS												
Public Sector	-21.17%	19.94%	-0.78%	-22.00%	2.69%	-6.38%	27.78%	16.77%	5.27%	-0.56%	1.08%	3.30%
Private Sector	-2.21%	13.10%	2.77%	-3.29%	-1.98%	4.76%	-2.33%	8.35%	4.63%	-1.24%	0.45%	-0.22%

Select the analyzed Dataset

Sample Dataset

◉ Enter scenarios using % change
◯ Enter scenarios using actual values

Add Scenario:

Scenario 1

List of Saved Scenarios

Scenario
Scenario 1
Scenario 2

Save As

New   Delete
Edit   Save

COSO Application Techniques, Exhibit 5.10: Scenario Analysis and Stress Testing

Scenario analysis assesses the effect on an objective of one or more events. **Stress testing** assesses the impact of events having extreme impact. Stress testing differs from scenario analysis in that it focuses on the direct impact of a change in only one event or activity under extreme circumstances, as opposed to focusing on changes on a more normal scale as in scenario analysis. Stress testing generally is used as a complement to probabilistic measures to examine the results of low likelihood, high impact events that might not be captured adequately by distributional assumptions used with probabilistic techniques.

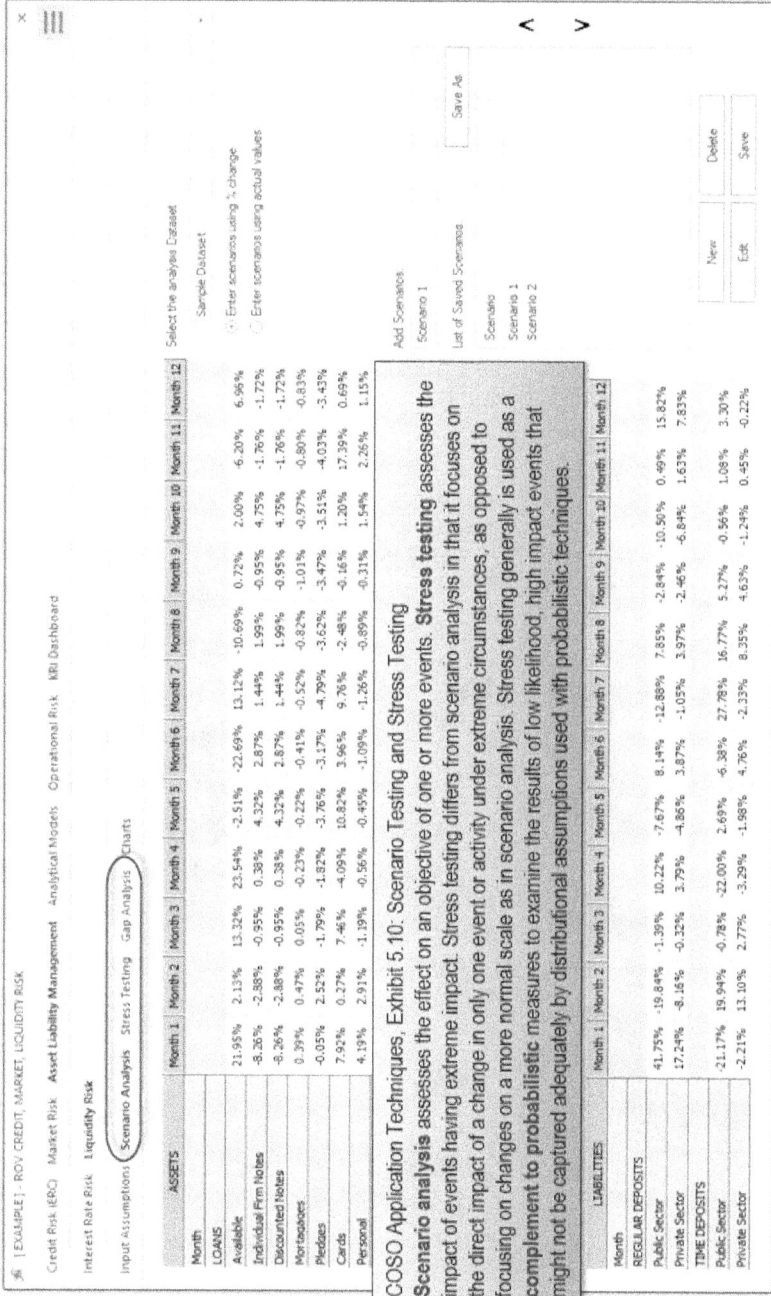

Figure 4.28: CMOL Module's Scenario Analysis and Stress Testing

Gross Value at Risk (VaR)

Horizon	VaR 99.00%	VaR 95.00%
1 Day	2,679,921	1,894,849
5 Day	5,992,486	4,237,012
10 Day	8,474,655	5,992,040

Internal Historical Simulation Value at Risk (VaR) 99.00%

Horizon	Total Values	Bonds Only	Currency Only
1 Day	1,784,836	1,817,804	55,871
5 Day	3,991,015	4,064,733	124,932
10 Day	5,644,147	5,748,400	176,681

Internal Historical Simulation Value at Risk (VaR) 95.00%

Horizon	Total Values	Bonds Only	Currency Only
1 Day	1,352,838	1,348,769	38,157
5 Day	3,025,037	3,015,939	85,323
10 Day	4,278,049	4,265,182	120,665

Update

Asset Positions and Details

Asset	Daily Volatility	Current Position	Current Weight	99.00% VaR 1 Day	99.00% VaR 5 Day	99.00% VaR 10 Day	95.00% VaR 1 Day	95.00% VaR 5 Day	95.00% VaR 10 Day
Asset Name 1	1.06%	26,073,072	30.65%	643,403	1,438,693	2,034,620	454,921	1,017,234	1,438,586
Asset Name 2	2.61%	3,187,500	3.75%	193,273	432,173	611,184	136,655	305,569	432,140
Asset Name 3	1.50%	28,710,170	33.75%	999,427	2,234,787	3,160,466	706,649	1,580,115	2,234,620
Asset Name 4	1.78%	15,720,097	18.48%	652,132	1,458,212	2,062,223	461,093	1,031,035	1,458,103
Asset Name 5	1.25%	0	0.00%	0	0	0	0	0	0
Asset Name 6	1.29%	0	0.00%	0	0	0	0	0	0
Asset Name 7	1.03%	0	0.00%	0	0	0	0	0	0
Asset Name 8	1.15%	0	0.00%	0	0	0	0	0	0
Asset Name 9	1.39%	0	0.00%	0	0	0	0	0	0
Dollar	0.68%	3,456,494	4.06%	54,809	122,557	173,322	38,753	86,654	122,548
Euro	0.74%	7,908,463	9.30%	136,876	306,065	432,841	96,779	216,404	306,042

COSO Application Techniques, Exhibit 5.8-5.9: Loss Distributions, Back Testing, Sensitivity Analysis
Certain operational or credit loss distribution estimations use statistical techniques, generally based on non-normal distributions, to calculate maximum losses resulting from operational risks with a given confidence level. Back-testing [historical simulation] typically consists of periodic comparison of an entity's at-risk measures with subsequent profit or loss. Back-testing commonly is used by financial institutions. Sensitivity analysis is used to assess the impact of normal, or routine, changes in potential. events.

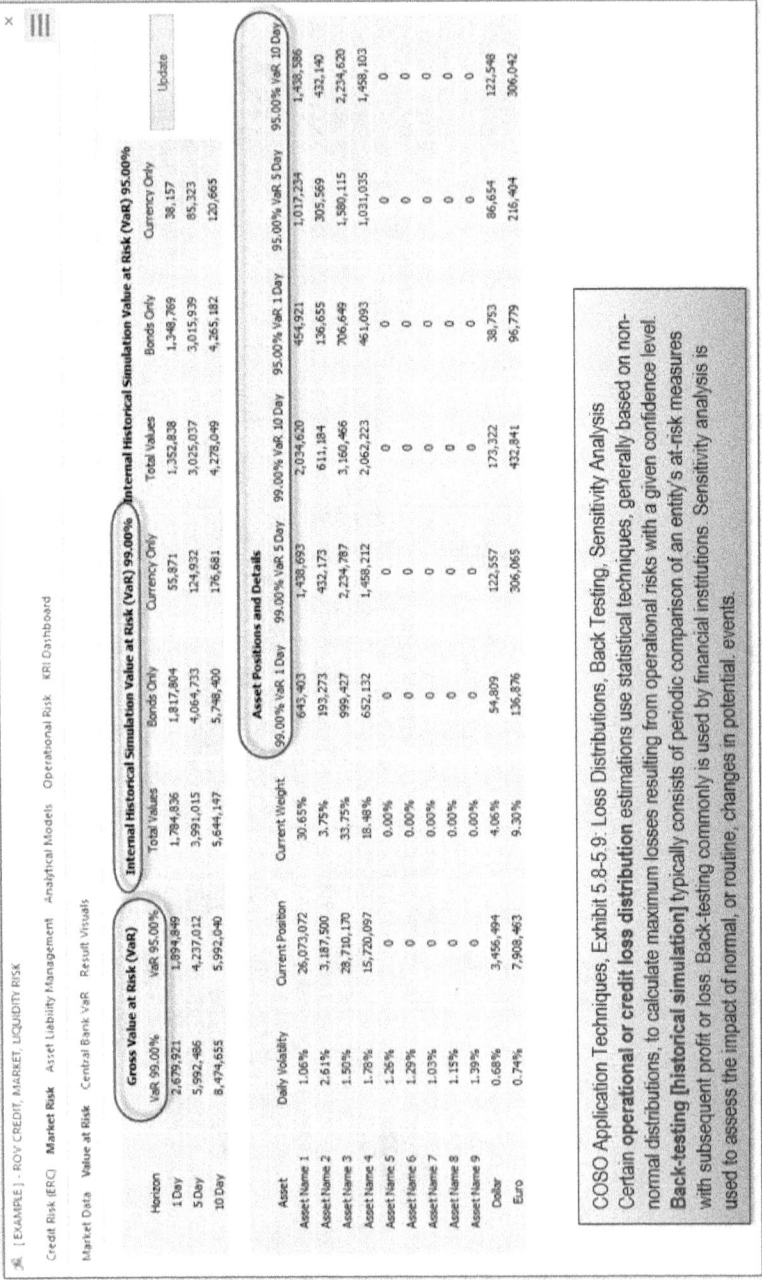

Figure 4.29: CMOL Module's Value at Risk and Back-testing Historical Simulations

SOFTWARE DOWNLOAD & INSTALL

As current versions of the software are continually updated, we highly recommend that you visit the Real Options Valuation, Inc., website and follow the instructions below to install the latest software applications.

- **Step 1**: Visit **www.realoptionsvaluation.com** and click on **Downloads** and **Download Software** (Figure A). You will be prompted to log in. Please first register if you are a first-time user (Figure B) and an automated e-mail will be sent to you within several minutes. (If you do not receive a registration e-mail after you register, then please send a note to support@realoptionsvaluation.com.) While waiting for the automated e-mail, browse this page and see the free getting started videos, case studies, and sample models you can download.

- **Step 2**: Return to this site and LOGIN using the login credentials you received via e-mail. Download and install the latest versions of **Risk Simulator** on this Web page. The download links, installation instructions, and Hardware ID information are also presented on this page (Figure C).

- **Step 3**: After installing the software, start Excel and you will see a Risk Simulator ribbon. Follow the instructions provided on the Web page to obtain your Hardware ID and e-mail it to support@realoptionsvaluation.com. Mention the code **"MR3E 30 Days"** and you will be sent additional download links and a free extended 30-day license to use the Risk Simulator, Modeling Toolkit, and CMOL software applications.

www.realoptionsvaluation.com/getting-started-and-modeling-videos/

Testimonials | FAQ | Global Partners | Contact Us

English | Chinese (Simplified) | French | German | Italian
Japanese | Chinese (Traditional) | Korean | Portuguese (Brazil) | Russian | Spanish

Real Options Valuation

CQRM CERTIFICATE | TRAINING | CONSULTING | SOFTWARE | BOOKS | DOWNLOADS | PURCHASE |

SOFTWARE DOWNLOADS

GETTING STARTED AND
MODELING VIDEOS

PRODUCT BROCHURES

SAMPLE MODELS

WHITEPAPERS AND CASE STUDIES

DOWNLOAD CENTER

You can also visit our mirror download site if you have problems downloading from this page

Welcome to Real Options Valuation, Inc.'s download center. Here you will be able to download _____ versions of the software you have purchased (license information required to install these full versions), product brochures, case _____ple training videos to help you get started in using our software, as well as sample Excel models to use with Risk Simulator and Re_____ _____ _____ _____ftware.

GETTING STARTED AND MODELING VIDEOS

The following are some live-motion and voice narrated videos which are playable on your computer using Windows Media Player or other video players capable of WMV playback. You can simply click on any of these links below to view the streaming videos.

ROV SOFTWARE GETTING STARTED VIDEOS

We also have some more detailed Risk Analysis and Risk Simulator software getting started videos that you can download and watch. These videos total about 2 hours. For even more detailed training, please check out our set of 12 Training DVDs (over 30 hours) or our hands-on Certified in Risk Management seminars (4 days). The following are updated detailed getting started videos on Risk Simulator, featuring all the new tools such as Auto ARIMA, GARCH, JS Curves, Cubic Spline, Maximum Likelihood, Data Diagnostics, Statistical Analysis, Modeling Toolkit, and more...

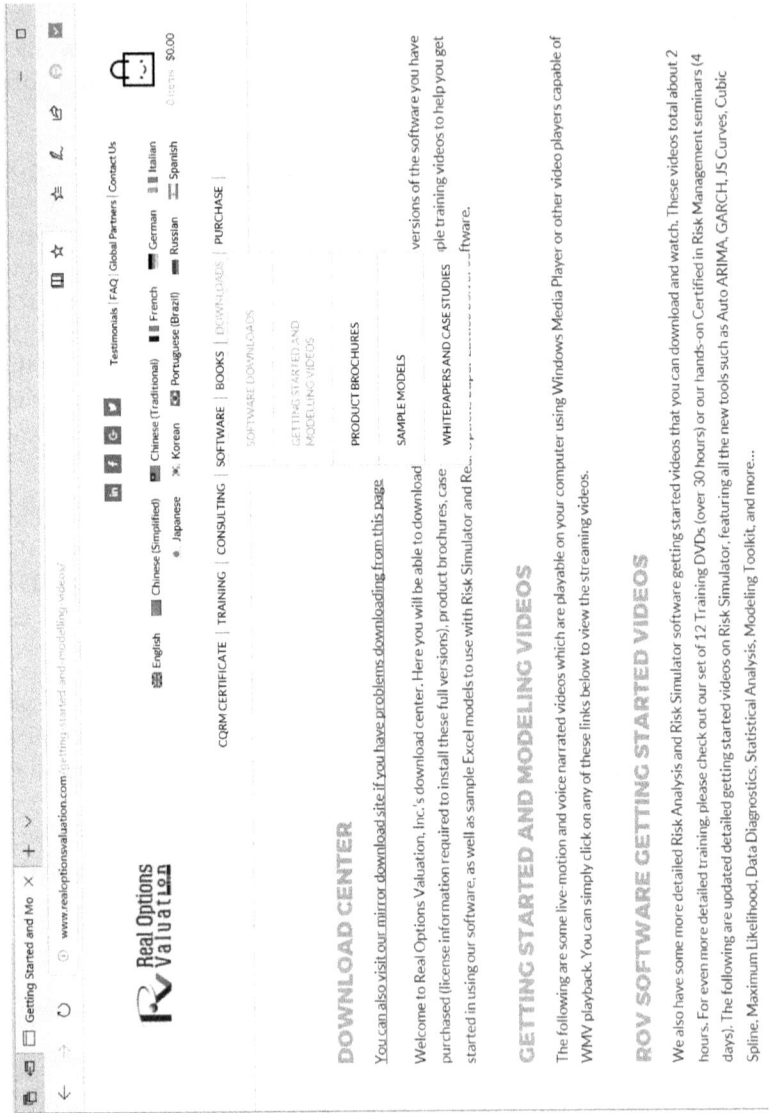

Figure A: Step 1 – Software Download Site

DOWNLOAD CENTER

You can also visit our mirror download site if you have problems downloading from this page

Welcome to Real Options Valuation, Inc.'s download center. Here you will be able to download trial versions of our software, full versions of the software you have purchased (license information required to install these full versions), product brochures, case studies and white papers, and sample training videos to help you get started in using our software, as well as sample Excel models to use with Risk Simulator and Real Options Super Lattice Solver software.

YOU ARE REQUIRED TO LOGIN TO VIEW THIS PAGE.

Username

Password

| LOGIN | REGISTER |

Figure B: First-Time Visitor Registration

English ▤ Chinese (Simplified) ▤ Chinese (Traditional) ▌▌French ▌▌German ▌▌Italian
● Japanese ※ Korean ▧ Portuguese (Brazil) ▤ Russian ▭ Spanish

Real Options Valuation
CQRM CERTIFICATE | TRAINING | CONSULTING | SOFTWARE | BOOKS | DOWNLOADS | PURCHASE |

FULL & TRIAL VERSION DOWNLOAD:

Download Risk Simulator 2018 – Auto Installer

Download Risk Simulator 2018 – Auto Installer (mirror site)

Download Risk Simulator 2018 – For 32 Bit Excel

Download Risk Simulator 2018 – For 32 Bit Excel (mirror site)

Download Risk Simulator 2018 – For 64 Bit Excel

Download Risk Simulator 2018 – For 64 Bit Excel (mirror site)

Download OLDER version of Risk Simulator 2014 [WIN x64 and Excel x32 edition]

Download OLDER version of Risk Simulator 2014 [WIN x64 and Excel x32 edition] (mirror site)

This is a full version of the software but will expire in 15 days, during which time you can purchase a license to permanently unlock the software. Please first uninstall all previous versions of Risk Simulator before installing this newer version.

To permanently unlock the software, purchase a license and e-mail us your Hardware ID (after installing the software, start Excel, click on Risk Simulator License) and e-mail admin@realoptionsvaluation.com the 16 to 20 digit Hardware ID located on the bottom left of the splash screen). We will then e-mail you a permanent license file. Save this file to your hard drive, start Excel, click on Risk Simulator | License | Install License and point to the location of this license file, restart Excel and you are now permanently licensed. Installing the license only takes a few seconds.

SYSTEM REQUIREMENTS, FAQ, AND ADDITIONAL RESOURCES:

- Windows 7, 8, and 10 (32 and 64 bits)
- Microsoft Excel 2010, 2013, or 2016
- 2GB RAM Minimum (4 GB recommended)
- 600 MB Hard Drive
- Administrative Rights to install software
- Microsoft .NET Framework 2.0, 3.0, 3.5, or later
- MAC OS users will require either Virtual Machine or Parallels running Microsoft Excel

Figure C: Download Links and Hardware ID Instructions

INDEX